AFTER OSLO

AFTER OSLO

NEW REALITIES, OLD PROBLEMS

Edited by
GEORGE GIACAMAN
and DAG JØRUND LØNNING

Pluto Press
LONDON • CHICAGO

First published 1998 by
PLUTO PRESS
345 Archway Road, London N6 5AA
and 1436 West Randolph, Chicago,
Illinois 60607, USA

British Library Cataloguing in Publication Data
A catalogue record for this book is available from
The British Library

ISBN 0 7453 1243 8 hbk

Library of Congress Cataloging-in-Publication Data
After Oslo : new realities, old problems / edited by George Giacaman
    and Dag Jørund Lønning.
        p.   cm.
    Includes bibliographical references.
    ISBN 0–7453–1243–8 (hbk)
    1. Arab–Israeli conflict —1993– 2. Palestinian Arabs—Politics
    and government. I. Giacaman, George. II. Lønning, Dag Jørund.
    DS119.76.A38 1998
    956.05'3—dc   97–44922
        CIP

Designed, typeset and produced for Pluto Press by
Chase Production Services, Chadlington, OX7 3LN
Printed in the EC by TJ International, Padstow

CONTENTS

NOTES ON CONTRIBUTORS

Azmi Bishara is a Member of Knesset, the Israeli Parliament, and a Researcher and Board Member of Muwatin, The Palestinian Institute for the Study of Democracy.

Nils A. Butenschøn is Professor of Political Science at the University of Oslo.

Jan de Jong is Geographer and Consultant for the Saint-Yves Society, Jerusalem.

George Giacaman is General Director of Muwatin, The Palestinian Institute for the Study of Democracy, and Professor of Philosophy and Dean of Graduate Studies at Bir Zeit University.

Jamil Hilal is Visiting Senior Research Fellow at Muwatin, The Palestinian Institute for the Study of Democracy.

Lena Jayyusi is Chairperson of the Department of Communications at Cedar Crest College, Allentown, Pennsylvania and Visiting Senior Research Fellow at Muwatin, The Palestinian Institute for the Study of Democracy.

Dag Jørund Lønning is Research Fellow at Chr. Michelsen Institute, Bergen.

Fouad Moughrabi is a professor and Head of the Department of Political Science at the University of Tennessee.

Amon Raz-Krakotzkin is a professor at Ben Gurion University.

Graham Usher is Staff Correspondent for *The Economist* magazine, based in Jerusalem.

PREFACE

The famous handshake in Washington on 13 September 1993 between PLO leader Yasser Arafat, the late Israeli Prime Minister Yitzhak Rabin and Foreign Minister Shimon Peres, has been celebrated by almost the entire world as a symbolic catalyst for a final and peaceful solution to the long conflict between Israelis and Palestinians. Despite continuous violence, Israeli settlement expansion and severe human rights violations by both parties to the negotiations, the international media, politicians and academics have continued to refer to the Oslo accords, which produced the handshakes, as 'the peace process', thus, metaphorically, denoting 'a controlled, gradual and expansive movement forwards and/or upwards'.[1]

And new realities *have* been created. A range of new actual achievements has been produced, facts which the contending parties have no option to ignore. These include first and foremost the Israeli recognition of and signing of treaties with the PLO, the establishment of a Palestinian Authority with parts of the Occupied Territories under its control, the return of the Palestinian leadership in exile and the election of a Palestinian Legislative Council.

Nevertheless, old problems have deepened and continue to dominate Israeli–Palestinian relations. For the Palestinians, especially, the post-Oslo accords era has meant severe economic deprivation and restrictions on movement. Furthermore, bantustanisation looks increasingly to become permanent as more and more land and natural resources have been taken for settlement expansion or apartheid-style 'bypass roads'.

This volume has two analytical objectives. First, it represents a critical and analytical assessment of the Oslo process, of some of its social, political and human consequences and results for the region in general and on Palestinian society in particular. Second, it also attempts to conceptualise and understand the continuous crisis in the area since the agreements were signed.

As different contributions show, the effects of the Oslo accords in terms of creating *peace* have been meagre at best. The lack of a real international response to continuous Israeli colonialist expansion and to the gradual development of a new political autocracy in the Palestinian Authority areas has caused extreme frustration at Palestinian street level.

With a thorough focus on reasons for, and the discourse of, frustration, this volume attempts to demonstrate that a peace process which does not give a satisfactory answer to the legitimate demands of an occupied people will fail. Unending popular revolts are a clear reminder that only by identifying and challenging oppression at all levels can a lasting and comprehensive peace be established between Israelis and Palestinians. An unjust and undemocratic process can only be supported at gunpoint, and, at best, postpone violence and war.

This volume is the result of an ongoing cooperative research and exchange programme between Chr. Michelsen Institute, Bergen, Norway, and Muwatin, The Palestinian Institute for the Study of Democracy, Ramallah, Palestine.

The programme is supported by the Royal Norwegian Ministry of Foreign Affairs, to whom the two institutes extend their gratitude. This book has also been made possible through a generous grant from Den Norske Bank's Jubilee Fund for Chr. Michelsen Institute.

The editors further wish to express their gratitude to Øystein Rygg Haanæs, Head of Information at CMI, whose initiatives, interest, dedication and late nights of work have been vital in the realisation of this volume.

Dag Jørund Lønning
Chr. Michelsen Institute
Bergen

April 1997

George Giacaman
Muwatin,
The Palestinian Institute
for the Study of Democracy
Ramallah

NOTE

1   Van Teeffelen, Toine, 'Development Discourse. The Case of Palestine' in Inge Boer, Annelies Moors and Toine Van Teeffelen (eds), *Orientations. Changing Stories. Postmodernism and the Arab World* (Amsterdam, 1996).

1 IN THE THROES OF OSLO: PALESTINIAN SOCIETY, CIVIL SOCIETY AND THE FUTURE

George Giacaman

The two Israeli–Palestinian agreements (Oslo I and II as they came to be called) represent the terms of settlement after the defeat, or more specifically, after the acceptance of defeat by the Palestinians. The acceptance of defeat was a process with many stages inasmuch as the Oslo agreements themselves constitute a process that continues to unfold and may not clearly end in its results and implications. The process was made possible by diverse factors, including the collapse of the Soviet Union and the Gulf war. Yet the Oslo agreements' main distinctive feature is that they ushered in a new reality, and henceforth any Israeli–Palestinian contestation over land, rights, sovereignty and the future will have the agreements as one of its main points of reference.

No less significantly for Palestinians, the new reality involved the creation of a Palestinian Authority with some jurisdiction over the two-and-a-half million Palestinians living in the West Bank and Gaza. It also included the establishment of an elected Palestinian Council with executive and legislative authority constrained by the agreements. A host of new questions, most of them still open, were posed to Palestinians, such as the relation of the Palestinian Authority to the PLO and of the Palestinian Council to the Palestinian National Council which is part of the PLO structure. But the more important questions revolve around the nature of the new Palestinian political system that is still in the process of development, its relation to Palestinian society and to the people that live under it, the new role of Palestinian political parties and other organised groups in society, and the ability of

the new system to salvage national rights from the throes of an
agreement made in an atmosphere of resignation.

BEGINNINGS

For a conflict that has spanned a century since the first waves of
Zionist settlement in the 1880s, the road to Oslo has been long. It
has been a history of limited successes and major defeats.
Palestinian demands and expectations progressively grew more
modest as time went by: from an attempt to retrieve the whole of a
lost homeland, to the 'secular democratic state' for Palestinians
and Jews, to the 'two-state solution', to a limited autonomy under
the Oslo agreements, with further negotiations concerning the
future under adverse conditions for Palestinians. The 'illusion of
endurance of settler regimes' turned out to be less illusory, at least
in Palestine, than many thought and hoped in the early 1970s.[1]
Yet the more proximate factors that made the Oslo agreements
possible began, ironically, with the results of the Palestinian
Intifada in the late 1980s and early 1990s.

As a mass popular movement against occupation, the Intifada
posed a novel challenge for Israel. The first priority in the field
was military containment, but this could not be fully accomplished without higher civilian casualties among Palestinians,
more than were politically acceptable given world attention. The
Intifada was therefore able to break the political stasis imposed by
Israel since its invasion of Lebanon in 1982, which had resulted in
the removal of the PLO leadership to a more distant exile in
Tunis. The Intifada could not be completely subdued by military
means alone, and political initiatives appeared necessary.

Eager to utilise the political opening made by the Intifada, the
PLO moved to formalise its acceptance of Israel as a state, a position
it adopted gradually from the mid-1970s through the 'two-state'
formula. The move brought it closer to entry in the political process
since acceptance of Israel as a state within the 1967 boundaries was
understood to be a minimum condition. This took place at the
meeting of the Palestinian National Council in November 1988 in
Algiers. Two main decisions were taken. The first included the
recognition of Israel as a state through the acceptance of the

principle of partition of Palestine. The second included the recognition of Israel within the 1967 boundaries through the acceptance of UN Security Council Resolutions 242 and 338.

Consensus politics had been a salient feature of PLO political life, at least when it came to strategic issues and in particular those related to Palestinian national rights. The Algiers conference introduced a change. The first decision was taken by consensus. The second, relating to Israel's borders, was taken by a majority vote. Consensus on the second would not have been possible given the position of some of the groups within the PLO. But the need to formulate a political position in line with the 'international consensus' was overriding. It was thought to be mandatory if the PLO was to be part of any political process resulting from the Intifada.

This was not the beginning of due process by majority vote, but in retrospect, the beginning of the breakdown of due process altogether in PLO political life. Thus when the Oslo agreements were signed, the Palestinian National Council was never called to ratify them. Whatever life it possessed before then quickly expired, especially after the election of a new Palestinian Council in January 1996 under the terms of the Oslo agreements.

In response to the Intifada, with the Gulf war as an important contributing factor, the Bush Administration in turn perceived a need for political movement. Former Secretary of State James Baker had already started a process of shuttle diplomacy several months before the eruption of the war in the Gulf, basing his approach on the Shamir plan of May 1989. Heading a Likud-led coalition, former Prime Minister Yitzhak Shamir, under US prodding as a result of the Intifada, had submitted a 'peace plan' that envisioned a 'two-track' approach to peace: an Arab track and a Palestinian track. However, Mr Shamir never tired of repeating after he announced his plan that the main item in it dealt with peace with the Arab states rather than with the Palestinians.

Mr Baker's shuttle diplomacy continued after the war. Its aim was threefold: to make the Shamir government take its plan seriously, to find a place in it for Palestinians and to get Palestinians and Arabs to accept it, at least as a starting point. The result was the 'Madrid formula' in terms of which Palestinians were to be represented as part of the Jordanian delegation.

The Madrid conference was convened at the end of October 1991. In the following two years, several rounds of negotiations took place but remained deadlocked, in part because the Palestinian leadership, then in Tunis, was not a direct party in the negotiations. In contrast to the Likud-led government, a Labour government under Rabin and Peres was willing to trade recognition of the PLO with an agreement it could defend domestically. The result was the Declaration of Principles signed in Oslo on 13 September 1993 between the PLO and Israel. This was followed by the Agreement on Palestinian Interim Self-Rule, the 'Gaza–Jericho' agreement signed on 4 May 1994. A few days later, on 10 May, Palestinian police entered the Gaza Strip.

VIRTUALLY NEW REALITY

For most Palestinians living in the West Bank and Gaza, the new political reality became more concrete only after the Palestinian Authority assumed control over the main cities and towns, and joint control with Israel over most of the population in Palestinian villages. This took place within one month following the signing of 'Oslo II' in Washington on 28 September 1995.

A central feature of the new reality brought about by Oslo is that it was no longer possible for Palestinians and Israelis to engage in politics totally outside the framework of the Oslo accords. This applies both to Palestinian relations with Israel and to internal Palestinian political life. Prime Minister Netanyahu discovered this soon after his election in June 1996, with the crucial difference that the Oslo cards were decked on his side with US backing at every turn. It also took a bloody conflagration in late September of the same year and an ensuing, but brief, international isolation to make him modify his position on the Oslo agreements.[2]

On the Palestinian side, the new reality precipitated a major crisis in Palestinian political life, and for parties in the opposition in particular. Their inability or refusal to enter, in some fashion, the 'new politics' had a detrimental effect on the development of Palestinian civil society after Oslo, and on the achievement of Palestinian national rights or what was possible under the 'negotiated process'. Whereas Israel is a state with a question about its borders but not its existence, crucial questions remain at least partially open about the political future of Palestinians and about the structure, nature and future of the society now being formed in part of Palestine. To the analysis of some of these issues we will now briefly turn.

SOCIETAL ORGANISATION

In its pre-modern form, societal organisation in Palestine existing in relative independence from the state has had a long history. By this I mean forms of association that are ethnic, tribal or kinship-based, functioning in relative autonomy which varied in accordance with the ability of the central government to extend its authority to the various regions formally under its control. Considerable local autonomy, for example, was possible at different periods under Ottoman rule. Various communities organised aspects of their life with custom and tribal law as central elements contributing to their cohesion.

Modern forms of association based on voluntary membership increased in the twentieth century. The Zionist–Palestinian conflict was a contributing factor. In the inter-war period new political parties emerged whose main focus for political work was the continuing and increasing Zionist colonisation of Palestine. These parties however were largely led by notables from well-known land-owning or urban families. As a result political life and rivalry acquired a traditional family and clannish colouring. Nevertheless, this period also witnessed an increase in other forms of association such as unions, charitable societies, clubs, professional associations and the like.

This trend continued through the 1950s and the early 1960s, in part spurred by the dispossession of 1948. It also prepared the ground for the qualitative changes that began in the early 1960s and remain with us in one form or another to the present day. The emergence of the PLO brought a qualitative change to specific aspects of Palestinian political life and organisation. It brought political diversity and a clearer definition of ideological pluralism within Palestinian society and introduced modern party association with a concentrated focus on Palestinian national issues. The PLO was not led by traditional landed families. Membership in the groups and parties within the PLO was open, and, for ill or for good, upward mobility within parties was possible based on the rules of the game of party politics. This was not always a democratic process, but success did not require a pedigree. Thus it was possible for many from rural backgrounds or from refugee camps or from the ranks of the poor to rise to positions of prominence in the PLO and within Palestinian society in the West Bank and Gaza. Many were later to become the 'new elite' within the system established by the Palestinian Authority after Oslo, especially those loyal to Yasser Arafat who were allowed by Israel to come from Tunis after the accords were signed.

All major parties within the PLO had extensions in the occupied territories and supporters in mass organisations such as unions, student groups, women's groups and various 'committees' throughout the West Bank and Gaza.[3] The PLO also gave a boost to the formation of new non-governmental organisations (NGOs) and charitable societies whose main work was service delivery and relief work for different sectors in society.

In general it can be said that the PLO gave support to the process of societal organisation of varied forms under occupation. This was also accompanied by rivalry between the groups of which the PLO was composed, a rivalry that often hampered the work of civic organisations, or duplicated it unnecessarily. Nevertheless, organised groups working within the developing sphere of civil society became a clear feature of Palestinian society, especially during the past two decades.

ANTINOMIES OF THE PLO 'MODEL'

The PLO 'model' therefore harboured within it two antinomial and contradictory elements: a pluralistic civil society-in-the-making lodged within the confines of a proto-state, the PLO. For, by definition, the sphere of civil society is the non-state sphere, or that which exists in relative independence from the state. Yet in the absence of a state and in the conditions of the diaspora, the antinomy of state/civil society endured as a temporary necessity and as a means of shouldering national responsibilities, in what was hoped would be a transitional stage.

Thus the PLO was not only a proto-state composed of political formations, but also contained within its structures labour unions, student unions, teachers' unions, women's unions, writers' unions, productive enterprises, research centres and NGOs.[4] The requirements of the national struggle and of survival in the diaspora appeared to mandate such a mobilisational effort. An all-encompassing organisation also seemed essential for the expression and preservation of a collective identity, for a definition and preservation of the self in juxtaposition to a community uprooted and to a society destroyed.

But once a new Palestinian entity emerged on the ground in Palestine after Oslo, the threat to civil society from such a unitary model and history became quickly apparent, especially in light of the disarray of the opposition within the PLO and the resultant weakness of political parties, as well as the requirements of the agreement with Israel.

Early public signs of the tensions endemic to the unitary model however, pre-date Oslo and can be clearly pinpointed. On 14 December 1990, a conference was held in Jerusalem devoted to social issues related to women with the Intifada as a backdrop.[5] Representatives of different political parties attended, thus giving legitimacy to the public discussion of issues related to women aside from their connection to the national struggle. It was the first Palestinian conference with local PLO participation to view women's issues as being of significance in their own right. Hitherto, issues related to the national question were viewed as taking precedence over all others. Indeed, an active suppression of public discussion of women's problems was the accepted norm among parties and groups within the PLO, including leftist ones. Such issues were deemed divisive since inevitably questions related to patriarchy were bound to be raised. The convening of the conference no less significantly also signalled disillusionment with what the national question had come to, thus asserting the need to address issues long postponed on account of the struggle for liberation. It was a harbinger of things to come, including Oslo and the crisis of political parties.

PARALYSIS OF POLITICAL PARTIES

The Madrid conference was the first watershed to herald the crisis of political parties. As a result of their opposition to the Madrid formula (that is, having the Palestinian delegation represented as part of the Jordanian delegation, in addition to other factors), most Palestinian parties found themselves outside the political process but unable to stop it or influence its direction.

The second crucial watershed, also leading to the total paralysis of opposition parties within the PLO, was the formation of a Palestinian Authority as a result of the Oslo agreements. Not only were they not part of the new Palestinian political entity being formed on the ground, but most did not join the elections for the Palestinian Council held in January 1996. The elections for the Council were the only available opportunity at that time to enter the new system. In addition, the opposition could neither mobilise public support against the election, nor run on platforms opposed to the Oslo agreements. Indeed, the elections generated heated debates within most parties and some were aired in public at conferences and in newspapers. In the end, the winners were the 'hard-liners', comprising mostly the leadership outside the West Bank and Gaza. Hence, most parties which were members of the PLO (as well as Hamas, which is not) found themselves not merely outside the political process, but outside politics altogether.

The crisis of Palestinian political parties, however, had begun earlier. For a few years the Intifada helped mask the impasse they had reached. Unable to realise their programmes for a 'just, comprehensive, and permanent' peace, most parties, especially those on the left, were unable or unwilling either to change their programmes or to follow 'pragmatically' the lead of Yasser Arafat.[6]

By the late 1980s and early 1990s it was clear that most parties, especially those on the left, were quickly losing whatever mass base they had or could mobilise during the Intifada.[7] The phenomenon was not restricted to the West Bank and Gaza and could be seen clearly in Palestinian communities in the United States and Europe as well. Much organisational work done there during the Intifada or earlier quickly collapsed with the flight of members and loss of supporters. Loss of a clear cause, lack of hope, perception of the end of the national project, and the limited results of the Intifada were all factors (though heroic in more than one respect, finally the Intifada was an expiring splutter lighting the road to Oslo).

Meanwhile, it was clear that the PLO was no longer a functioning body, especially after the establishment of the Palestinian Authority in parts of the West Bank and Gaza. The historic leadership of the PLO, represented by Mr Arafat, was now in charge of Palestinian society, without the presence of an organised opposition working within the new system, or able to influence it from without. With a Palestinian authority on the ground but without the presence of political parties with a mass base in the opposition, the tension inherent in the duality of state/civil society finally reached its point of crisis.

THE PERIL OF THE MODEL

The unitary model of the PLO, applied to the emerging political entity in the West Bank and Gaza, threatens to engulf society in the absence of organised societal strength in the form of effective opposition parties and mass-based movements. The essence of the model stems from the mobilisation aims of the PLO towards a community in dispersion. But once the model is transposed in order to govern a population living on its own land, its latent totalitarian traits quickly come to the fore.

The all-encompassing totality of the model envisions society 'organised' into 'General' and 'Higher' unions, associations, organisations, societies, and councils, at the top of which, after Oslo, the Palestinian Authority presides. The irony of having the government establish a 'Higher Council for Non-Governmental Organisations' in the spirit of the unitary model, appears to have escaped its founders.[8]

What apparently confuses matters is the 'transitional' nature of the situation in which the Palestinian Authority operates. Most of the main Palestinian national issues remain outstanding and relegated by Oslo to the 'final status talks'. These include the fate of Palestinians scattered in the diaspora, the right of return, the borders of the State of Israel, the right to self-determination, and Jerusalem. Such a context lends itself to the transposition of the unitary

model to the new situation under the pretext of achieving mobilisational goals. In addition, many political and social activists appear to
face a genuine dilemma, especially after the election of the Netanyahu government. Internally, on issues related to human rights, civil
liberties, the rule of law, accountability and civic organisation, they
feel constrained to play an oppositional role. But given the conflict
with Israel and the indeterminate future for Palestinians, they feel
equally constrained to play a supportive role and are not averse to
mobilisational aims for that end.

Nevertheless, this has not prevented limited oppositional
efforts in spite of the relative weakness of organised strength in
Palestinian society at present. Such an effort took the form of
contests over draft laws, human rights issues, academic freedom
and civil rights. Union and working-class issues have not figured
prominently, in part because the majority of the labour force is
dependent on work in Israel with a sizeable portion of the
remaining labour force dispersed on different locations in the
West Bank and Gaza. Thus lack of access to work accentuates the
political as opposed to the class factor, which in turn is used by
Israel as a bargaining counter with the Palestinian Authority.

A single but significant exception was the strike waged by
government school teachers in March 1997, many of whom receive
subsistence wages. The leadership of the official General Union of
Palestinian Teachers did not support the strike which was led by
'Teachers' Committees' with no specific loyalty to the Palestinian
Authority. As the strike progressed, the leadership of the General
Union found themselves in the difficult position of being opposed
to the demands of the vast majority of the constituency they were
supposed to represent, thus risking their own delegitimisation.[9]

This was a clear case of the contradiction inherent in the unitary
model. It was also clear that change in the model would only come
about through contestation over the terrain of civil society.

CIVIL SOCIETY

The revival of the concept of the 'civil society' in the early
1970s and its popularisation by the media in the context of the
struggle of the Polish Workers' Movement against the state has

left a wealth of material written on the subject. As a rallying cry, the phrase has been inducted into the service of various causes in Asia, Latin America and the Middle East. But writings on the subject, including those in Arabic, show no agreement on some of the components, institutions and actors within this sphere. Should political parties be included? Should ascriptive and primordial forms of association be included? Are totalitarian groups dedicated to the diminution of such a sphere to be considered agents of 'civil society'? Is a capitalist economy an essential component?[10]

Such questions raise issues that go beyond the scope of this chapter. I merely note that any definition of the phrase, given the history of its evolution and the changes attendant on what it denotes, must of necessity contain a normative starting point, stating what the phrase ought to mean in a specific historical context and giving a justification for its usage.[11]

Under authoritarian regimes, and in the Palestinian case in particular, any expansion in the sphere of civil society must appear desirable. Authoritarian regimes, particularly in the Middle East, do not normally seek to restrict economic activity, in contradistinction to political activity, civil liberties and the right to unionise and organise. Any attempt to bring about change in society must therefore give precedence to the protection of political and civil liberties and to respect of human rights as necessary conditions for further change in society. In the Palestinian context, political parties in the opposition, together with other organised groups with a vested interest in change and in the protection of civil liberties and human rights, appear as main agents in the endeavour to expand the sphere of civil society.

It must be clear as well that civil society cannot endure without the protection of democratic structures. This is the lesson to be drawn if one were to survey the situation in many a country in the world today, including a majority of Arab countries. Hence, in the Palestinian case, the question concerning the prospects for the development of civil society can be rephrased as a question concerning the prospects of democracy in Palestinian society. I will briefly discuss stages in the process and refer to actors and agents necessary for its development.

Historical Analogies

The history of the development of civil society in the West is
instructive and in some of its aspects relevant to the Palestinian
situation. The rights of citizenship that are now taken for
granted in many countries in the West came about gradually
and as a result of the struggle of groups and classes that were
denied those rights. The history of the development of civil
society in the nineteenth and twentieth century, in Western
Europe in particular, was a history of struggle for the
achievement of specific rights. The rights of unionisation,
association, freedom of speech, free press, but most importantly
the right to organise political parties and to vote, were all
denied to large sections of the populace, principally the working
classes. It took large-scale general strikes in Austria in 1896 and
1905, in Finland in 1905, in Belgium in 1902 and 1913, and in
Sweden in 1902, to secure universal voting rights. In Britain,
the first Reform Act of 1832 left five out of six adult males (let
alone women) without the right to vote, and only in 1918 was
universal political citizenship recognised.[12] Securing social and
economic rights was no less a matter for struggle. Some success
was achieved, but conditions varied from one country to another
with ebbs and flows continuing to the present day.

However, the rights of citizenship are inseparable from the
development and expansion of the sphere of civil society. For, if
honoured, rights as claims with correlative duties for the state
increase entitlements and expand the sphere of freedom of action
in society. Equally important is the fact that securing those rights
came about as a result of the effort and struggle of social forces and
organised groups with a vested interest in their political, social
and economic inclusion in society.

Keeping in mind that historical analogies can be misleading,
there is nevertheless reason to argue that Palestinian society at
the present stage of its development is, at least in one respect,
comparable to some European societies during the nineteenth
century. The development of civil society in the Palestinian
context will only come about as a result of the work, effort and
struggle of organised groups and social forces active in society.

Here the analogy with Europe ends, since we are not talking about the inclusion of classes that have been outside the scope of full citizenship. Rather, the problem lies in the fact that the concrete realisation of the rights which Palestinians formally agreed all Palestinians ought to have is subject to the vagaries of authoritarian politics.[13] What are absent are the structural guarantees necessary for the security and durability of those rights, hence the connection between democratisation and the development of civil society. Without constitutional and legal guarantees, but more importantly, without the separation of powers, independence of the judiciary, rule of law, accountability and rotation in government, any expansion in the sphere of civil society will remain vulnerable.

Twofold Dilemma

The problem then is twofold. The first is internal and concerns the nature of the Palestinian Authority and its relation to society. The second relates to the agreement with Israel and to the pressures that are brought to bear by Israel on the Palestinian Authority that are detrimental to the process of democratisation. It has been the demand of both the Labour and Likud governments in Israel that the Palestinian Authority play a policing role among its own population without regard to civil and human rights.

The confrontations that have taken place since September 1996 are a bleak reminder not only that peace has not been achieved, but also that there is a connection between the process of democratisation and the achievement of a political agreement that is acceptable to Palestinians. The stronger the resentment of the political situation, the more internal suppression is required to keep the population at bay.

A political agreement that is widely perceived by Palestinians to be unjust and to the detriment of their national interest will not make it possible for any Palestinian authority to be democratic if it were to remain wedded to such an agreement. Ultimately it will come into conflict with its own population on issues related to national rights and national future. To admonish the Palestinian Authority to respect human rights and to govern democratically, without reference to Palestinian national rights and to the failings of the current political process, is to pay only lip-service to those causes.

In the long run it will be not be possible for Palestinian society to develop in a democratic direction without a political settlement which a majority of Palestinians feel satisfies a minimum of their, by now, modest aspirations. Hence, the development of civil society in Palestine will neither take place in a political vacuum nor proceed on a track unrelated to the question of national rights.

NOTES

1. I. Abu-Lughod and B. Abu-Laban (eds), *Settler Regimes in Africa and the Arab World* (Wilmette, Illinois: Medina University Press, 1974).
2. Sparked by the opening of a tunnel adjoining the Al-Aqsa Mosque in Jerusalem on 24 September 1996, the clashes left more than 60 Palestinians dead, mostly civilians, and over one thousand wounded. Fourteen Israeli soldiers were killed, and nearly fifty were wounded.
3. On the development of mass organisations under occupation, see Lisa Taraki, 'Mass Organizations in the West Bank' in Naseer Aruri (ed.), *Occupation: Israel Over Palestine* (Belmont, Massachusetts: AAUG Press, 1989) pp. 431–63, and 'The Development of Political Consciousness Among Palestinians in the Occupied Territories, 1967–1987' in J. Nassar and R. Heacock (eds), *Intifada: Palestine at the Crossroads* (New York: Praeger Publishers, 1990) pp. 53–72. For a detailed study of labour and women's movements in the West Bank and Gaza, see Joost Hiltermann, *Behind the Intifada* (New Jersey: Princeton University Press, 1991).
4. For a useful study of the development of institution building within the PLO in the diaspora, see Laurie Brand, *Palestinians in the Arab World* (New York: Columbia University Press, 1988). The author refers to some of the problems and limitations of popular organisations, including a relatively narrow power base because of dependence on groups and parties within the PLO rather than the popular union's membership (p. 222). My point is that this is endemic to the unitary model and reflects the antinomial nature of its components, a fact to be seen with greater clarity after the establishment of the Palestinian Authority.
5. See the proceedings of the conference, *The Intifada and Some Women's Social Issues* (Ramallah: Bisan Centre, 1991; in Arabic).
6. See my 'What is Political Action? On the Crisis of Political Parties at the Present Juncture', in *Pluralism and Democracy: The Crisis of the Palestinian Political Party* (Ramallah: Muwatin Publications, 1996; in Arabic). See also other contributions to the same volume.
7. On the flight of activists from parties to NGOs, see Reema Hammami, 'NGOs: the Professionalization of Politics', *Race and Class*, Vol. 37, No. 2 (1995) pp. 51–63.

8. Such a Council was established in the West Bank and Gaza in January 1997.
9. Their position oscillated from opposition to the strike, to guarded support, to a call to stop the strike after a 10 per cent increase was given to teachers. The strike finally ended after a ministerial committee was formed to study the matter in more detail. One argument used to end the strike focused on the need to face the 'common threat' posed by increased settlement building by the Netanyahu government.
10. The literature on the subject is already vast. For a useful overview see J. Cohen and A. Arrato, *Civil Society and Political Theory* (Cambridge, Massassuchetts: The MIT Press, 1994) pp. 15–82. See also Ellen M. Wood, *Democracy Against Capitalism* (Cambridge: Cambridge University Press, 1995). See in particular Chapter 8, 'Civil Society and the Politics of Identity'. This is one of the best critical short pieces on the subject as it applies to Western countries. Her conclusions however do not necessarily apply to Third World societies.
11. For a brief elaboration of this point see my 'Civil Society and Authority', in M. Budeiri et al., *Critical Perspectives on Palestinian Democracy* (Ramallah: Muwatin Publications, 1995; in Arabic) pp. 103–16. See also A. Bishara, *A Contribution to the Critique of Civil Society* (Ramallah: Muwatin Publications, 1996; in Arabic) pp. 9–24.
12. A. Seligman, *The Idea of Civil Society* (New York: The Free Press, 1992) pp. 103–4.
13. For instance, the rights and principles contained in the Declaration of Independence adopted by the Palestinian National Council at its meeting in Algiers in November 1988. For text, see *Journal of Palestine Studies*, Vol. XVIII, No. 2 (Winter 1989) pp. 213–16.

2   THE OSLO AGREEMENT: FROM THE WHITE HOUSE TO JABAL ABU GHNEIM[1]

Nils A. Butenschøn

INTRODUCTION

At the time of writing, in the early spring of 1997, the so-called 'Oslo process' seems to be at a dead end. It all started – officially – with the signing of the first Oslo Agreement on the White House lawn on 13 September 1993; it may all end – in reality – on a hilltop in the outskirts of occupied East Jerusalem called Jabal Abu Ghneim (Har Homa in Hebrew). The Israeli government is preparing this ground for yet another Jewish settlement on occupied land in defiance of protests from even its closest allies.[2]

The road from the lawn to the hilltop has been a dramatic one indeed – in the diplomatic corridors and on the ground – in terms of bloodshed, hopes and despair. A Palestinian National Authority (PNA) under the firm control of Yasser Arafat, the veteran leader of the PLO, has been set up in the Occupied Territories, a political structure which far from resembles even the most modest of existing Palestinian liberation doctrines. Looking back today, the signing ceremony in Washington happened in a distant past and is slowly disappearing beyond the horizon.

What follows is not primarily an analysis of the Oslo process from 'the lawn to the hilltop'. The main purpose is to put the 1993 Oslo Agreement into the context of Palestinian and Israeli strategies. The presumption is that both leaderships, after months of secret deliberations, voluntarily decided to present their own peoples and the rest of the world with a *fait accompli* in the form of a declaration of principles. There was undoubtedly a clear and strong motive on both sides to reach an agreement on a common platform for a projected peace process. In this fateful decision to pursue 'the peace of the brave' there was a rare element of equality between Israeli and Palestinian leaders, a recognition of interdependence which brought them into the same boat politically speaking. Thus, the Oslo Agreement (also called 'Oslo I') must be taken to reflect a solution to strategic problems and dilemmas as seen from the point of view of both Palestinian and Israeli leaderships at the time. Whether the leaders understood and represented the fundamental interests and rights of their people remains an open question.

The present chapter, then, relates basically to the first of the three stages which logically constitute the Oslo process. This is the stage of initial diplomacy which established the principles and strategies for a negotiated solution, including a timetable for implementation. This was not peace, but a mutual expression of peaceful intentions.

The second stage represents the establishment of an interim 'peace regime' – that is, the fabric of institutional and security-related arrangements deemed necessary for erecting a Palestinian infrastructure within the confines of the Agreement. This stage was introduced by the Cairo Agreement of May 1994 which cleared the way for the first Palestinian National Authority presence in Jericho and Gaza, followed by several other agreements. The most important of these is the Interim Agreement of September 1995 ('Oslo II') which details the institutional and security arrangements in the Occupied Territories, including the distribution of territorial and functional jurisdiction between the PNA and the occupying power. It also specifies a timetable for further Israeli withdrawal, and negotiations for a final settlement.

The final stage is the stage of conflict termination whereby the 'permanent status' of the Occupied Territories, Jerusalem, Jewish settlements and the Palestinian refugees is to be decided, and a comprehensive peace treaty ('Oslo III') implemented. According to the original timetable, the final status negotiations should have started by May 1996 to allow a peace treaty to be signed three years on, but continuing political crises have brought the process to a standstill. Currently there is no sign of a credible initiative that could lift the process into its final stage.

THE OSLO AGREEMENT: A CHARACTERISATION

The Oslo Agreement will have to be included as one of those
famous (or infamous) documents in the history of the Palestinian
conflict which symbolises the beginning of an era (and the end of
another). Other such documents are the Balfour Declaration of
1917, which introduced British protection and subsequently
League of Nations authorisation of Zionist colonisation in Palestine; the Partition Resolution of the United Nations General
Assembly in 1947, imposing the principle of partition and a
separate Jewish state in Palestine; the UN Security Council
Resolution 242 of 1967, which introduced the 'territory-for-peace'
principle guiding all subsequent Middle East peace diplomacy
(but not mentioning Palestinian rights), and the Camp David
Agreements between Israel and Egypt (and the United States)
which paved the way for separate peace accords between Israel and
Arab parties, effectively breaking the principle of a united Arab
front in the conflict. Will the Oslo Agreement be the first of such
historical yardsticks to introduce the age of Palestinian national
independence, or is it just another piece in the long line of
historical betrayals of Palestinian rights – this time with the active
support of the recognised leadership of the Palestinian people
themselves?

The answer to this question is in my opinion not a straightforward one, and cannot be given only on the basis of a reading of the
text of the Declaration of Principles. We need a *contextual* analysis
which refers the Oslo Accord both to alternative action that could
have been taken at the time and to its consequences as we have
seen them unfolding in the peace process. But even such analyses
will not easily bring us close to a conclusive answer since we will
have to rely heavily on hypothetical speculation: What alternative
action could have been taken in 1993 and what would have been
the consequences? How do we judge the implications of the Oslo
Agreement, and which criteria are applicable? The ambiguity of
the situation is strengthened by the fact that the peace process
unfolds in directions no one can completely control or predict; it
may have consequences which neither Israeli nor Palestinian
leaders intended or foresaw in 1993. This uncertainty is reflected

in heated debates and political struggles within both Israeli and Palestinian society, as well as in individual acts of terror by those on both sides who see the Oslo process as an existential threat to their future.

The Oslo Agreement is a declaration of principles which lays the foundation for a limited, interim Palestinian self-rule in those areas of Palestine occupied by Israel since 1967: the West Bank, including East Jerusalem, and the Gaza Strip. This includes about 20 per cent of the Palestine that the United Nations decided to separate into two states in 1947. Today, the Occupied Territories have a combined population of about 2.1 million (out of a total Palestinian population of about 6.4 million).[3] The Agreement does not define the political nature or territorial extension of the future Palestinian entity, but entails stipulations with regard to mechanisms and deadlines for a step-by-step implementation of peace. Most importantly from a legal point of view, the Declaration of Principles refers to Security Council Resolutions 242 and 338 as its source of legitimacy. The implication is that the Declaration does *not* replace the UN resolutions pertaining to the legal status of the territories as 'occupied territories', the exact delimitation of which is subject to contending interpretations. Article 1 reads as follows:

Article 1: Aim of Negotiations
The aim of the Israeli–Palestinian negotiations within the current Middle East peace process is, among other things, to establish a Palestinian interim self-government authority, the elected Council (the 'Council'), for the Palestinian people in the West Bank and the Gaza Strip, for a transitional period not exceeding five years, leading to a permanent settlement based on Security Council Resolutions 242 and 338.

It is understood that the interim arrangements are an integral part of the whole peace process and that negotiations on the permanent status will lead to the implementation of Security Council Resolutions 242 and 338.

The agreement covers basically the same main questions which were raised in the open talks in Washington prior to the Oslo Agreement: the arrangements and mechanisms for the transfer of authority from Israel as the occupying power to the Palestinian

Authority. The open talks were initiated by the United States after
the Gulf war and initially convened in Madrid in October 1991.
The significance of the Oslo negotiations as a diplomatic achievement is that Israel and the PLO were able to agree on the
contentious issues which had blocked the official negotiations,
particularly those which related to the question of the jurisdiction
of the elected Council, the location and nature of Palestinian
administration, security arrangements and so on.[4] In Washington,
the problem was the *setting* of the talks: the PLO was not officially
represented and the world press sat ringside. Watchful oppositions
on both sides prevented the negotiators from establishing the level
of mutual trust necessary for testing the opponent's seriousness
and commitment to the kind of risky compromises which were
needed. Nevertheless, at this time of post-Gulf war frailty, the two
sides had a strong desire to find a way out of the deadlocked
situation, sufficiently strong to free themselves of the obstacles in
Washington and start a real coordination of positions. A number
of informal initiatives emerged, some of which were private
initiatives by well-meaning individuals, others having tacit involvement by responsible persons from one or both sides. The
breakthrough came in one of these secret channels, working
parallel to the official one and organised by a small Norwegian
team of social scientists and foreign ministry officials.[5]

The central elements of the Declaration of Principles (DOP) as
signed in Washington can be summed up as follows:

• The agreement covers a period of five years with the establishment of a Palestinian Interim Self-Government Authority.
  Gradually, this authority will replace the Israeli occupation
  authorities in specific spheres, starting with education and
  culture, health and social welfare, direct taxation and tourism.
  (By mid-November 1994, these areas were formally transferred
  to the Palestinian Authority as agreed in the 'Early Empowerment Accord' signed at Erez Checkpoint, Gaza, 29 August
  1994.) Israel will continue to exercise the powers and responsibilities not transferred to the Council.

• The Israeli withdrawal will start in Gaza and Jericho, based on
  an agreement on its practical implementation.[6] (The Cairo

Agreement concluded 4 May 1994. PNA offices opened in July of that year.)

- In order to give the self-governing authority a democratic mandate, elections for a Council will be held as soon as possible. Until the inauguration of the Council the transfer of authority and jurisdiction to the Palestinians will be of a preparatory nature. The elections will take place under international supervision. (General elections were to be held by July 1994, but were not carried out until January 1996.)[7]

- The Council's jurisdiction covers Gaza and the West Bank, which are thus to be considered a single territorial unit, whose integrity will be preserved during the interim period. The jurisdiction does not include Jerusalem, Israeli citizens or the Israeli settlements and military locations, nor external security or foreign affairs. Even after the initial Israeli withdrawal from Jericho and parts of the Gaza Strip, and the establishment therein of a Palestinian authority, Israel reserves the right to defend existing Jewish settlements and to 'use roads freely in the Gaza Strip and the Jericho area' for military and civilian transportation.[8]

- Negotiations for a lasting peace will start no later than the third year of the interim period (May 1996).[9] These will resolve the remaining questions such as: Jerusalem, refugees, settlements, security arrangements, borders, relations and cooperation with other neighbours, and other issues of common interest. These negotiations will not be prejudiced or pre-empted by agreements reached for the interim period.

- Parallel to the Self-Government Authority, various Israeli–Palestinian committees will be set up under a Joint Israeli–Palestinian Liaison Committee which will supervise the implementation of the interim arrangements in all areas.

In the week prior to the signing ceremony in Washington, there was an important exchange of letters between PLO leader Yasser Arafat and Prime Minister Yitzhak Rabin, with the Norwegian

Foreign Minister Johan Jørgen Holst serving as messenger. Arafat explicitly recognised the State of Israel within its pre-1967 borders and the Security Council Resolutions 242 and 338. He declared that the conflict should be solved through negotiations and renounced 'terrorism and other acts of violence'. Furthermore, he undertook to submit to the Palestine National Council (PNC), the PLO's supreme authority, for formal approval 'the necessary changes' in the Palestinian Covenant (PLO Charter) which negated Israel's legitimacy as a state. (The PNC was convened in Gaza in April 1996 for this purpose without voting on a conclusive text, but referring the matter to a working group.)

In a separate letter to Foreign Minister Holst he stated that the PLO called upon the Palestinian people in the West Bank and Gaza Strip to 'take part in the steps leading to the normalisation of life, rejecting violence and terrorism', that is, to call off the Intifada, the Palestinian uprising which started in December 1987.

In his letter, Rabin declared Israel's recognition of the PLO as 'the representative of the Palestinian people', and expressed willingness to negotiate with the PLO within the framework of the peace process, without however referring to the UN resolutions or recognising the right of the Palestinian people to a separate independent state.

As these letters indicate, the Oslo Agreement is not an agreement between equal partners. It is an agreement between an occupying power and an occupied people without this fact being explicitly recognised in the text. Arafat's concessions on behalf of the PLO are staggering and much more far-reaching than Rabin's on behalf of the Israeli government – however significant the Israeli recognition of the PLO may be. The PLO called off their armed struggle and civilian uprising against the occupation without getting any guarantee for the right to national independence and statehood in return. As Naseer H. Aruri puts it, 'the situation in the West Bank and Gaza becomes occupation by consent.'[10] It is still up to Israel to set limits on how far the Palestinian 'liberation' may go, a humiliation that the PLO had to accept to get an agreement. Israel had no reason, given the circumstances, to accept an agreement which did not in a fundamental way reflect the balance of power between the parties.

The question is whether the peace process itself is likely to result in a basic shift in the balance of power in favour of the Palestinians (as claimed by the anti-Oslo Israeli right-wing and pro-Oslo Palestinians), or if the outcome of the process in the final analysis will be framed on the basis of whatever Israel believes to be its vital national interests (as claimed by pro-Oslo Israelis and anti-Oslo Palestinians). Israel has not irrevocably renounced its sovereignty over the Occupied Territories; but then again, neither has the PLO. As demonstrated during the Intifada, relative power is not easily measured in such conflicts.

This brings us to the conclusion so far that the Oslo Agreement is unique in the sense that it brings together for the first time the main adversaries of the Palestine conflict into a direct, mutually recognised, relationship, *within* the existing imbalance of power. In order to stabilise its own position and its legitimacy as a state in the Middle East, Israel finally recognised its political dependence on an understanding with the PLO and the Palestinian people. The PLO for its part recognised its impotence relative to Israel and concluded: 'If you can't beat them, join them.'

It follows from this that the Oslo Agreement changes the agenda of the Palestine conflict. The main issue is no longer whether power in historic Palestine should be shared between its indigenous Arab population and the organised Jewish-Zionist settler society, but rather how and on what terms it should be shared. Essentially, this is the implication of Israel's and the PLO's recognition of each other – not as friends and allies or as equal partners, but as legitimate adversaries.

As a foundation for building peace, the Oslo Agreement represents a vulnerable strategy. By explicitly taking the final status issues out of the talks and putting them in front of the peace train – using the interim arrangements as a shield – these issues have in fact built up in front of the actors and seem in the present situation to be almost insurmountable. In theory, they were to be left for future talks, but the political reality is that they have been on everyone's mind all the time and have dominated the agenda all the way – drawn into the open as it was by the ambitions of the Declaration of Principles. The Oslo accords have fostered the mobilisation of nationalism in both camps: it has brought the Palestinian conflict back to Palestine and made it more acute than it has ever been since the establishment of the State of Israel.

Many will agree that such a step would have had to be taken sooner or later but whether it could have been done in another way remains – again – an open question.

Future historians will probably see the Oslo Agreement as the starting point of the final struggle on the ground between Jewish and Palestinian nationalists for what each consider to be their homeland. The present situation is a process of conflict, not a peace process; it is a process whereby each square mile, village and city of the Occupied Territories and each symbol of authority and sovereignty of the land is contested. In the following sections I will try very briefly to explain how the two parties have brought this situation upon themselves by the logic of their own strategic priorities since the fateful war of June 1967.

THE ROAD TO OSLO: PALESTINIAN AND ISRAELI PERSPECTIVES

The acceptance of the Oslo Agreement, a document which was first thoroughly assessed by the top leaders through months of secret negotiations and later approved by responsible political bodies on both sides, must be viewed as a rational act by both Israel and the PLO. A swift retrospective look at the main streams in Palestinian and Israeli thinking since 1967 on possible solutions to the Palestine problem gives us a framework for understanding these decisions as logical outcomes of deliberate policies. Furthermore, such a retrospective also gives insight into the dilemmas and paradoxes that arise from these decisions.

The PLO's Path towards the Recognition of Israel

The PLO was established in 1964 for the purpose of liberating Palestine. The Palestinian Covenant (the PLO Charter) as adopted in 1968 clearly negates the legitimacy of the State of Israel and projects a future Palestine as the free homeland of the reunited Palestinian people, freed from organised Zionism and imperialist conspiracies. Developments since then can be described as a movement in two directions which apparently contradict each other. One points towards the fulfilment of Palestinian national aspirations, the other towards a Palestinian adaptation to a permanent subjugation under Israeli hegemony.

Over the past thirty years, since the Arab–Israeli war of June 1967, the Palestinians have fought their way back onto the centre-stage of the conflict. Security Council Resolution 242, which was the political outcome of the war, did not even mention the political rights of the Palestinians; they were not regarded by the international community at the time as a party to the conflict in their own right. And indeed, they had no recognised representative of their own to advocate their case internationally. Today, the question of Palestinian national rights is viewed universally as the core issue in the Arab–Israeli conflict and the PLO is recognised as the only legitimate representative of the Palestinian people. Through their intrepid steadfastness – *sumud* – the Palestinians under PLO leadership have confronted their enemies, and convinced the world from a position of physical weakness and moral strength, first from bases in Jordan (until 1970), then from Lebanon (until 1982), and last but not least from within the Occupied Territories (since the mid-1980s). Interestingly, corresponding to the process whereby the legitimacy of Palestinian national claims gained international support step by step, the PLO moderated its strategic doctrines of liberation from a fundamentalist 'all or nothing' position (reflected in the PLO Charter) to the 'almost nothing' position (reflected in the Oslo Agreement).

Before we try to make sense of this paradox it is essential to bear certain factors in mind that have restricted Palestinian opportunities for pursuing a struggle for liberation:

• The Palestinian people are geographically dispersed and live under very different political, legal and social conditions. About half (some 3 million people; the numbers are inexact) live in exile, most of them in refugee camps in Jordan and Lebanon. Another 30–40 per cent live in the occupied areas (including East Jerusalem), partly in well-established cities and villages, partly in refugee camps. The remaining 15–20 per cent (depending on the method of calculation) constitute a minority in Israel. (Today, a total of approximately 4.5 million Jews live in Israel and the Occupied Territories.)

- The dispersion of the Palestinian people has created disparate ideas about and visions for liberation and a 'free Palestine'. The Palestinians in exile, as traditionally represented by the PLO and the guerrilla organisations, have had *the right of return* (and the re-creation of Palestine as a predominantly Arab country) as their central objective. The Palestinians in the Occupied Territories, led by the local middle class and the intellectuals, have gathered behind the demand for *Israeli withdrawal* from the Occupied Territories and for the establishment of a Palestinian state alongside Israel. The Palestinian minority in Israel has demanded *equality before the law*, laws that would secure their equal opportunities with those of the Israeli Jews.

- The lack of a national territory has made a united liberation struggle all but impossible. The PLO was for many years compelled to organise its activities from neighbouring states, with or without the blessings of the host countries. This created a conflict-ridden dependence on Arab regimes that triggered several open and armed conflicts, for example, 'Black September' in Jordan in 1970 and the civil war in Lebanon in 1975.

- The Palestinians had bad luck in the choice of enemy: Israel has always enjoyed security guarantees from dominating Western powers, making it in fact a regional great power, a position confirmed time and again over the last few years by the United States.

Ideologically, the PLO is a legitimate child of the radical Arab nationalism of the 1950s and 1960s, which had Egyptian President Gamal Abdel Nasser as its foremost leader. As an organisation, Arafat's PLO is a product of the war of 1967, where Israel won a crushing victory over the neighbouring Arab countries. The war, which brought the entire country of Palestine under Israeli rule, illustrated to the Palestinians that the Arab states were not able to liberate their homeland for them; they had to rely on their own strength, based on the conviction of the legitimacy of their claim. Furthermore, the battle near the Jordanian village of al-Karameh in the spring of 1968, where Palestinian guerrilla soldiers rendered surprisingly strong resistance against a superior Israeli attack force, became a major psychological turning point for the Palestinian idea of liberation by armed struggle. This cleared the way for Yasser Arafat's organisation Fatah and other commando groups to win a controlling majority of the PLO's political bodies in January 1969. (The PLO was founded in 1964 on an initiative from the Arab League, and lawyer Ahmed Shukairy, an Arab League loyalist, became its first leader.)[11]

The PLO's doctrine of liberation has been revised several times, from the revolutionary enthusiasm following the battle at al-Karameh in 1968 to the sober talks with the proclaimed arch-enemy in Oslo 25 years later. Step by step, the PLO has limited its declared objectives for liberation and approached a position that Israel could accept as a basis for negotiations.

Originally, PLO doctrine resembled that of the FLN, the national liberation front in Algeria. The FLN had been waging its own war of liberation since the early 1950s against French rule and settler colonialism. Following independence in 1962 most of the one million French colonists left the country and returned to France. Now the Palestinians wanted to liberate their homeland from European settlers and to put an end to colonial attempts at changing the country's cultural and demographic character. Applied to practical policies, this meant that the Jews had to return to where they came from, that the Palestinian refugees were to be repatriated, and that a new progressive Arab society was to be built. This perspective, sometimes called 'the Algerian model',[12] laid the foundation for the Palestinian National Charter, the PLO's constitutional document from 1964, revised in 1968. Article 6, for instance, states (in its 1968 version) that 'Jews who had normally resided in Palestine until the beginning of the Zionist invasion will be considered Palestinians.' When exactly the Zionist invasion started could of course be subject to discussion, but not the principle that most of the present-day Israeli-Jewish society, created by the Zionist invasion, is without legitimate historical claims to the land.

Palestine was not Algeria, however, and the Israelis were different from the French *colons*. Among other things, the Israeli Jews had no alternative homeland which was committed to give

them entry and citizenship, and which could be a proper address
for the Palestinian demands.

In 1968, shortly after the war, Palestinian intellectuals initiated
a debate on how this understanding could be incorporated into the
ideology of the Palestinian struggle. Their view was that the
Palestinians had become innocent secondary victims of the
persecution of the Jews by the Nazis and other Europeans, and
that the Palestinians could not shape their own future unless they
paid attention to this special historical trauma. The Israeli Jews
had come to stay and thus they had to be incorporated into the
vision of a liberated Palestine. This became the nucleus of a new
doctrine, known as 'the democratic state'. In October 1968,
Fatah's congress declared that the objective for the liberation was
'a democratic, progressive, non-sectarian state in which Jews,
Christians and Muslims would live together in peace and enjoy
the same rights.'[13]

Theoretically, this model had several strong points. It was
entirely in accordance with the universal theory of the democratic
state which had become established since the French Revolution,
in which all the citizens within a territory are equal in the eyes of
the law and in relation to the institutions of the state. It was
constructive in the sense that historical injustices were made
irrelevant for the distribution of future rights. Furthermore, it was
balanced by requiring that not only Jews, but also Palestinians,
had to renounce their demand for exclusive rights to the land, in
favour of an equal citizenship.

The model had a short life politically, however. It had only
limited support in the Palestinian community and it raised a long
series of intricate questions concerning its practical implementation. From 1969 onwards, the PNC passed a number of resolutions
which reflected the democratic state idea, but it was never
incorporated as a doctrine into the PLO Charter. That would have
required a basic revision of the Charter. This was suggested, but
the effort encountered numerous political and practical obstacles.
Besides, the model was completely without foundation in Israeli
reality and public opinion. The Israelis and their Western
supporters described the idea of a democratic Palestinian state
which was to include the Israeli Jews as an expression of
anti-semitism because it did not recognise the legitimate existence

of any separate Jewish national identity. How could a democratic state be built in Palestine if a considerable part of the population, namely the Jews, did not want to take part in the project, but instead insisted on remaining 'Israelis'? The answer, which has been repeatedly given by the PLO, was that those Jews who did not want to take part in the process were free to leave. But then we are no longer talking about a democratic process based on respect for the integrity and equality of all the projected groups, but rather about the imposition of a *fait accompli* as far as the Jews are concerned.

The October War in 1973 was initiated by Egypt's President Anwar El-Sadat in order to create a new and more favourable basis for negotiations with Israel. Egyptian forces reconquered the east bank of the Suez Canal, in itself an important psychological victory.[14] But liberating Palestine was not on the agenda, and the Palestinian national movement was still outside the diplomatic and political processes which could be decisive for their own future. The Palestinian leadership thus launched a new diplomatic offensive for Arab, Islamic and international recognition and at the same time raised a question which was extremely controversial in the context of internal PLO politics: should the PLO indicate a willingness to consider a step-by-step strategy for liberation, starting with whatever parts of Palestine could be liberated? A fragile compromise was reached at the twelfth PNC congress in Cairo in the summer of 1974. A political resolution was passed, the critical paragraph of which read:

> The PLO will struggle by every means, the foremost of which is armed struggle, to liberate Palestinian land and to establish the people's national, independent and fighting sovereignty on every part of Palestinian land to be liberated. This requires the creation of further changes in the balance of power in favour of our people and their struggle.

The political essence of this resolution was that the PNC introduced the principle of a territorial solution, the foundation for what has become known as 'the two-state model'. Certainly, the PNC emphasised that the objective was still the liberation of the whole of Palestine, but this liberation might have to go through stages, including the establishment in the land of a national authority before a full-fledged liberation became a fact. The leap from the democratic state to the two-state model is considerable, but not entirely illogical. It can be argued that the most far-reaching compromise is expressed in the democratic state model, since it accords the same rights to Jews living in Palestine (that is, Israelis) as to Muslims and Christians (that is, Palestinians). Considering the fact that the democratic state model did not bring the PLO any closer to the negotiating table, and that the prospect of the armed struggle against the Israelis succeeding was bleak indeed, an alternative formula could be more effective: indicate a willingness to coexist with the Israelis as separate communities in the land. If power could not be shared within the framework of a *unified* state, then an alternative organisational formula had to be found. Logically and in fact, this opened the whole debate about stages of liberation, a possible mini-state, interim arrangements, diplomacy and so on. In any case, the combined effects of the diplomatic offensive and the new political strategy cleared the way for Arafat to address the UN General Assembly in November 1974 and for further international recognition.

The two-state solution did not become official Palestinian policy until 1988, when the PNC passed resolutions which a) recognised the validity of UN General Assembly Resolution 181, the Partition Resolution of 1947, implying for the first time in Palestinian history the recognition of the legitimacy of a Jewish state in Palestine; b) recognised the validity of Security Council Resolution 242 and thus a *de facto* recognition of the State of Israel within its internationally recognised borders (that is, the cease-fire lines of 1949); c) declared the establishment of the State of Palestine with Jerusalem as its capital and Arafat as its president. The first two of these decisions provided an entirely new legal and political basis for PLO diplomacy; the last could of course not be implemented and was mostly of symbolic significance.

After their defeat in Lebanon in 1982–83, it is reasonable to believe that it was the Intifada that gave the Palestinians enough self-confidence to abandon formally the established objective of liberating the whole of Palestine, and to concretise the concept of a state to pertain to the Occupied Territories. Arafat had acknowledged the weak bargaining position of the PLO, and this time put all his cards on one horse: to save what could be saved of the homeland through talks with Israel and the United States.

Time worked in favour of those forces in Israel that wanted an annexation of the Occupied Territories. The areas were gradually annexed by Israel through the settlement policy and the integration of the Territories' economy and infrastructure.

Thus the PLO in fact abandoned its rights to 80 per cent of the Palestinian homeland in order to save the remaining 20 per cent. It would have to be in this 20 per cent that a future independent Palestine could take form, if at all, side by side with Israel.

The symbolic creation of the State of Palestine, with Arafat as president, may be read as an attempt at self-binding, in advance of possible talks. With this declaration, the PLO committed itself to claiming that the borders of its state and the principles of unabridged national sovereignty were inviolable. This position was also reflected in statements by the Palestinian delegation to the talks in Washington under the 1991 Madrid formula, where the PLO was not officially represented. The Declaration of Independence certainly helped 'President' Arafat gain the support of Palestinians, but it lacked political substance in relation to the international community. Israel was not willing to accept Palestinian national self-determination as a basis for negotiations, a position they upheld throughout the official talks, so the efforts in Washington to attain a Palestinian–Israeli Declaration of Principles were at a stalemate. But 'the Oslo channel' enabled the parties to communicate freely about the elements of a mutual declaration. In this process the PLO gave substantial concessions beyond the resolutions of 1988. The PLO affirmed its willingness to give up the armed struggle and 'other acts of violence' (that is, the Intifada), and to assume responsibility for the arrangement of self-government, even before having received recognition for a state of its own within specified borders. The self-binding effect of the Declaration of Independence did not, after all, carry much weight.

Arafat's Palestinian critics believe he thus crossed beyond a threshold without a national mandate or authority: he played the last Palestinian card without assurance of corresponding reciprocity. Arafat had given Israel, the strongest part, an efficient veto against any Palestinian move towards the realisation of their historical rights. Under the conditions created by the present peace process, Palestinian liberation is subject to Israel's agreement. Furthermore, given the lack of national Palestinian consensus over the Oslo process, and the imposition of a huge PNA police force, replacing the Israeli military occupation, there is a real danger of a Palestinian civil war and a new Israeli occupation. According to this view, Arafat is about to make the PLO an instrument of Israel's policy of domination, and to reduce himself to a sort of 'Palestinian Buthulezi' emulating the leader of the KwaZulu homeland under South African apartheid.

From his point of view, Arafat had for a long time believed that the only hope for future Palestinian independence lay in the occupied areas. In other words, the struggle had to be moved from the foreign front to the home front. Everything had to be done to end an Israeli occupation which not only strangled all normal economic and community activity, but even threatened the very existence of Palestinian society in the remaining parts of Palestine. Through the settlement policies, the confiscation of land and water resources, and a military regime that isolated the Palestinian population centres from each other and the world at large, Israel had created conditions that many Palestinians (and Israelis too) feared would end in a catastrophe of the same magnitude as the one in 1948–49. For the Arafat faction, the Oslo Agreement represented a starting point for a new Palestinian national vitality; and it was in their view the best that could be achieved under the existing conditions to stop further Israeli expansionism. The alternative was continued confrontation with Israel. But, if this were to take place, from where should such a struggle be waged?

During the war in Lebanon in 1982–83, the invading Israeli forces swept the Palestinian semi-state off the map. After King Hussein had driven it out of Jordan in 1970–71, Palestinian resistance had grown strong in a weak Lebanon. In 1983, Arafat was forced to move the PLO headquarters to Tunisia, hopelessly distant for the purpose of leading a war of liberation for Palestine. The Palestinian uprising which started towards the end of 1987 also contributed to shifting the centre of gravity to the Occupied Territories, away from the exile communities. The Intifada supplied the Palestinian resistance with a new moral dimension and determination.

Arafat's decision to sign the Oslo Agreement cannot be considered a dramatic break with the PLO's politics in the previous years. How otherwise should we explain Arafat's ability to muster the necessary support for the Oslo process in the PLO's decision-making bodies and in the 1996 elections? Customary applications of manipulative and non-democratic means are not, I believe, a sufficient explanation. The opposition, particularly the democratic and left-wing opposition, has not been able to present a credible alternative, and has – however reluctantly – followed Arafat's lead. We must not forget, as outlined above, that the most far-reaching concessions, that is, the recognition of the principle of partition and UN Resolution 242, were already implicit in decisions taken by the PNC. Arafat's fateful decision, therefore, to go along with the Israelis, should reasonably be viewed as the logical conclusion of the well-established Palestinian politics of adjustment, which has tended towards negotiations for the last 23 years. By 'logical conclusion' I mean a position which reflects the relative bargaining strengths between Israel and the PLO, a conclusion Arafat had to strain to reach in order to achieve an agreement. Time will show whether his decision represents a dead end or a new beginning for the Palestinian people's enduring struggle for a decent life.

Israel's Way Toward Recognising the PLO

When Israel occupied the West Bank and the Gaza Strip, as well as the Sinai Peninsula and the Golan Heights in 1967, the whole of pre-1948 Palestine had come under Israeli control. For the Israelis, a question immediately arose: what to do with the conquered areas?

The question was crucial for Israel's future as a state. Fixing borders is always essential for a nation's security, resource base and communications. But the newly conquered Palestinian territories had a significance to Israel – by virtue of their strategic and symbolic values – which meant that the decision whether to keep the Occupied Territories or not reopened a classic debate in the history of the Zionist movement: what is the objective and meaning of a Jewish state, how is this state to be secured in the future and how do we relate to the non-Jewish population? Translated into the field of practical policies after the 1967 war, these questions all focused on the definition of the future status and national identity of the territories. Do they belong to the Jews by historical right, or to the State of Israel because they were conquered in a war of self-defence? Or do they belong to the Arabs, even to the Palestinians? The Israeli government decided not to commit itself to a very specific position on these questions, with the important exception of East Jerusalem, which was formally annexed by Israel in July 1967.

A dividing line in Israeli politics has since then been related to the conception of the Territories, either as an inseparable part of the Land of Israel (*Eretz Israel*), or as an additional territorial basis for Israeli security and a bargaining chip in negotiations with the Arabs for a lasting political settlement of the Arab–Israeli conflict.

The large political parties in Israel were unanimous in their opinion that Israel should not withdraw to the pre-war lines ('the Green Line'). There was also wide political agreement that Israel must not allow the creation of a Palestinian state between Israel and Jordan or recognise the PLO; this position was a natural corollary to the fact that Zionist and Israeli leaders had always opposed the principle of national rights for the Palestinians. On these issues there was a national consensus, which continued right up to the signing of the Oslo Agreement and the Israeli recognition of the PLO.

In truth, the Israeli government did not take the full step of accepting the right of Palestinians to form a state of their own. Nevertheless, the recognition of the PLO as the representative of the Palestinian people implied that Israel had crossed a crucial threshold in the direction of what most observers believed to be a step-by-step Israeli acceptance of shared sovereignty over Palestine. Most Western governments now believe that it will become difficult for Israel to oppose the creation of a separate Palestinian state after having accepted the principle that the Palestinians constitute a separate nation and that the PLO is a legitimate political movement in the Occupied Territories.

After 1967, two main trends of thinking crystallised in Israeli politics as far as the occupied areas were concerned, one may be termed 'strategic pragmatism' and the other 'frontier nationalism'. The first trend was essentially formed around the Labour Party, which was in power until 1977; the other was anchored in the coalition of right-wing and national-religious parties which formed the government from then until 1992.

Probably the best-known document conveying the strategic approach was presented in a draft in July 1967 by the late Foreign Minister and Deputy Prime Minister Yigal Allon (of the Labour Party), and hence known as the Allon Plan. Its purpose was to identify the significance of the Territories for Israeli security and strategic needs and come up with suggestions for territorial arrangements. As far as the West Bank and the Gaza Strip were concerned, Allon envisioned a 'territorial compromise' with Jordan. Israel was to appropriate those areas that were of special strategic importance for the country, notably the Jordan Valley rift and the Judaean Desert, while leaving areas heavily populated by Palestinians to Jordan (or a Jordanian-Palestinian state) – with the exception of Jerusalem.[15]

A first concern in the ideology of the Allon Plan was for Israel to establish secure and defensible borders. The West Bank would be well suited as a buffer zone against an Arab invasion from the east. Allon therefore held the opinion that Israel had to secure permanent control over the Jordan Valley as an essential line of defence. The control of Jerusalem was to be secured through a larger annexation of the land surrounding the city. The southern part of the Gaza Strip was also to be annexed to prevent the area from serving as a gateway for a possible Egyptian attack. In the course of 1968, the Israeli government started the construction of semi-military settlements in those zones that the Allon Plan had marked for Israeli annexation.

Second, Israel should not seek to incorporate the Palestinian inhabitants of the Territories, which would weaken Jewish demographic superiority. For the left-wing Zionists, including the Labour Party, this was a concern of the highest priority. They wanted Israel to remain a state for Jews, but they also wanted a democratic state. If these two desires were to be reconciled, then the borders of the Jewish state had to be redrawn in such a way as to include as few non-Jews as possible in the appropriated areas. The Palestinians already constituted approximately 15 per cent of the population of Israel proper. If all the occupied areas were annexed by Israel, this proportion would rise to about 35 per cent, and over time it would increase even more due to the higher

Palestinian birth-rate. If non-Jews were to be granted political
rights equal to those enjoyed by Jews, Israel's identity as a Jewish
state and the natural homeland for world Jewry would be
threatened. If Israel as a state was to remain organised on the basis
of an ethno-political programme, an increase in the percentage of
non-Jews would require a corresponding increase in control
mechanisms and restrictions on the rights of these people.

Then, as now, the dilemma for the Labour Party was that they
wanted to control the land, but not the people of the Occupied
Territories. According to Israeli demographers,

> ... the total number of non-Jewish children born annually in recent years
> in Israel and the territories together, substantially exceeds the number of
> newly born Jewish children. There are, at present, more non-Jewish chil-
> dren than Jewish children under the age of six in Greater Israel.[16]

These statistics do not include the Palestinian refugees either.
Allon's idea of a territorial compromise was an attempt at getting
around this dilemma. For Israel it would of course be an
advantage if they could get King Hussein to keep the Palestinians
in check, rather than having to do the job themselves. However,
things did not go according to Allon's plan.

The other main trend in Israeli politics relevant for our
discussion, that of the right-wing 'frontier nationalism', used the
war of 1967 as basis for a broad mobilisation around the demand
for the creation of a 'Greater Israel'. The war had opened a
window of opportunity to make old Zionist dreams come true and
drastically expand the frontiers of Israel. It was unclear where the
borders were to be drawn, but the projected Greater Israel surely
included the Territories occupied in 1967, while some versions
even included South Lebanon and the present State of Jordan. For
the right-wing Zionists, it did not seem a very relevant point that
Palestinians and other Arabs lived in these areas. In contrast to
the left-wing Zionists, they have always placed more emphasis on
the 'quantitative' aspects of Israel's strength – that is, military and
territorial control – than on the 'qualitative' aspects of Jewish
society and its relation to democratic values. Their view is that
after the Territories have been annexed and power has been
consolidated, the demographic problem can be solved by mass

immigration of Jews and by creating conditions to 'encourage' the emigration of Palestinians – or even by outright ethnic cleansing, such as took place during the war of 1948–49.

When Menachem Begin and the right wing came to power in 1977, the Allon Plan was put aside as a guideline for policy in the Occupied Territories. A new intensive phase in the Israeli politics of expansion was initiated; the long-term objective was to incorporate all of the West Bank and the Gaza Strip into Israel. This colonisation was not limited to strategically exposed areas; policies included efforts to encircle the Palestinian population centres and thus isolate them from each other. The West Bank became riddled with zones for Jewish settlement and the tempo of land confiscation increased (in line with the so-called Drobless Plan of 1981). By creating closed military zones, Israel had within five years obtained direct control over more than 40 per cent of the land area of the West Bank and 30 per cent of the Gaza Strip. These areas were no longer accessible for Palestinian use.

The situation was becoming serious for the Palestinians. From 1947 to 1983, the portion of Palestine under the control of Jewish institutions, and thus closed for Palestinian use, had grown from less than 10 per cent to about 85 per cent. In 1984 Meron Benvenisti, a known Israeli expert on the occupied areas, claimed that an Israeli annexation of the areas was inevitable; the process was irreversible.[17]

What neither Benvenisti nor anyone else envisioned was 'the human factor', the desperate protest by common Palestinians against this development. The PLO's attempt to organise a guerrilla struggle to liberate the homeland had failed. The PLO never represented any military challenge to Israel, and each time they sent a commando group into the country, Israel scored propaganda points in the Western media, especially when PLO actions resulted in civilian casualties. The *fedayin* were not only branded as 'terrorists', but described as the arch-terrorists of our time.

What changed this state of affairs more than anything else were protests by civilian Palestinians, in the form of an uprising (*intifada*) that ignited every remote corner of the Occupied Territories. The symbol of *this* Intifada was fearless stone-throwing youths facing heavily armed Israeli soldiers. But the

Intifada was much more than that; it was the creation of social, cultural and educational institutions, and efforts aimed at economic self-support. The Intifada created the seeds of a new Palestinian civil society. As the years passed, the Intifada took on a life of its own and people tried to make themselves as independent from the occupation and the occupying power as possible. Through a steadily stronger coordination of activities via the PLO in Tunisia, the Intifada actually became a practical framework for the construction of a Palestine state.

Defence Minister Yitzhak Rabin's attempt to crush the uprising became the most difficult war effort he had ever led, and certainly the least successful. The harder the measures he let his soldiers take (like breaking the arms of stone-throwing youths and blowing up their family homes), the more it cost Israel in terms of international support, and the harder and more bitter the resistance grew. An Israeli commando group entered Tunisia in 1988 and assassinated Khalil Wazir (Abu Jihad), the PLO's second-in-command and responsible for the Occupied Territories. Still, the Intifada was not destroyed. A survey dated 5 September 1989 by UNRWA, the United Nations organisation responsible for Palestinian refugees, based on daily reports, revealed that since the outbreak of the Intifada Israeli soldiers had killed 206 people and injured 27,959 – an almost inconceivable number – most of them youths, in the Gaza Strip alone.[18]

As the person responsible for the Israeli military occupation forces and the strategy against the revolt, Rabin met with strong local and international opposition, and was pressured to find a way out of the impasse. The Intifada also made a deep impression upon the Israeli population. Many felt threatened by the revolt and the hatred expressed against Israel as the occupying power, and supported the hard line. Others were shocked by the brutality of the Israeli soldiers and warned that Israel would destroy itself morally if it kept on suppressing another people in such a way. Peace activists in Israel wrote off Rabin as an unusually cynical and brutal leader.

But even Rabin must have realised that a change of course was necessary. In 1992 he ran for election on a programme promising a peace agreement within six to nine months, and received enough trust to form a fragile coalition government. It is well known that

Rabin was reluctant to give his support to the secret negotiations in Oslo. However, according to Avi Shlaim, 'despite his caution, Rabin moved a very long way in a very short time. In June he did not take the Oslo channel at all seriously; in August he wanted to go all the way.'[19] Perhaps only a person with Rabin's credentials as a ruthless defender of Israel's defence interests could sufficiently neutralise the right-wing opposition and bring the Israelis along with him on the journey. The roles of Charles de Gaulle during the war in Algeria and of F. W. de Klerk in South Africa may form tentative parallels.

In Algeria and South Africa a total abolition of, respectively, the French and the white Afrikaner hegemony took place. After 1962, about one million French settlers withdrew from Algeria, which France had for decades tried to integrate as a part of the French state. In South Africa the apartheid regime was abolished as a result of negotiations and democratic elections took place in 1994. F. W. de Klerk has passed through an apparently easy conversion from 'racist' to 'democrat', and became vice-president to his arch-enemy of 27 years, Nelson Mandela.

In the case of Israel and Palestine there is still not much to indicate that Israel intends to surrender real control over the occupied areas, and still less to indicate that it will surrender the Zionist system itself. So far, the peace process from an Israeli point of view is all about normalising Israel's existence in the Middle East. This was particularly important to former prime minister and peace architect Shimon Peres. His vision is that of a 'New Middle East' whereby Israel and the Arab countries develop normal economic, diplomatic and cultural relations. What Peres asks in reality, however, is that the Arabs should give up all economic and political sanctions against Israel; he does not even consider that Israel should give up its system of ethnic hegemony. This is certainly also in line with American thinking.

In this broader strategic picture, the purpose of Palestinian self-rule, from the Israeli point of view, will remain to unburden Israel of the role of direct occupation; it hopes to transfer the politically and economically expensive task of maintaining peace and order to a Palestinian leadership which is loyal to Israel. What Israel needs – and what it has tried for a long time, but in vain, to build up in the Occupied Territories – is a loyal Palestinian leadership with enough authority to be accepted by the Palestinian population. Palestinian self-rule, then, has to be developed subject to and compatible with vital Israeli national interests, particularly in the security field. Israel would not proceed if these conditions of Palestinian self-rule were not laid out by Israel. Rabin was absolutely clear about this before accepting the Oslo Agreement.[20] Perhaps the Israelis believed, and still believe, that the Palestinians can be convinced that this is the best they can achieve, and that the alternative is to become disintegrated as a society. The Israelis may close off the Occupied Territories at any time as a collective punishment with devastating economic consequences for Palestinian workers and a dependent Palestinian economy. In brief, if Israel can convince the Palestinians that they are powerless and will continue to stay powerless, then the Palestinians may realise the futility of further resistance, accept their destiny and contribute to building 'peace' and 'stability' in the Middle East – in the manner that Israel and the United States want them to.

It remains an open question how 'cooperative' Arafat is in the role Israel seems to have defined for him, or how far he may go without cutting himself off totally from his own people. The tug-of-war for Arafat's loyalty continues to rage between his negotiating partners on the one hand and the Palestinian rank and file on the other.

A closer look at the self-government arrangements as they are now unfolding indicates that Israel is leaving little to chance. Israel stresses its claim for control not only through physical and military monitoring and its presence in the Palestinian areas, but also when it comes to the development of the various institutions of the PNA. Parallel to Yasser Arafat's government, a number of joint committees with Israeli and Palestinian representatives have been set up to monitor and coordinate efforts related to the development of Palestinian self-government. Considering all the problems related to the interim arrangements, this may be a natural and necessary structure, but it also gives Israel a good opportunity to influence the practical work involved in establishing a Palestinian structure in such a way that it benefits Israeli interests.

From an Israeli point of view, there is still the risk that the Palestinians may use the restricted self-government they have acquired to arm themselves militarily, politically, institutionally and economically for a future demand for a state that might threaten Israel's security; or even worse, resurrect the dream to liberate all of Palestine. As correctly pointed out by the Israeli right-wing opposing the Oslo accords, Israel's problem in the future might be how to restrict and prevent a Palestinian political entity, which has the sympathy of the world, from developing out of Israel's control, having already recognised the principle of Palestinian national rights. Will not Israel, sooner or later, be forced to grant full equality of rights to the Palestinians? From a Palestinian perspective, this reasoning may warrant Arafat's signing of the Oslo Agreement.

CONCLUSION

It follows from my reasoning above that the time perspective is crucial when we are evaluating the strategic implications of the Oslo accords. The arch-enemies, Israel and the PLO, have openly entered into short-term cooperation in order to build a lasting foundation for what they see as their long-term interests. The parties' long-term objectives are still very much in conflict. The parties can cooperate in the short term because both see it as the only option for realising their long-term objectives. This means that at least one side is making the wrong prophecies, and that the battle ahead will mainly revolve around the question of whose long-term interests will triumph. An important point here is that there are limits to what Israel can attain on the basis of its relative military superiority. The strength of the Palestinians is that they have 'justice' on their side, simply because they have been deprived of fundamental rights. And this deprivation is not made less, or indeed irrelevant, even if we accept that today's oppressors were once the oppressed. Experience shows that a people's perseverance in the battle for their rights can overcome even the strongest superpower.

The Oslo Agreement, then, establishes hopes for a peaceful, eventually even a just solution, but that is not for the foreseeable future. The Agreement indicates a transition from an epoch of total war to – well, to what? Probably a new epoch of conflict, a conflict that in many ways will resemble the conflict in Southern Africa during the time of apartheid. As a dominating settler state in 'an ocean of natives', Israel will probably still feel threatened and hold on tight to its unilaterally proclaimed right of military intervention in the region, demonstrated so many times in the past. The Palestinian self-governed Territories will, at least in the foreseeable future, hardly attain any greater degree of genuine self-government than the black homelands used to have in apartheid South Africa. Israel will undoubtedly seek to incorporate the Palestinian entity into its strategy for economic and military regional dominance. Unless a radical change in the economic and social conditions of the self-governed areas takes place, they will become reservoirs of cheap labour for the Israeli economy. For ordinary Palestinians, life will still be governed by pass laws and nervous, heavily armed Israeli soldiers.

The Oslo Agreement is bad for the Palestinians and good for the Israelis to the extent that it preserves Israeli domination in Palestine and the Middle East. Under the prevailing conditions the Palestinians are unlikely to achieve anything more than a pro forma independent 'Palestinostan', if at all, as the outcome of the projected final stage of the Oslo process. On the other hand, in a wider perspective, the Oslo Agreement may have been the Palestinians' last chance for creating a new infrastructure as the basis for a long-term liberation struggle within Palestine's own borders. An eventual 'apartheid' structure will create a resistance of its own and motivate a new Palestinian vision of liberation.

If we conclude, therefore, that in the long-term perspective, the agreement may be bad for Israel as an exclusive Zionist state and good for the Palestinians and their hopes for real liberation, it is only because the situation for the Palestinian cause after the Gulf war was critical. A new start, however painful and difficult, was needed. The emerging political order in Palestine may indeed resemble an apartheid structure, which in my opinion realistically reflects the nature of the political system in Israel and the current Israeli–Palestinian balance of power. And because it reflects a reality, I believe that this way of describing the situation will, eventually, be accepted – not only by the victims of this development, the Palestinians and Arabs, but also by the West and a growing number of Israelis. This is where I see hope for the future today.

NOTES

1. This chapter is based on my booklet *The Oslo Agreement – Peace on Israel's Conditions?* (Oslo: Gyldendal, 1994; in Norwegian).
2. This is not the first time, I must admit, that the Oslo process has been declared finished and dead. But this time the crisis seems to be deeper than on previous occasions. The last remnants of mutual trust which till now have saved the process have disappeared. A whole new concept for building peace, different from the Oslo strategy, will probably have to be introduced in order to get the political process going again.
3. These figures are based on D. Artz, *Refugees into Citizens: Palestinians and the End of the Arab–Israeli Conflict* (New York: Council on Foreign Relations, 1996), quoted in R. Brynen, 'Imaging a Solution: Final Status Arrangements and Palestinian Refugees in Lebanon', *Journal of Palestine Studies*, Vol. XXVI, No. 2 (1997) p. 54.
4. For a comparison of documents, see Institute for Palestine Studies, *The Palestinian–Israeli Peace Agreement. A Documentary Record* (Washington, D.C.: IPS, 1994). See also Haidar Abdul-Shafi, 'A Political Reading of the Declaration of Principles' in *Challenges Facing the Palestinian Society in the Interim Period* (Jerusalem: Jerusalem Media & Communication Centre, 1994).
5. See Jane Corbin, *Gaza First – the secret Norway channel to peace between Israel and the PLO* (London: Bloomsbury Publishing, 1994); Nils Butenschøn, 'The Oslo Agreement in Norwegian Foreign Policy', *CIMES Occasional Papers* (Durham: Centre for Islamic and Middle Eastern Studies, University of Durham, 1997).
6. In the agreement, 'withdrawal' is used only to designate the Israeli withdrawal from Gaza and Jericho. Future withdrawals from the Occupied Territories are termed 'redeployment' in order not to 'prejudice' future negotiations on the final status of the Territories.
7. For a discussion of the elections, see N. Butenschøn and K. Vollan (eds), 'Interim Democracy: Report on the Palestinian Elections 1996', *Human Rights Report No. 6* (Oslo: Norwegian Institute of Human Rights, 1996). See also articles by L. Andoni and K. Shikaki in *Journal of Palestine Studies*, Vol. XXV, No. 3 (Spring 1996).
8. Annex II, Agreed Minutes to the Declaration of Principles on Interim Self-Government Arrangement.
9. As a right-wing coalition under the leadership of Benjamin Netanyahu came to power in Israel in May 1996 on an anti-Oslo platform, these negotiations were postponed indefinitely.
10. N. H. Aruri, 'Early Empowerment: The Burden Not the Responsibility', *Journal of Palestine Studies*, Vol. XXIV, No. 2 (1995) p. 39.
11. For a discussion of the founding of the PLO see for example H. Cobban, *The Palestinian Liberation Organisation. People, Power and Politics* (Cambridge: Cambridge University Press, 1984).
12. M. Muslih, 'Towards Coexistence: An Analysis of the Resolutions of the Palestine National Council', *Journal of Palestine Studies*, Vol. XIX, No. 4 (1990). See also Alain Gresh, *The PLO: The Struggle Within* (London and New Jersey: Zed Books, 1988).
13. Quoted in A. Gresh, *The PLO*, p. 32.

14. The political outcome of the October War did not become apparent until the Camp David Agreements in 1978 and the Israeli–Egyptian peace treaty of 1979.

15. For a discussion of the Allon Plan, see for example M. A. Heller, *A Palestinian State: The Implications for Israel* (Cambridge, MA: Harvard University Press, 1993) pp. 34–7.

16. Jaffee Center for Strategic Studies, *The West Bank and Gaza: Israel's Options for Peace* (Tel Aviv: Jaffee Center for Strategic Studies, 1989) p. 204.

17. M. Benvenisti, *The West Bank Data Project. A Survey of Israel's Policies* (Washington and London: American Enterprise Institute for Public Policy Research, 1984).

18. Quoted in T. Anda, 1989, *Intifada – Opprør mot Israel* (Oslo: Universitetsforlaget, 1989; in Norwegian) p. 48.

19. A. Shlaim, 'The Oslo Accord', *Journal of Palestine Studies*, Vol. XXIII, No. 3 (1994) p. 32.

20. See for example A. Shlaim, 'The Oslo Accord', p. 32.

3   THE OSLO PROCESS AND
THE ARAB WORLD

Fouad Moughrabi

INTRODUCTION

This chapter will examine the impact of what is commonly
referred to as the 'peace process' on the Arab region. Egypt and
Jordan have already signed peace agreements with Israel. The
Palestinians have also signed several agreements and are in a
continuous negotiating mode with the Israeli government. Most
Arab governments, including Syria, have decided that a peaceful
settlement of the conflict with Israel is a strategic objective. Some
of them have opened their borders to Israeli tourists, signed joint
ventures with Israeli companies and permitted the Israeli government to open trade and diplomatic offices. Others have adopted a
wait-and-see attitude. Some have slowed the process of normalisation as a protest against Israeli intransigence. With some excep-
tions, however, the majority of the public in most Arab countries
remains mostly hostile to a normalisation of relations with Israel.

Arab reaction, both at the level of governments and of public
opinion, is conditioned by several factors. One is the nature of
peace. Is it peace based on territorial compromise or on the
absolute security requirements of the Israeli government? Will the
people of the region benefit from peace and if so, how? A second
factor is that the nature of government response differs from that
of the public. The governments are being pressured by international agencies to engage in structural adjustment, to privatise
their economies and to enact liberal economic reforms. As a result,
large sectors of Arab society suffer severe dislocation, unemployment and higher levels of deprivation.

New York Times columnist Thomas Friedman, reflecting the prevailing view among American policy-makers, argues that those who

are frustrated by this new restructuring turn to Islamic fundamentalism, take to the streets and denounce their governments' relations with Israel because that is 'the most effective and evocative way to delegitimise the regime for raising bread prices'. Friedman goes on to say that the governments respond by distancing themselves from Israel without lowering the price of bread.

There is no question that Arab governments have historically used anti-Israel sentiment as a cynical way to gain legitimacy in the eyes of their public. At the same time, however, Arab governments have suffered a serious crisis of legitimacy which has more to do with the kinds of socio-economic and political policies they have pursued than with their failure to challenge Israeli aggression. How accurate is it to claim that a critical attitude towards Israel on the part of Arab public opinion derives from feelings of frustration resulting from efforts at restructuring? This paper will analyse these complex factors and try to make some projections for the future.

TO NORMALISE OR NOT?

Less than one week after the signing of the Hebron Agreement, a full-page advertisement appeared in the *New York Times* with the headline 'Peace' in English, Hebrew and Arabic, and the slogan, 'It's a beautiful sight to see.' It seems that Israel, Jordan and the Palestinian Authority had teamed up to reassure American tourists that their countries were safe, wondrous and beautiful. The advertisement reads: 'Children are playing in the parks of Jerusalem', and 'There is a new spirit in the streets of Bethlehem.' One could see 'Welcome to Jordan' in the smiles of every shopkeeper in Amman. The Israeli Minister of Tourism was convinced that Egypt would also join the effort. The Jordanian government had apparently invested a considerable amount of money in new facilities and in training programmes in anticipation of waves of tourists following its peace treaty with Israel.

Should peace break out, tourism could bring obvious advantages to the countries of the region. Given the nature of present arrangements, however, it is more likely that an economically advanced Israel will benefit significantly more than the Arab countries. One analyst recently concluded that, in the absence of proactive planning and Arab coordination, 'Israel will get the tourists and will determine how long, how much and where they spend their tourist dollars. The Arabs will get day trippers at most. Most tourists will come to Israel and make short forays into Arab land. The Jordanians are already experiencing some of the negative effects of this arrangement.'[1]

Prior to the Israeli elections which brought the Likud back to power, several important developments occurred as a result of the 'peace process'. On 27 May 1996, a Tunisian interest group opened an office in Tel Aviv and an Israeli trade mission opened in Qatar. On the same day, an Israeli trade delegation arrived in Oman to discuss trade and economic links. Indeed, it seemed for a while, that the gates of the Arab world were opening wide for relations with Israel. The process of normalisation, which Israel and the United States government have been insisting on, appeared to be moving even more rapidly than expected, as various Arab governments and Arab businesspeople hurriedly tried to cultivate new relations and to strike new deals with the State of Israel. So far, publicly acknowledged deals are limited. Some analysts, however, maintain that there are quite a few deals which have been made discreetly and others that are still in the planning stages. Salem Jubran, a well-informed Palestinian journalist, suggests that some of the deals involve shadow companies set up in Europe or in the United States. Jubran quotes an Israeli economist from Haifa University who claims that Israeli exports to the Arab countries had reached nearly six billion dollars by 1996.

After Netanyahu's election, however, Algeria, Qatar and Tunisia said that they would consider slowing, but not reversing, the process of normalisation with Israel. During the Arab Summit on 22 June 1996, Egypt, Oman, Qatar and Syria agreed to link future normalisation with progress in the 'peace process'. Qatar cancelled the opening of a trade office in Israel but agreed to let the Israeli trade mission in Doha issue visas to Qatari businessmen who wish to travel to Israel. Tunisia followed through with plans to send a mission to Israel to investigate business prospects. On 21 July 1996 Egypt signed a deal with Israel to build an oil refinery in Alexandria and Oman opened a trade office in Tel Aviv on 11

August 1996. Finally, King Hassan of Morocco turned down a
request from the new Israeli prime minister to stop in Rabat on
his way back from Washington. The king apparently informed the
Israelis that he would meet with Netanyahu only after the latter
had met with President Yasser Arafat.

In June 1996, the first Arab Summit since the Gulf war took
place in Cairo. Sponsored by Egypt, Syria and Saudi Arabia, the
Summit was attended by 21 Arab leaders, excluding Iraq, which
was not invited. Syria wanted the Summit to adopt a statement
which called for an end to normalisation if Israel backed away
from 'land for peace' as a basis for negotiations. Jordan, Oman,
Qatar, Morocco and Tunisia apparently objected. The Summit
issued a statement which was deemed stronger than expected but
which fell short of calling for an end to normalisation. The
Summit communiqué (23 June 1996) stated the following key
points: a comprehensive and just peace in the Middle East
requires Israel's complete withdrawal from all occupied Palestinian territories, including Arab Jerusalem, enabling the Palestinian
people to exercise their right to self-determination and to establish
an independent state with Arab Jerusalem as its capital; the
withdrawal of Israeli forces from the Golan Heights to the 4 June
1967 line and full and unconditional Israeli withdrawal from
Southern Lebanon and the western Biqa; any violation by Israel of
these principles and bases on which the peace process is founded,
any retraction of the commitments, pledges and agreements
reached within the framework of this process, or any vacillation in
implementing them will set back the peace process and will entail
dangers and consequences that will plunge the region back into a
spiral of tension and will compel all the Arab countries to
reconsider the steps they have taken toward Israel within the
framework of the peace process.

Although what we have here are some admittedly fragmentary
developments, they do constitute some kind of trend. Some tentative
conclusions may, therefore, be drawn. In the first place, there is no
doubt that old Arab attitudes towards Israel have changed in a radical manner. Some of the Arab countries appear to be anxious to jump
over political obstacles in order to plunge into a new world. Others
are more hesitant. Therefore, there is a differential rate of change
among the various Arab countries. Despite this, however, Israeli

economic penetration of the Arab world is already deep enough to make it difficult to reverse. Some of the Arab countries can slow down the process but they are not likely to reverse it. In the second place, one must distinguish between states and people. Despite having signed a peace treaty with Israel, both Egypt and Jordan find significant opposition at the popular level to the process of normalisation. The same is true elsewhere in the Arab world where varying levels of popular opposition exist. In the third place, opposition to normalisation does not necessarily mean opposition to peace with Israel. There is enough evidence to suggest that the desire for peace among the Arabs is strongly and universally held. In addition, there is a generalised feeling that the tragic conflict between Israel and the Arabs must come to an honourable end in order to permit people to proceed with their search for economic growth and development.

What constitutes an honourable end to this conflict? How can we assess Arab reaction to the Oslo Agreements both at the level of governments and at the popular level? What projections can be made into the future?

THE ARAB RESPONSE: STATE AND SOCIETY

There is an Arab consensus concerning the modalities of resolving the conflict with Israel: the Palestinian dimension is still the core of the conflict. Most people in the region are willing to accept a settlement that includes Israeli withdrawal to the 1967 lines, the emergence of a sovereign independent Palestinian state with East Jerusalem as its capital, and the right of the refugees to return or to be compensated. In addition, most Arabs would like to see an Israeli withdrawal from the occupied Golan Heights and Southern Lebanon.

Most Arabs realise that the balance of power is such that Israel, which has nuclear weaponry, may be able to defeat all the Arab armies combined in conventional warfare. In other words, there is a conviction that a military solution to this conflict is simply out of the range of possibilities. In addition, there is a conviction that Israel is here to stay for the foreseeable future. Most people are willing to accept Israel as one of the states in the region but they are not willing to accept it as the hegemonic power. Consequently, some Arabs look with some anxiety at Israel's desire to penetrate the region economically and to become the dominant power. They view projections of a new Middle East as a way for Israel and other non-Arab countries (Turkey and perhaps Iran) to establish control over the Arab region.

There is a reluctance on the part of a variety of governments and business interests in the Arab world to link normalisation with Israel to the process of resolving the conflict with the Palestinians or with Syria and Lebanon. By all expectations, the next stage in the process of negotiation between Israel and the Palestinians will be extremely difficult. Issues such as Jerusalem, refugees, settlements and borders are the crux of the problem. In the negotiations with Syria and Lebanon, the issue of withdrawal from the Golan Heights and from Southern Lebanon, will be equally difficult. Here one must ask: how will the Arab governments react to Israeli intransigence on these matters?

To answer this question, one must first examine the nature of the Arab state system and its links with the global economy. In the first place, there is a serious crisis of legitimacy in the contemporary Arab world. The various states have failed miserably in their efforts at political and economic integration and development. Half-hearted efforts at democratisation have been halted and, in some cases, seriously reversed. Most of the regimes rest on a narrow social base and rely upon their armies and security apparatuses to enforce order. In the second place, the Arab countries are about to enter the twenty-first century in a state of deep economic crisis. For example, the Middle East is currently the 'least food self-sufficient area in the world'. In fact, all countries in the Middle East and North Africa with the possible exception of Mauritania, Morocco and Israel are net importers of food. Bromley argues that most of the regimes are entering 'a period of profound uncertainty as they adapt to pressures of structural adjustment and economic liberalisation'. He anticipates some success in some areas but the outlook for the populous states such as Egypt is rather bleak. It appears to be equally bleak even for the smaller oil-producing states. In the third place, there is

... a small elite which subsists at levels fully comparable to those of the West, but for the majority of the population in the region as a whole their poverty is exceeded only by that of the peoples of sub-Saharan Africa and the least developed parts of Asia.[2]

Except for Israel, which has recently surpassed some European countries in achieving a high per capita income, the overall economic picture for the region is therefore not very encouraging. In general, the countries of the region have participated less than those of other regions in the globalisation and integration of international capital markets. However, the flow of private capital has occurred more in countries which have embraced structural adjustment. This includes Egypt, Israel, Jordan, Morocco and Tunisia.[3]

The region trades mostly with the countries of the European Union (30 per cent of exports and 40 per cent of imports), with the United States (12 per cent of the region's exports and imports), and with Japan (16 per cent of exports and 8 per cent of imports). Intra-regional trade remains minuscule, accounting for 8 per cent of both exports and imports. Non-oil exports account for approximately a quarter of the region's exports, with Israel accounting for nearly half of this total.

The countries of the Middle East and North Africa experienced during the 1989–94 period an annual rate of population growth of about 3 per cent. This rate is higher in Kuwait, Libya, Oman, Qatar, Saudi Arabia and the United Arab Emirates. On the other hand, Iran, Bahrain, Lebanon and Tunisia have a rate below the 2 per cent mark which is the average for developing countries. For several countries, more than half the population is under the age of 15. At the same time, unemployment figures are higher than in other developing countries, except for the oil-producing countries of the Gulf Cooperation Council. Unemployment rates are over 30 per cent in Yemen and more than 50 per cent in the Gaza Strip.

There is a generalised feeling among policy-makers in the region that major reforms are needed before it can overcome the economic stagnation that has prevailed for several years. If such reforms are undertaken, and if a comprehensive, just and durable peace in the Middle East is achieved, it is quite likely that the region may enjoy a substantial peace dividend. So far, however, it is safe to say that the majority of the people in the region have not experienced the benefits of peace. In some cases, as in the Palestinian one, there has been a major deterioration in living conditions.

The mixed nature of Arab reaction to the 'peace process', which the rush to normalise relations with Israel indicates, belies some serious underlying fissures in the Arab state system. The Gulf crisis of 1990 in fact put an end to the old dreams of Arab unity. There is a generalised feeling that each country or, in some cases, each group of countries will have to fend for themselves. The countries of the Gulf continue to be afraid of Iran and feel safer in putting their fate in the US's hands. In this sense, they are more open to dealings with Israel, a country which they see as a potential strategic ally against Iran. Other countries, such as Tunisia, which have adopted structural reforms and which have become more connected with the global economy, see possibilities in improving trade with a vigorous Israeli economy. Similarly, Jordan, which has always been in a strategic alliance with Israel, wants to benefit from the new climate. Egypt, by contrast, is an entirely different issue altogether. Egyptian policy-makers see Egypt's role in a different way. They are opposed to Israel's attempts to establish economic relations with the region before the achievement of a just, comprehensive and durable peace. They will not tolerate an Israel which acts as a Prussia in the region; but they are willing to accept Israel as one of the many states in the area. In addition, Egyptian policy-makers will honour their peace agreement with Israel and will make some deals with Israeli companies in areas that benefit the Egyptian economy. They do not feel, however, that they have to embrace trade with Israel as a way of showing good intentions. And finally, Egyptian policy-makers are responsive to their public opinion, which so far has opted against normalisation of relations with Israel. Egypt suffered numerous casualties during its wars with Israel, including the deliberate killing of Egyptian prisoners of war by the Israelis.

As we prepare to enter the twenty-first century, the Middle East region stands at an important crossroads. Two clear options exist: on the one hand, the countries of the region can embark on major social, political and economic reforms in order to meet the legitimate aspirations of their populations. In addition, a comprehensive, just and durable peace may help legitimate this process and could produce a significant peace dividend. Or, they can continue on their present path of socio-economic and political stagnation along with a limited, unjust and temporary peace and, in the process, produce more costly and highly debilitating internal and perhaps even regional conflicts.

WHAT PROSPECTS FOR THE FUTURE?

It is by now quite clear that structural adjustment has become the new development paradigm. In a region dominated by the United States and highly dependent on the advanced economies, most of the Arab countries are embracing this new paradigm with all of its negative consequences: immense economic hardship for the poor, sharp increases in unemployment, declining access to public services, an exacerbation of existing inequalities in the distribution of wealth, and sharp increases in the cost of basic commodities such as food. In most countries, infant mortality rates have risen and levels of nutrition have fallen. Austerity measures usually lead to popular unrest (food riots in Jordan, for example) which is followed by even more political repression.

The sharp increase in levels of impoverishment comes at a time when some of the Arab countries are trying to resolve the Arab–Israeli conflict and to move towards what is called 'normalisation' of relations with Israel. This means that for a large sector of these societies the benefits of peace are highly questionable. Imagine how a Jordanian father who is unemployed and unable to feed his family feels when he sees hordes of Israeli tourists spending money freely and staying at luxury hotels in his country? This man is very likely to be a Palestinian whose family lost its land and home in 1948 and has lived in a refugee camp since then. He may even have relatives who were killed by Israelis. This man may have worked in Kuwait for many years and been able to provide for his family. Now he is stuck in Jordan with a large family, no money, no prospect of employment, unable to educate his children or to find decent medical care for them. As a Palestinian refugee who lost home and land in 1948, he sees that the prospect of returning or of being compensated appears dimmer than ever before.

This man may have been a conservative, non-practising Muslim most of his life. He may have fasted during the month of Ramadan and prayed on some occasions. Now, he finds that the only groups which advocate an improvement in his life and who speak on his behalf are the Muslim opposition groups. He joins one of them because they can provide him with a modicum of a safety net. They may offer him some basic foodstuffs, or some medical care in their volunteer clinics, or education for his children in their schools. He therefore becomes what is now commonly referred to as a 'Muslim fundamentalist'. He is opposed to 'normalisation' with Israel. He knows that the Israelis are the only ones who seem to be benefiting from the new 'peace'. These are the same people who have wronged him in the past and continue to deprive his people of their basic rights. He dreams of being able to pray in the Al-Aqsa Mosque in Jerusalem but knows deep down that he may never be able to do so. He simply does not wish to see Israelis roaming around his country, acting like the new privileged rulers of the world, while he and his family languish in poverty.

By contrast, imagine a businessman in Jordan, who may also be a Palestinian and who drives a Mercedes. He probably graduated from an American university years ago with an MBA. He has acquired what is known as a pragmatic outlook on life. He reads analyses by the World Bank and the IMF and seems to be convinced that structural adjustment is a necessary thing. He sees opportunities for trade and joint projects with Israeli companies. He may have invested in a textile plant which uses cheap Jordanian labour and materials to produce Gucci shirts for an Israeli manufacturer to be sold on the lucrative American market. He and his Israeli counterpart have a great deal in common; they speak the same language and share the same interest, which is to make money. He thinks this kind of activity will eventually filter down to people in the form of new investments and new jobs. He lives in one of Amman's new villas and travels overseas for shopping trips. He may even cross the Jordan River to go shopping at the Jerusalem Mall in Jewish West Jerusalem.. The house and land that he lost in 1948 have become a dim memory. For him life must go on and one cannot go back to the past. One must seize the new opportunities if one wants to prosper in the new climate.

This man has seen a slight increase in his living expenses. But he is making so much money that he hardly feels it. He is able to send his children to study in the United States where tuition and living expenses may run up to $25,000 a year or more. These children are able to return home for vacations once or twice a year.

The family takes at least one vacation during the year to some European country. This businessman thinks that his less fortunate counterpart poses a threat to his existence, is too radical in his demands and that he simply does not understand the complex new realities of the modern world.

An alliance between the new elites in both business and politics has produced in this era what may be called a pro-American lobby in the Arab world. This lobby wants to incorporate the economies of the Arab world into the global economy and is eager to implement the kinds of structural reforms that the World Bank and the International Monetary Fund are calling for. In addition, this lobby is vulnerable to political pressure from the US government. It is therefore willing to accommodate American insistence on normalisation of economic and political relations with the State of Israel, even in the absence of progress on the peace settlement front. The American logic is that such normalisation will create new facts and trends that will be difficult to reverse. In other words, the various Arab countries will have such a vested interest in economic relations with Israel that they will be willing to make the needed compromises.

The Arab elites, however, are cautious. On the one hand, they try to accommodate American insistence on creating more openings to Israel. They know that economic normalisation is likely to benefit Israel, which is by far the strongest and most developed economy in the region, more than their own economies. This means that the steps taken by various Arab countries are, in fact, more political than economic in nature. On the other hand, the Arab elites are worried that Israel's rigid position on key issues – the status of Jerusalem, the issue of the refugees, the issue of water resources, and the question of withdrawal from the Golan Heights and from Lebanon – may end up sabotaging the peace process. This will throw the region back into an explosive political situation. In this case, vulnerable Arab regimes, which are facing serious challenges from various opposition forces, may end up being overthrown.

There is a serious crisis of legitimacy in the Arab world. Even countries such as Saudi Arabia, once deemed stable and reasonably secure, are now facing mounting opposition. Two key factors are likely to compound this crisis. The first is the failure to produce a comprehensive, just and durable peace whose effects are felt at the popular level, leading to an improvement in peoples' lives. The second is the effect of social and economic dislocation resulting from the incorporation of the countries of the region into the global economy. Historically, the various Arab governments engaged in economic and political development schemes which effectively benefited the few at the expense of the majority. Large segments of their populations had been marginalised. During the era of petro-dollars when thousands of workers from the poor countries were able to work in the Gulf and send back remittances, the relative economic boom managed to hide underlying problems resulting from inequities in the distribution of goods and services. Now, with overall economic decline, these problems are coming to the surface and they are compounded by new pressures leading to mass impoverishment. Unless major reforms are undertaken, the political map of the region will probably be radically altered in the near future.

Palliative solutions, which fall under the category of symbolic politics, such as occasionally removing some officials charged with corruption (now fashionable in many Arab countries) are simply not enough. More substantive reforms are needed, including a move toward more democratic reform of archaic systems of governance and a more equitable distribution of income.

Are these various regimes able to respond to these challenges? Three options exist. One is the traditional repressive mode which these regimes have adopted for several decades. It appears to be the most likely approach that these governments will follow in response to the new challenges posed by the factors outlined in this paper. The second is the reform mode. Here one is more likely to see limited attempts at reform such as trying to curb some of the more visible and outrageous signs of corruption by public officials. Other aspects, however, will remain untouched. The third approach relies on radical transformation of existing systems of governance which means more violence, civil wars and intercommunal tension. This approach, already evident in some cases, is likely to spread as economic and social conditions deteriorate further. The Arab governments are most likely to adopt a combination of the repressive and the reform modes with more emphasis on the former. This means that conditions for the third mode are likely to develop even further.

CONCLUSION

What conclusions can we draw? The existing Arab state system is characterised by the persistence of archaic political structures and deep socio-political cleavages. In addition, the economic performance of the region lags behind that of most developing countries. In this environment, two major factors are being introduced: a peace process which aims to produce a comprehensive settlement of outstanding issues in the Arab–Israeli conflict, and a profound, fast-moving set of changes in the international economic environment including rapid movement towards liberalisation, globalisation and productivity-driven international competitiveness.

The peace process has led to some attempts at normalisation between Arab countries and Israel, including trade deals and joint ventures. Overall, these measures have so far benefited Israel, which is by far the strongest and most developed economy in the region. In the future, these steps will continue to benefit Israel more. In the area of tourism, for example, the Israelis will reap the majority of benefits from tourists who will fly into the country, spend most of their money there and take quick side trips to Arab sites. This means that the average person in the Arab world is not likely to benefit to a substantial degree from the peace process.

In addition, it appears more likely that the peace process itself, fundamentally flawed as it is, may indeed stall. As a result, the region could easily slide into tension and confrontation as the Israeli government of Mr Netanyahu proceeds with its current intransigent policy. Netanyahu's approach, which seems to be fully endorsed by the US government, relies upon the following conditions, the first being that Israeli security is an overarching requirement. There is to be no negotiation over Jerusalem and rapid occupation of the Arab part of the city with new Jewish settlements. A campaign of ethnic cleansing must be designed to drastically reduce the demographic presence of the Palestinians in the city. There will be no withdrawal from the Golan Heights and Syria must accept peace without land. Finally, there will be no withdrawal from any of the Jewish settlements in the West Bank as, instead, these settlements are expanded and more land is confiscated to the point where a settlement with the Palestinians may only amount to at the most a fifty–fifty sharing of the West Bank. It is difficult to foresee any progress on the peace front in view of the arbitrary conditions imposed by the Israeli government, and endorsed by the United States.

It is highly unlikely that a comprehensive, just and durable peace will be arrived at in the near future. Whatever peace dividend could have been generated is therefore not likely to materialise. The region will continue to be the most heavily armed area of the developing world. Possibilities of regional and internal conflict will continue to exist.

Possibilities of regional cooperation by the Arab countries, called for by the last Arab Summit, remain hypothetical at best. Inter-Arab trade is minuscule despite the existence of unusually favourable opportunities for integration. Political considerations continue to obstruct plans for regional Arab economic integration.

Arab countries are likely to continue the process of structural adjustment advocated by the International Monetary Fund and the World Bank. Unless major reforms are undertaken at the same time, however, the levels of impoverishment are likely to increase, making the region even more ripe for political turmoil and instability. Given the crisis of legitimacy and the enduring cleavages in Arab countries, it is more likely that the political map of the region will, in the coming few years, look quite different from what it currently is.

NOTES

1. Atif Kubrusi, 'The Economics of Peace: The Arab Response' in *Regional Economic Development in the Middle East: Opportunities and Risks* (Washington, D.C.: The Center for Policy Analysis on Palestine, 1995).
2. Simon Bromley, *Rethinking the Middle East* (Austin, Texas: The University of Texas Press, 1994) p. 172.
3. Mohammed El-Arian et al., *Growth and Stability in the Middle East and North Africa* (Washington, D.C.: The International Monetary Fund, 1996) p. 2.

4 A PEACE WITHOUT ARABS: THE DISCOURSE OF PEACE AND THE LIMITS OF ISRAELI CONSCIOUSNESS

Amnon Raz-Krakotzkin

In many ways the Oslo Accord marks a radical change in the Israeli political arena. From the Israeli point of view, the decision of the Labour government to recognise the PLO as the representative of the Palestinian people, and the meeting of Prime Minister Rabin with Arafat, were dramatic and revolutionary steps which reflected a change in the attitude towards the Palestinian question. It was not only a change of policy, but the breaking of a taboo. For many years, the demonisation of the PLO was an essential factor in the construction of Israeli consciousness. It played a role in designing and maintaining the image of Israel as a peaceful and innocent community attacked by demonic evil. It was a taboo which served in defining the borders of the Israeli consensus. Seeing the PLO as the representative of an ultimate evil was a source of legitimacy for the occupation and a motivation for the continuing settlement activity by both Labour and Likud governments. At the time that the Declaration of Principles was signed in 1993, all relations with PLO members were forbidden by law.

Representatives of the so-called 'peace camp' accepted the signing of the agreement with euphoria and enthusiasm, describing the event as 'the end of a hundred years of conflict' and the beginning of a new, redemptive age – the age of peace. The agreement was considered as an historical compromise, one which would inevitably lead to the establishment of a Palestinian state and to the 'solution' of the Palestinian question.

Many of those who had been struggling for years – in one way or another – against the occupation, celebrated what they considered to be their final and ultimate victory. For many others, who were used to the continued propaganda which demonised the PLO, it was shocking and confusing. Others on the right, and especially amongst the settlers, saw in this new beginning the collapse of their dreams and visions. And indeed, Rabin's very decision to negotiate with Arafat demanded a reformulation of the political debate, as well as a real psychological change.

Yet on the other hand, the dramatic decision did not reflect a change in how the conflict or the PLO were perceived by Israelis. The new policy was accepted, not because a new consciousness had evolved but because it seemed the only way to fulfil the long-standing political aspirations of Israel and to salvage the self-image which defined Israeli culture. Paradoxically, the terms of the Oslo Accord and the shift in the attitude towards the PLO were accepted by many Israelis because it helped them to preserve their identity and political goals. Israeli politicians involved in the negotiations did not present a different attitude towards the Palestinians to the Israeli public, but rather claimed that it was the PLO and Arafat who had changed.

The Israeli ambivalence can be understood by looking at the political attitude of Yitzhak Rabin himself. For the former chief of staff and defence minister, the shift in attitude towards the PLO was indeed unexpected. Yet it was not a result of a rethinking of the relationship between Jews and Palestinians but an understanding that this was an opportunity to achieve what he always considered to be Israel's interests. Although he regarded it as a terrorist organisation, Rabin's rejection of the PLO was not sentimental but a result of his conviction that negotiations with its representatives would lead to undermining what he considered Israel's strategic needs. In his memoirs he commented on a meeting he had when serving as prime minister in the 1970s with Matti Peled, a former general in his headquarters, who later became one of the first Israelis to meet with PLO leaders and to participate in the struggle for a two-state solution. Peled came to inform him about his talks with delegates of the PLO at a time when such talks were totally prohibited. Rabin did not regard Peled as a traitor, however, and his attitude to the subject was not emotional. But he thought that Peled's direction was not realistic and could not be accepted on the political level since it contradicted Israeli strategic interests.[1]

Rabin only changed his mind and agreed to come to an agreement with the PLO after the change in global-political reality and when he realised that this was a better way to serve the same strategic interests. Rabin was a follower of Yigal Allon, who after the 1967 war outlined a plan according to which the district of Jerusalem, as well as parts of the Hebron district and the Jordan Valley, would be kept under Israeli sovereignty. The remaining territory, according to this plan, would become an autonomous Palestinian area, with a link to Jordan. Rabin considered the Oslo framework to be one which would enable him to achieve, via different tactics, the policy he had always favoured. The decision to negotiate with Arafat was therefore based on the principles which he had always held and which directed his previous actions.

In itself this does not lessen in any way the implications of the accord both for the Israeli–Palestinian arena and particularly for the internal Israeli debate. Yet it enables us to define the parameters of the debate and its limits, and sheds light on the conflicting views within Israel.

The peace process has sharpened and reformulated the internal political disputation, which became at least temporarily violent, a development which reached its climax with the assassination of Rabin. Israel is divided into two camps in relation to political issues, especially regarding the Palestinian question: the left (or 'peace camp') versus the right (or 'national camp'). Yet, despite the very important differences between the supporters of the process and its opponents (differences which will be discussed later), it would be wrong to regard this debate as being between two different attitudes towards the Palestinian question. The debate reflects two different approaches to the question of Jewish sovereignty in Palestine and is formulated by two different terminologies. Yet, in spite of the significant differences, both camps share some basic assumptions. The prevailing distinction between supporters and opponents of the process is therefore misleading as it prevents a true examination of the attitude of those who enthusiastically support the process and regard it as the end of the conflict.

In general, the two approaches represent the two different
political languages in which Israeli culture is conducted: the
terminology of traditional religious language and the terminology of modern liberal discourse. The combination of these two
languages determines Zionist political culture in all its
appearances, while in each camp the emphasis is of course
different. The tension between these two sets of vocabulary
stands at the centre of many of the conflicts and contradictions
of Israeli culture. Yet it would be wrong to regard these
terminologies as strictly corresponding to each of the two
camps. True, they are used to reflect different attitudes, yet the
so-called liberal conception is also dependent on theological
terminology, as will be discussed later.

A close examination of the debate over the Oslo Accord shows
that first and foremost it was a debate over the values and definitions
of Israeli society. The enthusiasm with which the peace process was
received by liberal circles in Israel was not because of a belief that it
signified a real compromise between Israel and the Palestinians or
the recognition of the civil and national rights of the Palestinians,
but rather because it seemed to signify an opportunity to get rid of
them and consequently to recreate the concept of the 'vacant land'.
This view of the land as uninhabited was one of the main motifs of
Zionist historical consciousness. The various discourses which constitute Israeli culture regarded the land as though it had no history
outside its role in the Jewish myth and actively disregarded the 'non-
Jewish population'.

The debate continued and intensified the basic tensions which
characterise Israeli society and exposed some of the contradictions
within Zionist consciousness. It is therefore impossible to separate it
from the discussion of other aspects of the Zionist context: between
religious and secular Jews and between Ashkenazi Jews (of European
origin) and Mizrachi Jews (who immigrated from Arab countries).
The debate over the Palestinians was part of these disputations.

THE FULFILMENT OF THE ZIONIST UTOPIA

Following the signing of the Oslo Agreement, many writers,
supporters of the 'process', described their images of peace,

depicting different aspects of an imagined Middle East which they believed would be realised in the immediate future. The visions contained descriptions of prosperity, of open markets, of high-tech industry, large roads and economic development, of restaurants in Damascus and projects in Jordan. The event was considered to be the beginning of a new and redemptive era, paving the path for the fulfilment of all wishes.

However, none of the images and visions were concerned with the fate and the future of a single child in a refugee camp. The future of Gaza played only a secondary role in the various dreams and utopian images. It was not the realisation of the Palestinians' rights which was celebrated by the Israelis in Oslo but the full accomplishment of Zionism. The agreement, it seems, became a golden opportunity to return to the image of innocence. Zionism could once again be conceived by its believers to be free of injustice. The Oslo Accord gave them back their original notion of themselves, a notion which had survived until 1967 and, to a certain extent, up to the Intifada in 1988. The Intifada disturbed the self-image of the Israelis, undermining their image of themselves as victims, an image which was central to their consciousness. It altered their habitual disregard of the Palestinians and forced them to consider their rights in any discussion of 'Israeli-ness'. The Palestinian uprising emphasised the contradiction between the Israeli self-image and the reality of occupation, confiscation and brutality. This led more and more Israelis to the conclusion that there could be no solution except through negotiations with the PLO. Only under these circumstances, and not earlier, was this attitude adopted by many in the liberal camp. Until the late 1980s, bodies like Meretz (the party representing the 'Zionist left') and Peace Now did not recognise the PLO and did not accept the two-state solution. They accepted it only when they realised that this was the sole way to restore the previous images of their existence.

The most interesting point to observe here is the resemblance of the utopian images attributed to the 'peace' which was conceived in Oslo to images of the initial Zionist utopias. From its appearance in the late nineteenth century, Zionist culture produced many utopian visions, in which various ideals were

presented. These visions usually ignored the place where they
had to be actualised, namely Palestine and its population. The
images embedded in these visions played an important role in
the process of nation-building and in determining its cultural
values. Their authors imagined a new Jewish community in an
empty land, an idealistic Western society in which a new type of
Jew – emancipated, strong and productive – lived in an
'authentic' and 'progressive' way.[2] Popular songs about 'peace'
described prosperity in a land which is exclusively Jewish.
'Peace' was interpreted as not only the end of war but also the
termination of the 'enemy', its total disappearance. The Zionist
discourse retained the Palestinians only as 'a problem', a natural
disaster.[3] They were not considered an integral part of the
discourse on Zionist-Israeli identity. When they appear in the
description of the utopias, as in Theodor Herzl's *Altneuland*
('Old New Land', 1903), they are presented as natives, grateful
to the colonisers who will improve their circumstances.[4] This
can be regarded as a typical example of colonialist discourse. In
the 'classical' Zionist attitude, as it developed from the 1920s,
even this element was missing. The present was considered as
the return of the Jews to their homeland, and there was no
consideration of the land itself and its population. Palestinians
had been excluded from the vision long before their actual
expulsion, during the war in 1948, and their continuous
dispossession later.

The consciousness which led to the peace process can be
deciphered through the images of the vision. This consciousness
is concerned solely with the fulfilment of the Zionist dream on
both the political and cultural levels. Peace was considered the
end of a long nightmare, not for the Palestinians but for Israeli
Jews. It enabled the liberal circles who supported the process to
re-establish the self-image of Zionism as a pure and just entity.
The vision was never built on the principles of partnership and
equal rights; it did not include a vision of living together. Many
Israelis honestly believed that the agreement would bring relief
and sovereignty to the Palestinians. They truly regarded the
process as the end of the occupation. Yet, they did not develop
an attitude which regarded the Palestinian question as an
inseparable part of their context.

THE PRINCIPLE OF SEPARATION

This vision emphasises the principle which determined the core of the Oslo accords and which constitutes the Israeli consensus, namely the concept of 'separation'. The principle of separation was the essence of the logic of the Oslo Agreement from the Israeli point of view and is grounded in the consciousness described above. The idea of separation is evident both in the negotiations with the Palestinians and in the internal debate. Both 'right' and 'left' accept the desire for separation as a starting point. The debate was about how to achieve it. Groups in the radical right wing demanded a transfer of the Arabs, claiming that there is no possibility of the two nations living together. On the left the same arguments were used to justify a Palestinian state. Between these two solutions, there is a moral and political divide, yet it is important to understand that they both accept the same presumptions. The growing increase in support of the idea of a Palestinian state was thus not the consequence of the realisation of the Palestinian right for self-determination, but of the will to ignore Palestinian existence. The legitimacy given to the process stems from the fear of a bi-national state.

In that sense, the reality of separation which was formed after the Oslo Accord actually diminished the differences between the main political powers in Israel concerning the future of the Occupied Territories. The two leading political forces, Labour and the Likud, as well as most of the smaller parties in each block, all shared the same main principles: a rejection of a bi-national state as the major motivation to accept the solution offered in Oslo. They all agreed that Jerusalem and most of the settlements should remain in Israeli hands. Even the debate about a Palestinian state was, in a way, artificial. Superficially the distinction was between supporters of a Palestinian state and supporters of an 'autonomy'. But the attributes ascribed to these political entities are similar. The increase of the support in the establishment of a Palestinian state did not indicate acceptance of the values of equality and partnership, which was an integral element of the 'two-state' solution when it was proposed only by the small movements in the radical left. The acceptance of the term

'Palestinian state' was based on the reduction of its sovereignty long before that state was seriously discussed.

The dispute was between those who opposed the establishment of a state because they opposed its right to offer a return of Palestinian refugees and to have diplomatic relations with other countries, especially the Arab countries, on the one hand, and those who supported the idea of a Palestinian state since they believed it would be possible to define a state that would not settle refugees and could not have independent relations with any country on the other.

In other words, the debate was about terminology. While left-wing spokespeople used the term 'Palestinian state' more and more often, the right continued to talk about autonomy. Yet the difference is entirely semantic: the acceptance of the concept of a Palestinian state involved, for Israeli society, removing from that concept any notion of Palestinian national rights. The idea of a state, which once expressed the desire for emancipation, became a repressive concept, which would now serve to fulfil Israeli political goals. The idea of a state became merely the end result of separation. The word 'state' in Israeli discourse has become a euphemism for a kind of autonomy whose function is to separate the Palestinians from the Jews. The only real disagreement is on the degree of autonomy to be given to the Palestinians.

The Oslo framework has terminated the previous debate about the settlements. The Labour Party and the whole 'peace camp' have accepted the settlements as a fact of life, and in that sense they have accepted the Likud policy. On the other hand, the Likud has accepted the principle of autonomy, and therefore the essential principle of the peace process.

PEACE AND TRANSFER

One of the manifestations of the concept of separation can be seen in the policy of closure which followed the Oslo Accord. This policy had been established long before the agreement, and became almost permanent after the Gulf war in 1991. The Oslo agreements gave legitimacy to that policy. The closure was now described as a stage in the creation of a Palestinian state. Indeed, the closure was now associated with the establishment of the Palestinian authorities in parts of Gaza and the West Bank, and thus demonstrates how the agreement is seen from the Israeli point of view. It reflects the idea of separation and exposes its true meaning: apartheid.

In the days following the agreement, police patrols arrested many Palestinian workers who worked within Israel, especially in Tel Aviv, and expelled them back to Gaza, to the territories of the Palestinian entity. This was accepted as legitimate also by the supporters of the peace process, because it expressed the idea of separation. Series of bombings attacks made this policy not only reasonable but unquestionable. Tel Aviv became the only city in the West to which the entrance of Arabs was forbidden. In many ways, then, we can regard the attitude behind the peace process as close to the radical right in Europe: the steps taken before and after the Oslo Accord are exactly those demanded by Le Pen and his followers in France.

A PEACE WITHOUT HISTORY

The enthusiasm with which the agreement was accepted did not lead to any serious discussion of the essential questions concerning the conflict, or of the agreement itself. The public debate that ensued followed the logic of the agreement itself: it did not deal with the crucial questions that were relegated to the final status negotiations between the two sides. The political logic was that it was better to create confidence between the parties before dealing with the difficult aspects of the conflict: the question of Jerusalem, the right of return of Palestinian refugees and exiles, and the settlements. It was assumed that it was better to discuss these issues only later.

But the fact that these issues were not and are still not a subject of public debate is what maintains the Israeli perception and ignores the Palestinian one. It is (and always has been) one of the means by which separation was established. It emphasises the fact that the agreement was based on the Israeli view and on the demand that the Palestinians give up their own position.

The agreement also brought cultural activities under the auspices of 'peace' or 'coexistence', with the participation of both

Jews and Arabs. Many organisations that specialise in this kind of
activity are flourishing, funded by international organisations. Yet
this activity is rarely dedicated to a discussion of the central
issues. The presumption on which they work holds that we are
already in an age of peace, and that the process will inevitably lead
to the establishment of a Palestinian state. There is no attempt to
examine historical consciousness, to discuss the history of the
conflict, or even to question the policy of both Labour and Likud
governments, that is the closure and the development of settlements. In all these issues, at Oslo and afterwards, the Israeli
position dictated the framework of dialogue.

The question of historical interpretation is a crucial issue in regard to the Jewish–Palestinian conflict. That is not only an academic
or theoretical question, since the historical questions embody the
question of the permanent settlement between the two peoples. This
issue is certainly complicated, but its abandonment is another demonstration of the principle of 'separation' and therefore of the Israeli
conception, which excludes the Palestinian existence.

Paradoxically, this was expressed during these years in a debate
over the studies of the 'new historians' who critically examined
the history of Zionism and especially the expulsion of the
Palestinians in 1948. The research of scholars such as Benny
Morris, Avi Schleim, Ilan Pappe and others indeed changed the
focus, and created a new perspective. Yet the debate did not
involve political issues and remained at an academic level. Even in
its public and more popular appearances, the debate did not lead
to a change in the political attitude which would take the rights of
the Palestinians into consideration. Most of the participants in
that debate were among the supporters of the process, and even
they had not developed a different perspective. The discussion
remained concentrated on the nature of Israeli culture.

The fact that the process did not lead to a different perspective
concerning these issues is to be found in the fact that high-school
history programmes were not changed, even though the Ministry of
Education was headed, until the elections, by Meretz members Shu-
lamit Aloni and Amnon Rubinstein. The curriculum manifests the
principle of separation in yet another way: by separating the discussion of Zionist settlement in Palestine from the discussion of the
conflict, as if these issues are not the same. Students are taught that

the land was empty, without its history or that of its population outside Jewish existence and Jewish memory. The Arab existence is mentioned only in times of riots, which are described as evil attacks against the innocent Jewish settlements. There is no attempt to understand the conflict and the Palestinian stand. The expulsion of the mass of the Palestinians during the war of 1948 is not mentioned in the history textbooks.

It is not surprising that an education within this historical conception leads many Israelis to reject all Palestinian rights, and to ignore the Palestinian point of view. Unfortunately, it is this historical image which underlies the process. It leaves no room for the simple recognition that the Palestinians deserve equal rights. The precondition for the negotiations was that the Palestinians would accept the Zionist conception of history.

This is a crucial point for understanding the possibilities included within the framework of the Oslo Agreement. The attempt to retain the previous historical consciousness through the peace process rather than to re-evaluate it, has had severe political implications and it is determining the way the process is developing: while leading to the exit of Israeli forces from parts of the occupied territory, it extracts no price from the Israelis.[5]

RELIGION AND SECULARISM

Even though the principal concept of the Oslo Accord was accepted by a large majority and created a new consensus, at the same time it divided Israeli society and intensified tensions within it. It revealed a serious crisis in Israeli consciousness, and contradictions within Zionist ideology and collective identity. The assassination of Prime Minister Rabin was the climax of the reaction against the Oslo Accord, and in its own turn even aggravated the division in Israeli society.

The agreement was designed by the historical elite of the Labour camp, who were regarded as the representatives of the Ashkenazi (Jews of European origin) and the secular stratum. This definition is only partially accurate, yet it reflects the image emphasised by dominant groups in the peace camp, especially the 'Zionist left'. It was explicitly intended to serve the cultural

images of that elite and rested upon them. Yet, even though this
elite still possesses key positions in the economy, the judicial
system and the press, it has lost the absolute status it held before,
and is in a process of decline, a process afflicting also parts of the
traditional leadership of the right. This elite now has to face and
come to terms with other forces, which had been marginal until
the last decade, and which now emerge to undermine the
hegemonic status of the elites. These forces represent different and
sometimes rival groups and interests which could cooperate on a
common resistance to the cultural position which considered itself
as enlightened and liberal.

The debate was often described both by the supporters of the
Oslo Accord and by many of its opponents as a clash of two rival
world views, one religiously oriented and the other secular and
Western-oriented. That distinction refers indeed to a real phenomenon and points to an increase of the role of religion and
religious rhetoric in the Israeli discourse. In the years following
the signing of the agreement, the power and influence of religious
parties have increased. The most extreme resistance to the Oslo
Agreement undoubtedly came from religious groups.

Yet, even though this distinction reflects a real phenomenon, it
is also not entirely accurate, and in many ways misleading, since it
prevents us from examining the religious aspects of the so-called
'secular' stand. Besides, the distinction functions also as an
ideological construction, since it enables elements in the 'peace
camp' to promote their self-image as enlightened, and to describe
all religious people as primitive. In that way, this distinction
participates in the construction of reality and fulfils itself. It has
prevented discussion of the consciousness considered as 'enlight-
enment' and its mythical roots. The debate over the Oslo Accord
was regarded as a debate over hegemony in society, and as a battle
against all religious people (Jews and Moslems), who were
excluded from the definition of 'culture'. It therefore facilitated
and strengthened the formation of a new coalition between
different religious groups, and the continuing identification of
different religious groups with the 'national camp'.

The religious camp in Israel is composed of different, and
sometimes even opposing and rival religious groups: the Zionist-
religious, represented by the 'Mafdal'; the religious National

party, which is now dominated by the extreme leadership of the settlers; the ultra-orthodox circles, represented by Yahadut Hatora ('The Judaism of the Torah'); and Shas, which is not only a religious party but also a representative of oriental Jews, including non-religious (though the distinction between 'secular' and 'religious' is not always so clear concerning the Jews from Arab countries). Each one of these trends represents a different approach, and a different attitude towards the mainstream in Zionist culture, represented by the historical elites of both the Likud and the Labour Party.

Religious settlers determined the line which directed the opposition to the Oslo Accord from its beginning. They dictated the rhetoric and the effort to delegitimise the process and its designers. For some of them the peace process originated a real crisis, since it interfered with what was considered as the 'real' process, namely the process of redemption realised in the 'return' of the Jews to their 'promised land'.

Even among these sectors, one can observe contradictory attitudes towards the accords and the new reality. At the same time, many of them realised that in fact the agreement legitimised their existence in a way that has never happened before. In spite of radical and violent resistance, there was also a process of reorganisation and even growth of the settlements, encouraged by the Labour Party, especially in the areas which were planned to remain under Israeli rule even after any permanent agreement.

But this awareness did not influence the actions of the settler leadership. The public statement of their views was a total objection to the process and to its carriers. They created an atmosphere of violence which finally enabled the assassination of Rabin, and legitimised anti-Palestinian violence. The assassination was itself the climax of increased tension, and in its turn intensified it. The agreement was presented as an anti-Zionist act and its negotiators as traitors. Their campaign rested on two sets of arguments: on the one hand, religious arguments relating to the divine promise interpreted as a source of legitimation to the political annexation and for an absolute denial of national and civil rights of the Palestinians; on the other hand, an insistence on the demonic image of Palestinian leadership on the political level, at the same time making an analogy between the Palestinian

people and the Nazis. These two aspects were combined into a
mythical conception which determined their political activity.

The settlers introduced themselves as the authentic heirs of
Zionist founders, and their position as the one which was initially
that of the Labour movement. According to that interpretation, by
adopting its new policy, the Labour movement abandoned its own
values. And indeed, in spite of their Messianic radical approach,
the settlers' position should be regarded as a possible interpretation of the basic Zionist myth. It was based on the same elements
as those which constituted the Zionist identity: first, the historical
rights of the Jews in Palestine and second, the view of the
Jewish–Palestinian conflict as the battle of an innocent Jewish
community attacked by demonic evil. Zionism is essentially an
interpretation of a religious myth, which makes the religious/
secular dichotomy misleading. What is considered as secularisa-
tion is the reinterpretation of the religious myth in European-
modern terms. But religious narrative and religious sentiments are
still the ground of this historical consciousness, according to
which the present Jewish existence in Palestine is considered to be
their 'return' to their 'homeland', and the fulfilment of Jewish
history and of the prophesies. The new culture was based upon the
biblical promise, and regarded itself as the continuation of ancient
Israelite culture. The national-religious circles accepted the same
interpretation of Jewish history, but now returned it again to the
traditional terminology. By doing that, they have unravelled the
messianic potential to be found in the core of the Zionist myth
itself. The attitude of these religious groups did not reflect a
different identity from that of the Zionist secular one, but
expressed extreme conclusions of the same concept. Secularism
describes the abandonment of the Jewish law, the Halacha, but not
the role of religion in the constitution of the memory. Zionist
interpretation is radically different from what can be considered to
be the Jewish traditional concept of history, but still it was a
reconstruction of the Biblical Judeo-Christian myth.

It is true that the role of the historical myth in the shaping of
social practice had diminished in the years prior to the signing of
the Oslo Accord, which led to different social changes. Secular
'Israeliness' tried to emancipate itself from the mythical approach
as was established by the founders of Zionism. Yet that process

does not indicate the rise and formulation of a different approach among secular Jews in relation to the definition of Jewish existence in Palestine, one which could distinguish the present Jewish existence from the concept which regarded Palestine as the 'promised land'. These are still the concepts which are delivered in the educational system. All the elements which compose the collective memory of the settlers from Hebron are to be found in the Israeli textbooks. The debate between secular and religious does not involve the definition and legitimation of Jewish existence, but rather the status of religious law in determining the character of society and the state. In that sense, the challenge of right-wing settlers reveals the weakness and contradictions of the Israeli 'left'.

The presentation of the debate on 'peace' as one between secular and religious cultures also encountered significant changes within the ultra-orthodox camp, which was traditionally defined as non-Zionist and even anti-Zionist. During the last decade, and as part of their integration into the political system, these groups have also undergone a transformation and became closer to the Zionist religious groups. Though some of the leading ultra-orthodox rabbis continued to hold moderate political positions, social developments have led to the adoption of a radical-nationalistic rhetoric. The association of 'peace' with the secular anti-religious position inevitably led to the uniting or at least to the cooperation of various religious groups. This does not mean that the secular attitude was the only reason for that shift, but it certainly encouraged it. This shift should be regarded as a testimony to the crisis in these circles, whose attitude towards the state and Israeli society has been changed, threatening to destroy their unique and separate identity and institutions. But it indicates that the tension was not necessarily on the principle of compromise, but on its general cultural location within the debate. At the same time, the participation of orthodox groups in the campaign against the Oslo Agreement sharpened it as a recognised battlefield between Jewish attitudes and demonic gentiles.

The anti-religious sentiment of the Zionist left often even overlooked the Palestinian issue, and dominated the Israeli discourse. The association of these issues allowed the creation of Benjamin Netanyahu's coalition, which in itself is full of tensions and contradictions. The victory of this coalition was received by the 'peace camp' with anxiety, first and foremost because of the position of religious parties within it, not because of the future of the peace process. And indeed, the main issue which was emphasised by Meretz in its campaign was the anti-religious sentiments. Its role in the defeat of Peres is obvious.

The third religious block, the Sephardi religious represented by Shas, reveals another aspect of the conflict – the one between Ashkenazi Jews and the 'Oriental Jews' ('Mizrachim' or Jews of Arab origin). Shas became a source of identification also to non-religious Jews of Arab origin, who regarded it as their only representative in resistance to the Ashkenazi elites. Shas was a partner in Rabin's coalition, and its leader, Rabbi Ovadia Yosef, never hid his support of the Oslo process. He was one of the Rabbinical authorities who declared that there is no prohibition against giving back the Occupied Territories. Oriental Judaism offered a different approach from both that of the national-religious and the ultra-orthodox groups. It did not regard the present Jewish existence in Palestine (the Holy Land) as a messianic fulfilment of Jewish history, and at the same time did not hesitate to participate in political life. At least potentially, it offered a different conception which allowed its adherents to accept the existence of the Palestinians and to separate the discussion on Jewish identity from the political debate.

Yet, although Shas and its leader continued to hold the same attitude, it became increasingly close to the national camp, especially because of the anti-religious attitude of Meretz, based on the Ashkenazi elite. Meretz represents in the most extreme way the elites against whom the resistance of Shas was directed. The exclusion of Oriental Jews was one of the main practices through which the identity of these circles was defined. They were also considered as those responsible for the repression of Mizrachim, and their cultural and social rejection.

The presentation of the debate by liberals as one between two different cultural trends inevitably prevented the possibility of cooperation, and clarified the intentions behind the peace process. Shas attitude is still unpredictable, since it includes many contradictory positions: its voters include both moderate and right-wing people. But it is important to notice that the difference of opinions between this camp and the liberal circles was not on the political level. The tension was basically a cultural tension, related to the values of Israeli society.

The debate over the Oslo Accord even increased the tension between Ashkenazi and Oriental Jews, the most important split of Israeli society. Paradoxically, the circles of Meretz who were regarded as the supporters of the peace facilitated the emergence of the opposition against it. The values they possessed *vis à vis* the Oriental and religious Jews could not create a different collective position in support of the Oslo process.

CONCLUSION

It is impossible to predict where this crisis will lead in the future. But one can determine that the present borders of the political discourse prevent any possibility of a real compromise based on the recognition of the Palestinian rights and their point of view. The possibility that such an attitude will be developed is conditional on the creation of a new cultural consensus in Israel, a different definition of Jewish existence and sovereignty.

The discursive framework described and analysed above emphasises the lack of any considerable political position which could combine the discussion on Israeli–Jewish identity with the discussion on Palestinian rights. In all its appearances, including within the leftist circles, it remains a controversy over the terms of Israeli identity. The contradictions within this framework inevitably lead to the growth of the National camp.

The essential component which is missing in that discursive framework is the bi-national approach, namely one which does not separate the discussion on Israeli society from the Jewish–Palestinian conflict. Such an attitude does not refer (at least necessarily) to a bi-national state, since even a two-state solution can be established only on the recognition of that reality. To separate these discussions leads inevitably to apartheid, and to new ways to preserve Israeli control. Bi-nationalism, in its use here, refers to the position which aims to reach an historical compromise which is based on the rights of Palestinians as well as recognition of the Palestinian historical perspective. From the Israeli point of view, this is the precondition to a different political discourse. Without that, and even if the process is to continue according to its original framework, it will not lead to anything but to a separation based on apartheid values.

On the other hand, the present cultural position of the 'Zionist left', which excludes Oriental Jews and ignores the religious aspects of Zionist identity, prevents any possibility of a real change of the Zionist-Israeli perspective. A real change in their historical and cultural perception is therefore a precondition to any attitude which will enable a real 'peace process'.

NOTES

1. Y. Rabin, *The Rabin Memoirs* (Boston: Little, Brown, 1979).
2. Elboim-Dror, *Visions of Tomorrow* (Jerusalem, 1995; in Hebrew).
3. Like the most popular and 'consensual' poet Nomi Shemer, who wrote 'Machar' (tomorrow), which describes the day the soldiers will not have to fight any more. Shemer also wrote the canonical 'Jerusalem of Gold', which described East Jerusalem as a city with 'an empty market square', in the years before the occupation.
4. T. Herzl, *Old New Land – Altneuland,* (New York: Wiener Publishers/Herzl Press, 1941).
5. On the conflict and its perception among Israelis, see M. Benvenisti, *The Shepherds' Wars* (Jerusalem, 1989).

5 THE GEOGRAPHY OF POLITICS: ISRAEL'S SETTLEMENT DRIVE AFTER OSLO

Jan de Jong

'We screwed the Palestinians ...' – these were the words used by Shimon Peres, at the time a cabinet minister in the Israeli government, to characterise the so-called Interim Agreement concluded in September 1995 with PLO leader Arafat.[1] Known as the Oslo II Agreement it scheduled – after Gaza and Jericho – further Israeli redeployment from and self-administration to practically all Palestinian-inhabited locations in the West Bank and Gaza (except East Jerusalem).

The Palestinian leader chose to ignore this off-the-record remark and found opportunity to promote quite another interpretation of the agreement when Israeli forces were withdrawn from most Palestinian cities on the West Bank. In Nablus in front of jubilant crowds he proudly announced: 'Jenin, Tulkarm and Nablus are liberated. Qalqilya, Bethlehem, Hebron and Jerusalem will be next. ... We will build the Palestinian land with Jerusalem as its capital.'[2]

Meanwhile, some two years later, Peres has retreated from the political front stage after his electoral defeat by the Likud leader Netanyahu. Yet there is little doubt that his spirit will linger on over the post-Oslo landscape of Palestine. As its prime architect, Peres has laid the real foundations for that rapidly solidifying creation. The new Israeli premier has ensured continued building upon those foundations, not just in a figurative sense, but literally as well.

Whereas it took a full decade to increase the Jewish settler population of the Occupied Palestinian Territories (not counting East Jerusalem) from a scant 12,000 in 1979 to 75,000 in 1989, it took only five more years to double the last number to the 150,000 of today. Strikingly enough, the greatest increase began to manifest itself after the Oslo Accord had been signed in 1993. The current yearly growth figure of, on average, 10 per cent is enough to bring the total number of Jewish settlers in the Palestinian Territories, including East Jerusalem, to above one million in the year 2010.

While it is still difficult to assess the chances of this fully materialising, there is conclusive evidence that a solid consensus has emerged within Israeli politics in support of Netanyahu's vow to keep on building on the foundations of the Oslo Agreement. Little known by a broader public is how these foundations are firmly set upon a complete corpus of comprehensive planning schemes for roads, settlements, nature reserves and quarries, developed over the years. These schemes are now being stream-lined and optimised in anticipation of the expected territorial rearrangement of the Palestinian Territories as a result of the Oslo Accord. True to the Likud-engrained habit not to 'beat about the bush', Premier Netanyahu has explained that this will render only less than half the West Bank and Gaza available for Palestinian self-rule under the aegis of Israeli sovereignty while incorporating the remainder of the territories into the Jewish state.

Altogether these developments are prompting the urgent question as to whether the visionary spoils of the Oslo Accord, as outlined by Palestinian leader Arafat, can be considered realistic.

This article aims to offer material to help in formulating an answer to that question, taking full account of what should be considered the material foundations for the Oslo Accord, as can be recognised by a careful study of the Israeli planning schemes in combination with how these are, more vigorously than ever, turned into hard irrefutable 'facts on the ground'.

NATURAL RESOURCES

The current period of negotiations in the framework of the Oslo Agreement can be seen in the light of two concomitant, but different directions of growth: on the one hand that of the self-ruling Palestinian domain, and on the other that of the Jewish settlements, which as mentioned earlier, are witnessing accelerated growth. It is obvious that in between the two a borderline will emerge to demarcate two distinct administrative areas. Already, for decades after 1967, a considerable number of Israeli politicians, researchers and officials have thought hard how to achieve this demarcation. It has resulted in a series of Israeli-advanced options, not one of which was ever officially endorsed.

On the Palestinian side one single option was finally adopted in 1988, which entails complete Israeli withdrawal from all territories on the West Bank and in Gaza, occupied in 1967, in line with the interpretation to that extent of United Nations Resolution 242.

It is useful to review the principal options of both sides now that the final stage of intended negotiations has begun. This should be with one essential question in mind: what are the prospects of each option to assure both populations an equitable and equal measure of security and potential prosperity, now and in the future?

In this article, control of natural resources and infrastructure in the broadest sense is considered a crucial issue in answering that question. Lately, Palestinian leaders have increasingly alluded to South-east Asian Singapore as an enlightening example to be emulated. With roughly the same number of inhabitants and even less territory than currently under Palestinian self-rule, the state of Singapore has succeeded in building a high-performance economy in trade, services and manufacturing which offers its citizens a living standard that is one of the highest in the world. Could this not serve as a model for the Palestinian Territories in order to realise in the first place economic sovereignty for whatever minimal territorial configuration may be wrenched out of the final status negotiations?

Already at this point serious doubts should be raised concerning such a vision. To begin with, the differences between Singapore and the Palestinian Territories are much more profound than the supposed similarities on issues such as access to world markets, the technological, developmental and civil infrastructure within Palestinian society, or the input of a prominent self-conscious middle class. But probably the most crucial difference is that Singapore has no competing neighbour state such as Israel, itself aspiring to become the Middle East's exclusive Singapore which, with regard to

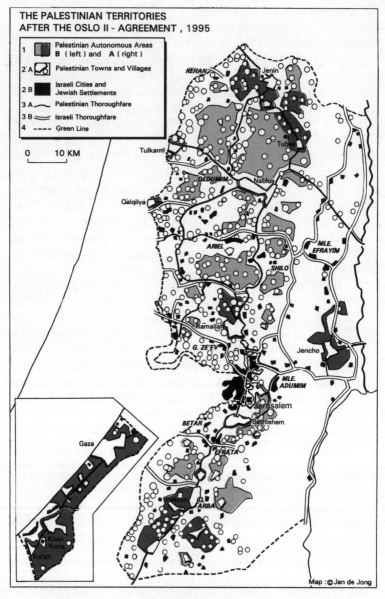

Map 5.1
The Palestinian Territories After the Oslo II Agreement, 1995

the Palestinian Territories, has laid, or is laying, a sole claim to the geographic assets needed to do so.

The Palestinian Territories, however, dispose of a practically as yet unexploited agricultural potential, with great possibilities for supplying the markets of the Arab neighbour states. Developing this potential could lay a realistic economic base to diversify and upgrade the Palestinian economy, without becoming too dependant on the vicissitudes of international financing, which has never demonstrated keen regard for the needs of the local population anyway. It is against this background that the main options for the final status of the Palestinian Territories will be discussed.

It is instructive to review these not just descriptively, but preferably also visually through the use of maps in order to better contextualise their essential features. In the following overview these features will be graphically characterised within the framework of crucial points in time (from 1967 and the situation of today, rounding off with a projection of the near future) and in space (the Palestinian Territories, gradually focusing in upon Jerusalem).

The method is explained with the first map in this overview. Map 5.1 characterises the situation after the Oslo II Agreement.[3] Before explaining how the essential map features are visualised, it is important to stress that, regarding the extent of Israeli redeployment and transfer of self-rule to Palestinian areas, the map has been updated to reflect the current situation (Summer 1997), depicting the announced next stage of Israeli redeployment and further transfer of Palestinian authority to rural West Bank areas. Roads and settlements, however, are pictured according to the situation immediately prior to the signing of the Oslo II Agreement. This is to enable better comparison with the drastic infrastructural changes since then, in order to arrive eventually at the situation targeted on the Israeli plan schemes, pictured at Map 5.5.

The central elements on Map 5.1, and the ones to follow, are the distinct domains of towns, villages, settlements and their surroundings, and in particular their administrative status. The grey-shaded area indicates what is and will be placed under full or partial Palestinian administrative authority.

The West Bank's main cities – Jenin, Nablus, Tulkarm, Qalkilya, Ramallah, Bethlehem and Hebron, excluding East

Jerusalem – are placed under full Palestinian self-rule, next to the rural areas and places within, which are shaded in darkest grey, comprising altogether Area A. Other towns and villages, as well as rural areas in light grey are designated as Area B placed under Israeli security control and Palestinian civilian self-rule (see: Legends 1 and 2 on Map 5.1). The Palestinians consider both areas to be a first step toward the hoped-for independent state, whereas the Israeli government of Netanyahu has already indicated that full Palestinian independence will be out of the question.

The remaining area, left white on the map(s) indicates what at this moment remains under direct Israeli administration. For the Palestinian Territories, enclosed by the so-called Green Line (Legend 4), this concerns the Israeli Military Administration.

The inhabited places within the administrative domains are distinguished as follows: the map shows Palestinian towns and villages (see: Legend 2A) and Israeli cities and Jewish settlements (Legend 2B). In order to get some idea of the structural cohesion of the respective domains the main thoroughfares are depicted, which connect the inhabited places. Distinction is made between roads primarily used by Palestinians and the ones available for Israeli settlers and armed forces. Comparison with Map 5.5 shows how the current situation is only the first stage in the construction of a complete network of so-called 'bypass' roads around Palestinian places.

As such the map offers a concise visual impression of what the next period of negotiations will be about. It needs only a glance to recognise the field of tension between the white outlined Palestinian places and surroundings, all under self-administration (except East Jerusalem) as 'cornerstones' for the targeted independent state, and the Jewish settlements in between as tangible signs of actual Israeli sovereign domination imposed on the Palestinian territories. It is also immediately apparent that there is insufficient 'cement' of self-administered rural territory to connect the autonomous areas as a first step toward Palestinian independence. The crucial question is how much of the remaining area, left white on the map, Israel will be prepared to transfer to Palestinian rule.

Politically, additional factors are also at play regarding the livelihoods in the inhabited places of both communities. The following figures provide an essential background to the numerical weight of these interests. The current population of the Jewish settlements within the Palestinian Territories enclosed by the Green Line comprises around 330,000 people. Roughly 70 per cent of it is concentrated within the relatively small triangle between Giv'at Ze'ev, Ma'ale Adumim and Efrata, around Jerusalem.

This makes the Jewish settler population not more than 12 per cent of the total population of the Palestinian Territories occupied in 1967. These are inhabited by an estimated 2.5 million Palestinians, with the density sharply increasing toward the west. Almost half of the Palestinian inhabitants (around 40 per cent) live concentrated within the Gaza Strip, that is, in less than 5 per cent of the Occupied Palestinian Territories.

PROSPECTS FOR PALESTINIAN INDEPENDENCE

The next map, (5.2, overleaf) shows the Palestinian Territories according to the situation prior to the war of June 1967.[4] After 1949 the West Bank had fallen under Arab sovereignty administered by Jordan, while the Gaza Strip was administered by Egypt. Within the depicted borders – running along the Green Line – it represents the Palestinian option for the claim to a sovereign state.

The map conveys the essence of what that option entails. In the first place the Green Line is depicted as an uninterrupted line to emphasise its character as a recognised state border. Also shown is the outline of the so-called Kendall Town Scheme for East Jerusalem as a crucial internal plan area, which will be elaborated below.

. What the map primarily aims to convey is the actual cohesion of the Palestinian Territories, which is only interrupted by the stretch of Israeli territory between the West Bank and Gaza. What thus remains in cohesion is essential to unleash its developmental potential. On the one hand, this relates to a territorially contiguous product and labour market, with unhindered access to neighbouring countries, and on the other to a low-cost system for the transport of products and persons. These are essential factors to further economic specialisation and to accommodate workers

Map 5.2
The West Bank and Gaza, 1967

rendered superfluous in traditional agriculture within the sphere of urban activities such as light industry, services and trade. The depicted Kendall Town Scheme for East Jerusalem – named after the city planner who designed it on behalf of the Jordanian government in the 1960s – would be instrumental to achieving that result. It pictures the projected urban development of the city as the centrally positioned Palestinian metropolis and the potential economic motor for the entire area.

Before discussing the main Israeli-advanced proposals for the final status of the Palestinian Territories it is important to characterise the essential changes that have occurred after three decades of Israeli rule over the Palestinian Territories. That is the theme of Map 5.3 (overleaf). It pictures as it were a mirror-image of the previous map and summarises the main elements obstructing the above outlined developmental prospects after 1967.[5]

On Map 5.3 the Green Line, according to the Israeli view, no longer distinguishes between two distinct sovereign areas but only between the regular jurisdictional area of Israel and that of the militarily administered 'territories', to which Israel upholds a sovereign claim. Next, the outline of the Kendall City scheme for East Jerusalem has been replaced by the extended municipal borderline fixed by Israel to incorporate the Arab city into West Jerusalem. These major changes are underlying the theme of the map, which concerns the profound changes in land tenure, holding and use since 1967. Again, the map shows the permanently cultivated Palestinian areas.

Next, the land area is depicted which since 1967 has been alienated from the Palestinian community by means of Israeli civil and military legislation (the hatched area on the map). This area was predominantly used as grazing land. Traditionally this category of land was mainly communally held by Palestinian villagers, except for portions claimed by the succession of Ottoman, British and Jordanian authorities as 'government land'. Communal Palestinian grazing land became easy prey in a process by which Israel declared as 'state land' whatever could not be claimed by individual Palestinian farmers and/or what was not regarded as being permanently cultivated.

The hatched areas on the map claimed by Israel as 'state land', comprising slightly more than 50 per cent of the West Bank and

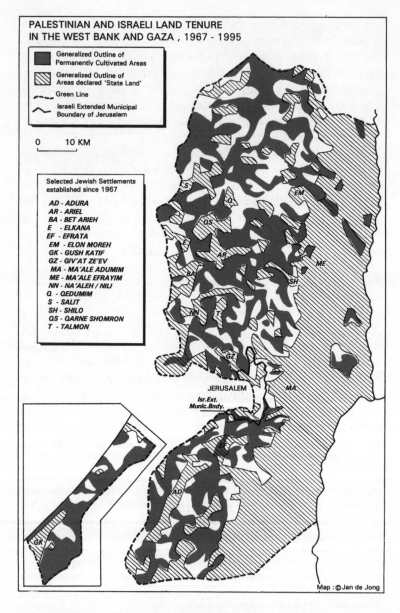

**PALESTINIAN AND ISRAELI LAND TENURE
IN THE WEST BANK AND GAZA , 1967 - 1995**

Generalized Outline of
Permanently Cultivated Areas

Generalized Outline of
Areas declared 'State Land'

Green Line

Israeli Extended Municipal
Boundary of Jerusalem

0   10 KM

Selected Jewish Settlements
established since 1967

AD - ADURA
AR - ARIEL
BA - BET ARIEH
E   - ELKANA
EF - EFRATA
EM - ELON MOREH
GK - GUSH KATIF
GZ - GIV'AT ZE'EV
MA - MA'ALE ADUMIM
ME - MA'ALE EFRAYIM
NN - NA'ALEH / NILI
Q - QEDUMIM
S - SALIT
SH - SHILO
QS - QARNE SHOMRON
T - TALMON

JERUSALEM
Isr.Ext.
Munic.Bndy.

Map : © Jan de Jong

Map 5.3
Palestinian and Israeli Land Tenure in the West Bank and Gaza,
1967–95

Gaza, stem to a considerable extent from the underdevelopment of Palestinian agriculture over the decades. Partly this resulted from the formerly slight pressure to produce more than what could be directly consumed by a sparse, self-sustaining and predominantly rural population. With a population that has tripled in size over the past fifty years the necessity to increase productivity drastically has nowadays become a most urgent matter. What, however, has been missing until today is an administration able to invest public funds toward developing the promising land potential through soil reclamation and irrigation. Not only is this lacking, but also the original Palestinian disposal of the Territories' water reserves has been drastically curtailed by Israel since 1967. The Palestinians are no longer able to tap their rightful share of the Jordan River's water, while Israel also extracts most of the West Bank's groundwater mainly for its own use. Altogether these are essential factors in explaining why the Palestinian cultivated land area has remained at the bare minimum, as depicted on the map.

But there is more to consider. Since 1967 Israel, as the *de facto* sovereign administrator of the Territories, has assumed the authority to issue development plans regulating the use of expropriated 'state land', as well as of the remaining Palestinian land plots, which to a large extent are held as private property. Over the years a stark difference has become obvious between the plans for the Jewish and Palestinian sectors. While Jewish settler organisations were generously allotted 'state land' to establish civil settlements for immigrating communities, residential zones for the rapidly growing indigenous Palestinian communities became increasingly scarce.

The Palestinian places outlined on Map 5.1 were the only living space allotted by Israel to a population which most likely will double to around 5 million by the year 2010. According to the proposed plan schemes, however, the Jewish settlements – pictured on that map to actual size – allocate a proportionally much larger area to communities of which the overwhelming majority has yet to arrive (see Map 5.5 for the projected settlement expansion). In that sense the partitioning of the economic and living space shown on Map 5.3 in what has generously been released for Israeli-Jewish use and what is left in that regard for the Palestinians becomes a striking phenomenon.

While the Palestinian population, as mentioned earlier, will double in size, their original living domain today has already been decreased by half. The induced losses in sources of livelihood are undoubtedly catastrophic. The economic potential of the territorial half left for the Palestinians, without the other half, claimed by Israel as 'state land', can be estimated as at most 25 per cent of the total.

When the first three maps are viewed once again, but this time in chronological order, beginning with Map 5.2 (the period before 1967), then Map 5.3 (1967–1995) and concluding with Map 5.1 (the situation after 1995), a scenario comes to light which will either result in a restoration of Palestinian independence (territorially reflected in Map 5.2) or in a situation projected on the combination of Israeli planning maps (see Map 5.5). The latter remains based on an adapted version of the territorial division of Map 5.3. That situation is reminiscent of the recently abolished South African system of so-called bantustans.

To assess the chances for both options to materialise requires a brief characterisation of the main proposals advanced on the Israeli side for the final status of the Palestinian territories occupied in 1967.

ISRAELI PROPOSALS

Over the decades a whole plethora of Israeli proposals have been formulated to address one single question: how to consolidate the essential spoils of the 1967 war, which had given Israel an exclusive *de facto* hold over all of historical Palestine, including the eastern core of its capital, Jerusalem.

It is most useful to concentrate on those proposals which reflect the predominant thinking in Israeli mainstream politics. A distinction can be made between proposals advanced before and after the signing of the Oslo Accord, the latter taking account of the anticipated Palestinian preparedness to accept a compromise solution under the Oslo-inspired motto 'Land for Peace'.

Map 5.4A pictures the oldest proposal advanced, which has served as a model for practically all subsequent proposals.[6] Known

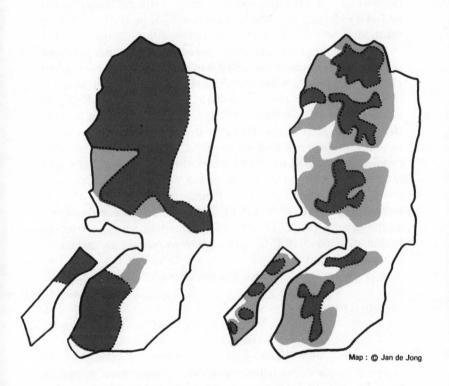

A   B

Map 5.4
Israeli Advanced Proposals and Options for the Final Status of the
Palestinian Territories
A The Allon Plan
B The Sharon Plan and The Enclave Proposal

as the Allon Plan, after the deceased erstwhile army commander
and cabinet minister who developed it in the late 1960s, it offers
essential clues to the fundamental considerations of Israeli politicians with regard to the Palestinian Territories occupied in 1967.
Although considered as a rightful part of *Eretz Israel*, incorporation of all of the conquered territories was found undesirable by a
substantial section of Israeli politicians. Allon represented the
current of opinion in the Israeli Labour Party which favoured
incorporation of just enough Palestinian territory to ensure Israel
of a lasting strategic and political dominance in all of the country
west of the Jordan river. This meant exclusion of most of the
densely populated Palestinian areas in order to safeguard the
character of Israel as a Jewish state. Balancing both motives
resulted in the territorial division pictured on Map 5.4A. The
areas to be returned to Jordan are shaded in dark and light grey
together. In later years it was, however, adapted in order to
broaden Israel's narrow territorial 'waist' east of Tel Aviv. This is
shown in light grey as reductions from the original configuration.
As can be seen, the plan's final version recommended the return to
Jordan of around half the Palestinian territories conquered in
1967, while incorporating within Israel the city of East Jerusalem
with its wider surroundings, the Jordan valley, the Hebron hills
and the southern Gaza Strip.

Map 5.4B shows how the Allon Plan was adapted in political
circles close to Labour, but in particular within the right wing
of the Israeli Likud Party. The map highlights two options
which took account of the Jewish settlements established in the
mid-1970s amidst the densely populated areas which, according
to Allon, should be returned to Jordan. Incorporating all the
then-established settlements, as a first option, would render the
minimal array of autonomous Palestinian enclaves pictured on
the map (only within the dark grey-shaded dotted outlines).
This was at the time the proposal of former army commander
Sharon,[7] today officiating as Minister of Infrastructure in the
Netanyahu government. Although strongly backed by militant
Jewish settler organisations, support for this proposal within the
Israeli public at large dwindled after experiencing the Palestin-
ian uprising from 1987 to 1991. This is mainly because it
violates the principle of maximum separation between the

Jewish and Palestinian populations and would be prone to invite
continued confrontation.

The urge to achieve maximum separation while retaining
maximum territorial control prompted another adaptation of the
Allon Plan, soliciting support within both the Likud and the
Labour parties, but also within less radical circles of the Jewish
settler movement. Known as the Enclave Proposal it advanced a
territorial configuration which would incorporate 90 per cent of
the Jewish settlers' residences within Israel, while at the same time
leaving almost an equal percentage of the Palestinian population
in independent enclave-like areas (indicated in light and dark grey
together). It was flagged as a forthcoming territorial compromise
that would reconcile the rights and aspirations of both populations. It was, however, difficult to overlook its overriding deficien-
cies, in particular, the exclusion of East Jerusalem from Palestinian self-rule, the territorial fragmentation of the West Bank and
the alienation of vital natural resource areas from Palestinian
independence.

The next maps picture the main proposals which were conceptualised after the signing of the Oslo Accord in order to elicit the
approval of Palestinian negotiators for a compromise solution in
line with the Allon Plan, but after alleviating major shortcomings
in the previous plans in light of the realities after the Oslo
Agreement.

Map 5.4C represents the proposal advanced by the Tel Aviv-
based Jaffee Center for Strategic Studies, conceptualised by its
former director Dr Joseph Alpher. It recommended restoring Arab
sovereignty to almost 90 per cent of the West Bank (only the areas in
dark grey including the hatched area), covering 85 per cent of its
Palestinian inhabitants. This would involve a regrouping of Jewish
settlements within contiguous so-called 'blocs' around Greater Jerusalem and west of Ramallah and Nablus, to remain under Israeli
administration and comprising 70 per cent of the Jewish settler
population. The hatched section roughly indicates the area where
Israel would continue to exercise a measure of security control, locally imposing some limitations upon full Palestinian sovereignty.
The major advantage claimed by this plan, in distinction to previous
proposals, was to leave the Palestinians with the bulk of the West
Bank as one contiguous area, and with unobstructed transport links

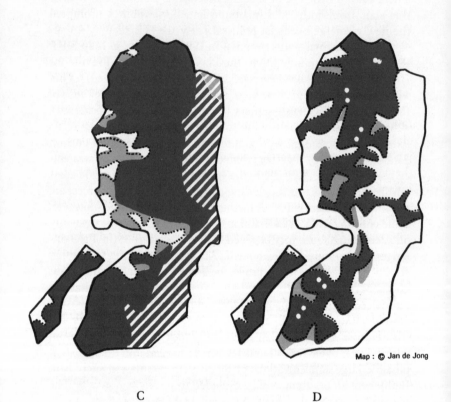

Map : © Jan de Jong

C   D

Map 5.4
Israeli Advanced Proposals and Options for the Final Status of the
Palestinian Territories
C Proposal of the Jaffee Center
D The 'Third Way' Proposal

to Jordan. Its major drawback again was the exclusion of East Jerusalem from Palestinian sovereignty. Closer inspection of the plan also revealed that the territorial contiguity outlined by Alpher was mainly a cosmetic affair, precisely because of the exclusion of East Jerusalem as the West Bank's one and only indispensable crossroads. There can be little doubt that the acknowledged shortcomings of this plan, from both Palestinian and Israeli viewpoints, prompted the newly emerged centrist political party the 'Third Way' to advance another final status proposal in 1995, pictured on Map 5.4D. Its description explained that 'the Plan is intended to provide for Israeli security and *developmental* needs ...' (emphasis added).[8] This would entail the incorporation of the living places of 93 per cent of the West Bank's Jewish settlers (East Jerusalem not considered), while at the same time leaving roughly an equal percentage of its Palestinian population within autonomous areas (depicted both in dark and light grey together) that 'can not endanger Israel strategically'. '... Greater Jerusalem, the Jordan Valley and strategic areas on the mountain ridge, including control of the water sources, are not to be compromised ...'. A further paragraph suggested, however, some consideration of Palestinian interests in stating the necessity of '... ensuring contiguity between the various parts of the Palestinian territories and the neighbouring Arab states ...'.[9] Precisely in that regard it was meant to improve the Enclave Map. But there was another crucial one, which could be inferred from the map that was publicised with the proposal. The major conclusion is that it suggested Palestinian self-rule for most of Arab East Jerusalem, implicitly referred to in the plan itself. It advocates the incorporation within Israel of Greater (that is Jewish) Jerusalem, but 'to the extent possible large concentrations of Palestinian population such as in Bethlehem and A-Ram, will be excluded from this region ...'.[10] The map indicates that this refers to most of Arab East Jerusalem as well, except the Old City. See the light grey sections near the West Bank's territorial waist, covering Arab East Jerusalem – except the Old City and the Jewish suburban settlements – with one small section fanning out northward, and another fanning out southward.

At this point it is useful to compare these two Israeli post-Oslo proposals in light of their potential to accommodate Israeli and Palestinian aspirations within the framework of the current negotiations. This is not least because conclusive evidence has surfaced that key elements of both plans have featured in a subsequent set of slightly altered proposals adopted by influential circles within the Labour and Likud leaderships. Before sketching these alterations it is instructive to summarise the differences between the original Alpher and Third Way proposals.

Alpher's plan obviously sought to upgrade the Allon Plan in order to make it more palatable to Palestinian negotiators, while sticking to its original basic tenets. Restoration of Arab sovereignty according to his adaptation would have no more than a limited meaning, and only in the context of economic linkage to Jordan. Just like the original Allon Plan it would fall short of enabling real separate Palestinian sovereignty. The map with his plan explains why. Just the alienation of the downstream valleys, west of Nablus, as vital water source areas, coupled with the absence of real transport links between the northern and southern West Bank, and not least the deprivation of Arab Jerusalem as the only potential Palestinian metropolis, would suffice to make separate independence a chimera.

Nevertheless, it appeared that the underlying principles of this plan did not escape Palestinian attention, that is real territorial (although in fact mainly functional) sovereignty instead of only self-rule, and if not unhindered road links throughout all of the West Bank, then at least links with the Arab hinterland across the Jordan River.

The Third Way plan may be understood as an attempt to emulate Alpher's plan, without having to alter the established Israeli defensive infrastructure in the Jordan Valley, as necessitated in the other plan. Although opting to transfer much less territory to Palestinian self-rule (48 per cent of the West Bank instead of Alpher's 89 per cent), it would, however, include substantially more Palestinian inhabitants (95 per cent instead of Alpher's 85 per cent). It would also provide better territorial contiguity in transport links, although tenuous in the extreme. But most of all the plan did not appear to shy away from Palestinian self-rule in and around Greater Jerusalem, limited though it was in substance. Despite these accommodations, it can be said to offer no better prospects for full Palestinian sovereignty than the other plan. Yet, it had the capacity to generate widespread support, even to generate maximum consensus, in Israel.

This consensus was not just within the ranks of the Labour

Party but increasingly also within the Likud, and probably most of all with the Israeli public at large. This was on account of the maximum separation between the two populations enabled by this plan, while offering to incorporate the greatest number of Jewish settlers within Israel, compared to all previous plans. But its political expediency extended further.

From an Israeli viewpoint it could be argued that this plan was the first largely to comply with the Oslo-induced principle of comprehensive self-rule for all Palestinian-inhabited areas. All previous plans, including that of Alpher, still presumed a continuation of Israeli rule over considerable sections of the Palestinian population, especially in and around East Jerusalem.

The Third Way plan could also claim, from the same rather formalistic viewpoint, to offer the best conditions of all plans for at least functional self-administration in the Palestinian areas, in providing tenuous but continuous roadlinks.

All in all it would enable Israel to present the border lines of this plan, largely accommodating the Palestinian aspiration for a practically contiguous, self-administered area covering almost the complete indigenous population in the West Bank and Gaza. This was up to the line where Israeli security considerations could be brought to bear, an issue which had never fallen on deaf ears in the Western world.

SEPARATION

What impact did these post-Oslo plans have on the concerned parties in the process, in particular on the Israeli government and the Palestinian Authority, and their public constituencies? Apparently none initially, when the (Oslo II) Interim Agreement was signed in 1995. But there is evidence that behind the scenes both plans began to influence perceptions and policies within the headquarters of the Israeli Labour and Likud parties and, reactively, of the Palestinian leadership as well.

Here it should be recalled what the Oslo process essentially is about. It is meant to create and demarcate Palestinian self-administered territory from Israel, but not completely. In other words: separation is the keyword, although mainly just in a

segregational sense. Both plans enabled different interpretations
of that notion. It could be more or less in scope; territorially,
demographically or administratively, or a mixture of all of these.
The Alpher Plan appeared to favour a territorially more stringent
separation, demarcated by a state boundary between a slightly
enlarged Israel (incorporating Jerusalem with the western water-
source areas) and the bulk of the Palestinian West Bank. The
separation targeted on the Third Way plan was much more
functional in scope, but not just. It emphasised precise borderlines
running criss-cross throughout the West Bank. These were,
however, not meant to distinguish Palestinian sovereign territory,
but rather 'cantonal' areas of self-administration.

The separation on the Alpher Plan was, however, demographically much less stringent (15 per cent of the Palestinian
population remaining under Israeli rule) than in the Third Way
plan (5 per cent).

But what kind of separation was favoured by Israel's political
leaders of the day? The areas in light grey on Maps 5.4C and D
are rough projections of the likely changes thought necessary
within the leaderships of Labour and Likud to achieve
territorial options that could move the Oslo process forward
politically. These were meant to muster the support of the target
constituencies needed to bring the process to its desired
conclusion.

The light grey adaptations on Map 5.4C aim to convey the
approach favoured by the 'Arabist' current within Labour, that
is, to make a territorial offer to the Palestinians – in addition to
that of the Alpher Plan – expected difficult to be refused by
them. The prospect of real statehood for the bulk of the
Palestinian territories would only come in return for a
Palestinian signature to formally endorse this revised, and from
an Israeli viewpoint, immensely improved version of the
original Allon Plan, based on a since then drastically reinforced
infrastructure of Jewish settlements and thoroughfares.

The approach pictured on the other map (5.4D) reveals a
different political orientation. Here, in contrast with the former
map, the areas in light grey are reductions from the proposed
original Third Way configuration. This was in order to secure
maximum support from crucial constituents within Israel proper,

in particular the armed forces and pragmatic Jewish settler organisations. The depicted reductions would leave the barest territorial backbone to enable functional Palestinian self-rule and make this Allon variation workable in primarily a practical sense. Once carried through, it was thought that it would create strong incentives for the Palestinian authorities to come to terms with it and ultimately to give their signature in formal endorsement of this result. This would be spurred by the need for normalised conditions and attract urgently needed financial investments from abroad. Despite the seemingly stark area-difference between these two approaches, the pattern similarity underlying both is much more substantial, but has been absent from the maps produced by the Israeli authorities for use at the negotiating table. This is the drastically growing infrastructure of Jewish settlements and thoroughfares on the West Bank. Both adapted options are designed to consolidate, extend and complete it as an inextricable domain of the Jewish state, acquiring a crucial position regarding Israel's overall national masterplan for habitation, roads and industries in the rest of the country.

The emerging domain of Jewish settlements on the West Bank is pivotal for extending and consolidating Israel's emerging metropolitan core of Greater Tel Aviv and Jerusalem, and for creating geographic depth for the Jewish state throughout the whole country as such. This is regardless of the domain's size, which is minimal in the first adapted option and maximal in the last one. A larger or lesser quantity of area surrounding the settlements has little bearing upon their functional impact as such. What really matters is the decisive metropolitan character of dense Jewish habitation and highway linkage, entirely dominating the Palestinian rural surroundings. In other words: the difference between the adapted options pictured on Maps 5.4C and D is mainly gradual in character. Both maps – in line with official policies of publication – omit this core Jewish settlement domain as the West Bank's real determining feature, conveying it only inferentially. Whereas the first option (Map 5.4C) looks accommodating from a Palestinian viewpoint, the second option (Map 5.4D) yields much stronger insights about the likely impact of the Jewish settlement domain.

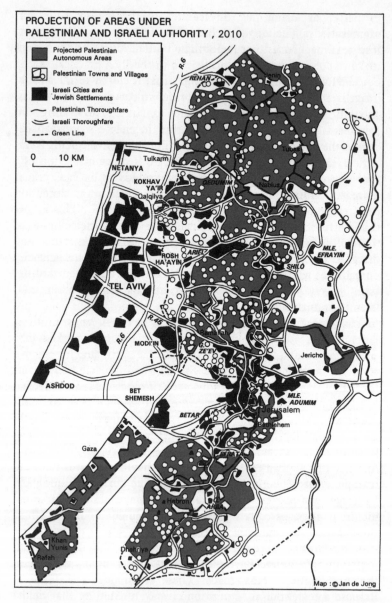

Map 5.5
Projection of Areas under Palestinian and Israeli Authority, 2010

Before exploring the real features of the Jewish settlement domain in interaction with that of the Palestinians, the topic of the next map, let us first review how both adapted options appear to have been advanced politically.

The Rabin-Peres government was initially clearly disinclined to stage a public debate about the future map of the territories. Instead all efforts were concentrated on quietly extending and reinforcing the required infrastructure to enable separation between the Palestinian and Jewish communities on the West Bank. The principal component of that effort was the construction of a network of so-called 'bypass' roads, consented to by PLO leader Arafat to expedite Israeli withdrawal from Palestinian population centres, and enable self-rule in these places.

The 1996 Israeli election campaign for a new Knesset and the post of prime minister brought the issue of the final status map back to the front pages of the news media. The tone appeared already set when the Likud leader Netanyahu suggested that the non-densely populated areas (dominated by Jewish settlements) should encapsulate the Palestinian areas as autonomous zones and not as a separate state.[11] Peres, officiating as Israeli prime minister after the assassination of his predecessor Rabin, remarked in a television interview on 6 March 1996: 'We will neither remove settlements, nor add new ones, that is the difference between us and the Likud.' Later on he advocated the consolidation of Jewish settlements within contiguous so-called 'blocs'.[12] He avoided, however, elaborating on what kind of sovereignty Israel should bestow on the remaining Palestinian areas, probably for two reasons. The first was in order not to damage the fruitful partnership with the Palestinian leaders, which was vital to complete the network of 'bypass' roads. The second and probably as important reason was that a Palestinian claim to full sovereignty of the allotted self-ruled areas was no cause for concern as long as that claim could only have a symbolic meaning. That would be guaranteed by the distinctive territorial pattern of separation materialising rapidly in the West Bank, mainly on account of the 'bypass' roads. These established a skeleton to impose a territorial configuration closely resembling that of the Third Way plan (see the network of bypass roads on Map 5.5, currently under construction). In that configuration the Palestinian territories are deprived of all essential natural resources and infrastructure needed for real sovereignty.

This raises the question of how the Palestinian leadership viewed the Israeli plans in connection with the changing realities on the ground. It appeared that their view remained fixated, across the emerging facts on the ground as it were, on the anticipated end result of the process, which was essentially 'a state' as such. Once established, it was expected to acquire the proper sovereign attributes currently not on the horizon. This fixation may have strongly coloured the Palestinian leadership's perception of the plans presented by Israel.

Apparently at first a slightly adapted version of the Alpher Plan was offered to the Palestinians. It seems to have been made more palatable by further contracting the settlement areas to half their original size, although not the settlements themselves (see the approximated light grey areas of reduction). It is not entirely clear whether this would also be in return for Palestinian consent to leaving all other Jewish settlements in place beyond the blocs. Viewing these as tiny enclaves on the map conveys a different impression from seeing them connected to the network of 'bypass' roads, rarely if ever printed on the Israeli-proposed final status maps.

In March 1996 the Israeli news media reported that an agreement had been reached between Cabinet minister Beilin and Palestinian negotiator Abu Mazen (Mahmoud Abbas) about the contours of a final settlement between Israel and the Palestinians. It stipulated that Israel could incorporate the living places of 70 per cent of the Jewish settlers (in the blocs), rendering 94 per cent of the West Bank for Palestinian administration, provided with the emblems of a state. Jerusalem, however, would remain under Israeli sovereignty. But Palestinians could obviously proclaim their capital 'Al Quds' in the city's eastern suburb (Al Eizarya-Abu Dis), while unofficial reports suggested prospects for Palestinian municipal self-rule in Jerusalem's Arab neighbourhoods, more or less according to the Third Way plan. Was this the breakthrough that opened a pathway to recover practically all (94 per cent) of the Palestinian territories occupied in 1967 indicated by the dark and light grey areas together on Map 5.4C?

Premier Peres hastened to put the agreement in its proper perspective as an unofficial understanding between the two

signatories, while emphasising the underlying unmapped principles. He stressed in particular the prospects it offered for Jews and
Palestinians to live together side by side, not in absolute territorial
separation, but rather in a segregated functional sense. Later
reports mentioned Israeli reservations for large-scale redeployment out of the Jordan Valley, upholding the right to lease most of
it, even if under nominal Palestinian administration. It thus
appears that the principal breakthrough only came from the
Palestinian side in endorsing the principle that Jewish settlements
in the West Bank were compatible with a 'Land for Peace'
compromise agreement.

The formation of a new Israeli government under the elected
Likud Premier Netanyahu in May 1996 initiated a disenchanting
and confrontational phase in the post-Oslo partnership with the Palestinians. A year would begin in which the Palestinian leaders were
gradually waking up to the harsh realities of what the process was
accomplishing both practically and jurisdictionally. The new Israeli
premier vigorously departed from the vagueries cultivated by the
previous government with regard to the final status of the Palestinian Territories. Already in July 1996 he confirmed his earlier statement that the emerging self-ruled areas would be 'less than a state
and not entitled to sovereignty'. To enhance their economic viability
he advocated contiguity between the territories, which as mentioned
above, was an important issue in the Third Way proposal.

It appears that officials of the Netanyahu government, a coalition
which included the Third Way party, recognised the *principles* of the
Beilin-Abu Mazen agreement as a suitable platform for a comprehensive Israeli final status option capable of bridging the positions of
Labour and the Likud. It is likely that the Palestinian concession
embodied in the latter agreement was seen as a convenient 'stepping-
stone' towards the imposition of a scaling-down of the territorial
accommodation with the Palestinians initially suggested in that
same agreement. That would preclude relocation of settlements in
delineating borderlines around intertwining Jewish and Palestinian
population blocs while dividing the empty territory between the two
sides. This conforms to the pattern of the Beilin-Abu Mazen agreement, but with a marked decrease of the unpopulated area to fall
under nominal Palestinian control. This would be, however, without a reduction of Arab citizens in the prospective Palestinian 'state-

minus'. All of this could be achieved by minor adaptations of the
Third Way plan (see the light grey-shaded reductions on Map 5.4D).

The strenuous effort to mobilise the majority of the Likud
constituency behind these principles may have caused considerable stagnation in implementing and negotiating further stages of
Israeli redeployment from Palestinian areas. After the disturbances in the wake of the Al-Aqsa Mosque confrontations in
September 1996 – meant to display Israeli commitment to hold on
exclusively to Jerusalem – the Netanyahu government came under
heavy international pressure to comply with the Oslo-scheduled
phases of further redeployment. Netanyahu may have gained
political clout for closing the ranks of his party and reconciling it
to a restricted interpretation of the Oslo Accord, which was to be
'translated' into a final status option that would preclude further
fundamental internal Israeli controversies.

In January 1997 this appeared to have been achieved in close
cooperation with the influential circle of Labour Party stalwarts
around former Premier Peres. Titled the 'National [Labour–Likud]
Agreement Regarding the Negotiations on Permanent Settlement
with the Palestinians', it became better known as the Beilin–Eitan
Agreement. It appears primarily as the conception of former
(Labour) minister Yossi Beilin accommodating the bottom-line
positions brought in by Likud's parliamentary faction head Michael
Eitan. Probably its principal point was that it sharply outlined an
extended Jewish core domain to be kept under Israeli control, dominating a Palestinian 'entity' in a geographic pattern that would constrain the potential scope for Palestinian statehood. Whatever label
would be attached to the Palestinian entity, a state in the regular
sense of the word, or a state-minus resembling the autonomous
republics in the former Soviet Union, it could on account of this area
pattern never acquire sovereign proportions. Months later the
Israeli news media featured a roughly sketched map, entitled 'Allon
Plus', which Prime Minister Netanyahu reportedly presented to
President Clinton. The core domain of Jewish settlements outlined
on that map largely conforms to the principles set out in the
Beilin–Eitan Agreement.

The decision in the spring of 1997 to start the construction of the
Jewish suburban settlement of Har Homa in East Jerusalem appeared as a clear signal that the Israeli political mainstream – most

probably also including the new Labour leadership around party
chairman Ehud Barak – is steering a further 'Oslo' course in which
the initially materialised partnership with the Palestinians seems to
have outlived its initial main purpose of primarily expediting the
physical and administrative separation between the two population
domains. It may herald a protracted phase in which only the barest
minimum of economic and security dealings is maintained.

Due to the Palestinian failure in not having developed and con-
sistently pursued a comprehensive, resourceful, publicly supported
Palestinian strategy to recover the West Bank and Gaza, also within
the restrictive framework of the Oslo negotiations, Israel has been
able to utilise the Oslo agreements within the frameworks of its own
strategic aims. Palestinian participation on the agreed terms of the
Oslo Accord has been instrumental in coming practically all the way
toward fulfilling the long-disabled Israeli vision first formulated by
Allon, to separate the Palestinian population of the West Bank and
Gaza from the only territorial assets needed to realise national self-
determination and secure the resources and means to attain prosperity and consequently peaceful coexistence with Israel.

CANTONISATION

At this point it is useful to review the determining geographic features of both the West Bank's Jewish and Palestinian domains in
closer detail, in particular with an eye on their projected final shape
in the near future. This is the theme of Map 5.5. Like the previous
maps in this overview, the residential areas and connecting roads are
primary landmarks. On this map these are depicted according to the
officially proposed planning schemes in order to present a realistic
view of the recommended structural expansion, that is to say, by the
Palestinian authorities within their jurisdictional areas and by Israel
in the remainder. It leaves this corpus of plan schemes as the real
foundation for the prospective territorial division depicted on the
map.[13] In that sense the projection of self-ruled Palestinian areas
mainly serves the purpose of reference, in most clearly exposing the
spread pattern of Jewish settlement blocs *vis-à-vis* the Palestinian
population areas. Even if the latter were to be slightly enlarged –
which is highly unlikely – it would leave the depicted settlements
and network of bypass roads intact.

Although this territorial division is still short of official approval
in the targeted formal Peace Treaty (Oslo III), it is likely to materialise in any case in implementing the approved planning schemes. If
no final agreement will be reached, then this division, closely similar
to the Allon Plus map, will remain as the outcome of the Oslo process. The only difference from the configuration pictured on Map
5.4D concerns the enlarged municipal area of East Jerusalem. Here
the situation remains depicted according to the original Third Way
proposal, leaving the eventual prospect of delegating Palestinian
municipal self-rule to most of Arab Jerusalem – except the Old City –
within the framework of Greater Jewish Jerusalem, which is detailed
below on Map 5.7 (page 113). Although currently out of the question,
it is important enough to keep in mind.

Just a glance at Map 5.5 shows how the Palestinian Territories
are in this projection divided into five cantonal clusters. One is
emerging in the north around the city of Nablus, followed by
three smaller ones in the centre around the cities of Ramallah,
Bethlehem and Jericho, and another larger one in the south
around the city of Hebron. These clusters are meant to be linked
by a Palestinian corridor road to a final one situated in the Gaza
Strip. This cantonal fragmentation is likely to have far-reaching
consequences. In the first place, it will deprive the Palestinians of
vitally important resource areas that remain under Israeli administration. This not only concerns highly productive arable land, but
also degraded land that could be reclaimed for cultivation or for
the purpose of construction. As mentioned earlier, these are
crucial resources for a doubling population with already today
insufficient means to sustain itself. The loss of these areas'
developmental potential is particularly serious. Adequate access to
the territories' ground and surface water in order drastically to
increase agricultural production and expand the arable land
surface is essential. According to the division projected on the
map, however, all important water-producing areas will remain
out of reach for the Palestinians.

Secondly, the Palestinian clusters will be subjected to a
territorial fragmentation much more serious then appears at first
sight. The consolidation of Jewish settlement blocs strongly
prejudices what cohesively remains for the Palestinian areas in
between. The map pictures the Jewish blocs as deep indentations,

of which the far ends are connected with bypass roads that are
projected straight through Palestinian populated areas. This
reveals a pattern of fragmentation not just of six larger clusters but
of several dozens of smaller territorial sub-units.

These are loosely tied together by local roads branching off
from the principal Palestinian thoroughfare running from Jenin
and Nablus in the north to Hebron and Dhahriya in the south.
That is the remaining fragile thread for the Palestinian Territories
to hang on to. They will be interrupted at numerous intersections
with bypass roads as key locations for security checkpoints.
Altogether these factors are likely to severely impede prospects for
the rehabilitation of the Palestinian Territories.

The inherent socio-economic potential of the Palestinian
Territories can be imagined along two axes of development. One
runs vertically along the traditional north–south route with a
predominantly rural orientation. The other stretches horizontally
between west and east, from Gaza via East Jerusalem to Jericho.
The latter has a distinct metropolitan orientation with major
prospects for trade, industry, services and tourism. Both ends of
this axis connect to Arab neighbour states with promising market
outlets. The two developmental axes cross at East Jerusalem as the
obvious node to ensure a productive interaction between the two.
Just one glance at the map reveals how the above outlined
potential will be severely constrained or even cut off at crucial
locations along both axes.

Undoubtedly the most resource-rich and economically promising Palestinian areas will be hit hardest by the pattern of cantonal
fragmentation. These are the water-producing areas in the west
and the east and the main Palestinian agglomerations. This keeps
the rich agricultural potential curtailed to its current minimum,
but also severely constrains urban development at the most
socio-economically promising locations. The latter result becomes
evident foremost in and around Arab Jerusalem and Gaza. Their
prospects of functioning as real Palestinian metropolitan gateways
toward the Arab hinterland, both east and west, are reduced, and
they are threatened with being cut off and absorbed by Tel Aviv
and West Jerusalem. Palestinian urban constraint is becoming no
less critical in cities like Hebron, Qalqilya, Ramallah and Bethlehem. On all sides these are squeezed in between Jewish settle-

ments, bypass roads or designated nature reserves. Already these cities are suffocating for lack of growing space, forcing up land prices tremendously, while local labour, service and product markets remain undersized.

These are circumstances strongly prejudicing the developmental outlines indicated above. Likely to remain is a provincial marginal economy caught within the emerging cantonal confines. This threatens to pre-empt the proper conditions for an adequate consumption market of indigenous products and services.

It is beyond the scope of this article to elaborate upon the socio-economic consequences of Palestinian cantonal fragmentation. Suffice to mention the current catastrophic upsurge in unemployment of which the structural character, in the face of failing geopolitical incentives to rehabilitate the Territories economically, is hard to ignore.

What appears to be lost on the Palestinian side seems to be gained by Israel. Map 5.5 is the first in this overview to situate the Palestinian Territories in the context of its surroundings, in particular the country's core area between the Mediterranean and the Jordan river. This is the proper perspective to take in comparing the processes of territorial and socio-economic contraction on the Palestinian side with expansion on these same points becoming apparent for Israel.

Map 5.5 pictures how the country's core area is increasingly being dominated by a coordinated formation of Jewish residences and roads, which can be identified as the emerging combined metropolis of Greater Tel Aviv-Jerusalem. Until recently its original metropolitan core had to remain constricted to Greater Tel Aviv on the coastal plain, with West Jerusalem as its economically marginal satellite city. The Green Line imposed a solid barrier to natural growth inward, even in the period after 1967. Without a political settlement of the conflict about the Occupied Palestinian Territories, the growth of remote Jewish settlements like Ariel or Efrata was limited, despite a highly attractive and affordable living environment. After the signing of the Oslo Accord, the barrier of the Green Line appears to have been cleared out of the way, or rather, to be bent inward around the fragmented Palestinian cantonal blocs. The map highlights the main elements required to turn the original metropolitan area of Tel Aviv one quarter to the right inward and become doubled in size.

The first element is the aforementioned network of bypass roads. The second is the large-scale expansion of urban and industrial areas in the so-called 'seam' area, what was until recently the almost unpopulated strip of land along the Green Line.

Targeted main locations are Kokhav Ya'ir, Rosh Ha'ayin, Modi'in and Bet Shemesh, known as so-called 'Star' settlements and altogether capable of absorbing about half a million Jewish newcomers. Both elements are decisive in opening up the natural hinterland of metropolitan Tel Aviv, in connecting it to that of Jewish Greater Jerusalem and integrating it into Israel. There is considerable pressure behind this process in light of the expected rise of Israel's population from 5 to 7 million by the year 2010.

It is instructive to trace the dimensions of this combined metropolis on the map. With the coastal strip above and below Tel Aviv as its baseline, it extends eastwards from Netanya to Ma'ale Efrayim in the Jordan Valley. From there it descends around Ma'ale Adumim to Efrata in the south, turning back via Bet Shemesh to the coast at Ashdod. Two projected main roads lead from, to and through the metropolitan area to link it with the rest of the country and the hinterland. The first is Highway 6, Israel's future infrastructural 'spine'. The second is Road 45, to link the country to the eastern Arab world and function as Israel's prospective metropolitan gateway and undoubtedly the country's primary economic asset.

At this point it is useful to summarise the main conclusions of Map 5.5. On the one hand, the 'Oslo'-induced process of separation between the two populations goes hand in hand with a further dissolution of the West Bank as the one remaining major Palestinian territorial unit. On the other hand, it means a substantial territorial consolidation of Israel within the country's natural borders.

Instrumental to this process is the emergence of the combined Israeli metropolis of Greater Tel Aviv–Jerusalem in the country's geographical core. The Palestinian residents within are likely to become a numerically and economically subordinate community compared to the Jewish metropolitan citizens. As a result, only three of the emerging Palestinian cantonal clusters are likely to remain as areas where the indigenous Arab population remains locally prominent: around Nablus, Hebron and Gaza. In this

territorial context all infrastructural assets likely to develop and
absorb the territories' socio-economic potential are being acquired
by Israel. In that case the Palestinian developmental potential is
likely to shrink to a provincial level, compelling a large section,
probably the majority of the Palestinian labour force, to integrate
in a dependent position within the Israeli economy.

With such a territorial division and stagnating Palestinian
developmental prospects, Map 5.5 pictures a scenario for implo-
sion. Both the Palestinian territorial domain and the prospective
resources for livelihood are reduced by half, against the background, however, of a virtual demographic explosion, where the
Palestinian population is expected to double. The future prospects
thus emerging are already acutely coming to light in the Gaza
Strip. There a crisis is flaring up because insufficient sources of
livelihood are opened up to compensate for the inaccessible or lost
potential for self-sustained economic development. Historical
records picture the villages and towns of the traditional Gaza
District (before 1948) as the most prosperous of the country. Since
then, Gaza has been reduced to one-third of the district's original
size, but with a population that has increased from the 150,000 of
half a century ago to the one million of today, expected to double
to two million in the next 15 years. A way out of this crisis is
painted by some in the colours of Singapore. According to such a
vision, all depends on large-scale financial investments in sectoral
projects, not necessarily connected. On account, however, of the
apparent cantonal limitations of this area, these will have little
macroeconomic self-sustaining and durable potential. A more
promising solution requires an entirely different approach. Gaza,
just like the other Palestinian areas currently becoming peripher-
alised, could largely recover on its own, basically on two conditions. First, when unobstructed access is provided to the hinterland in Palestine and the adjacent Arab neighbour states. Second,
when minimal but adequate allocation of crucial resources (such
as living space and water in Gaza) is allowed, now remaining out
of reach. It has been mentioned before that full linkage to the
Palestinian territorial core, in and around Jerusalem, is crucial for
outlying districts such as Gaza in order to avoid socio-economic
marginalisation.

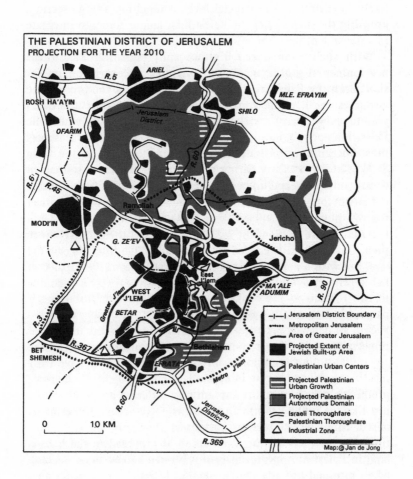

Map 5.6
The Palestinian District of Jerusalem; Projection for the year 2010

JERUSALEM, THE HEART OF THE PALESTINIAN TERRITORIES

The District

What in the case of Gaza has occasionally been dismissed as the result of a tragic incident may in effect be repeated in the Palestinian core district of Jerusalem, but this time according to an entirely different process – not as the result of violent political disturbances, and of massive population flight like in the late 1940s, but as the gradually materialising consequences of statutory planning.

Map 5.6 covers the traditional Palestinian district of Jerusalem, comprising close to 40 per cent of the West Bank, with roughly the same percentage of its Palestinian population. The map highlights the projected result of perhaps the most crucial Israeli regional planning scheme, known as the 'Metropolitan Jerusalem Plan'. It is set within a territorial frame extending beyond the district's borders (see map legend). The central plan area within is designated by Israel as 'Metropolitan Jerusalem' (see the dotted line), with 'Greater Jerusalem' as its real target area (indicated by the solid line), which is dominated by Jewish suburban habitation within the City itself and in the surrounding settlements.

Developed by an interministerial committee and completed in 1995, that is after the signing of the 'Declaration of Principles' (!), it provides strong clues to Israel's current geopolitical assumptions in taking full account of the anticipated outcome of the Oslo process.[14] Although not yet formally endorsed, it is in fact being feverishly implemented on a daily basis.

The map pictures the division of the projected Palestinian self-ruled domain according to the pattern of the previous map into three cantonal fragments: Ramallah, Bethlehem and Jericho. Considerable sections of these fragments have already taken shape according to the stipulations of the Oslo II Agreement. The remaining area, left white on the map, contains a number of Palestinian villages that are only autonomous within the built-up perimeter, but beyond are enveloped within the emerging domain of Jewish settlements remaining under Israeli administration. The

latter are depicted according to their proposed settlement planning schemes. It means that the major ones are targeted to expand
three- to five-fold. As indicated earlier, the network of bypass
roads, already practically completed in metropolitan Jerusalem,
will be instrumental in furthering this growth. On the map it is
depicted as a checkerboard containing and mutually separating
the Palestinian territorial fragments, which together had previously functioned as one cohesive area. That is now being replaced
by the drastically expanded Israeli metropolitan area. Consequently it threatens to marginalise the district's Palestinian
population in all imaginable aspects. Most advantages of the
infrastructural concentration of industry, transportation and services within one contiguous area will fall to Israel. The Palestinian
community is in fact only allowed to grow away from the
advantageous metropolitan core toward the district's peripheral
sectors.

The authorities on both sides have meanwhile understood that
the majority of the Palestinian labour force will entirely depend
on the Israeli metropolis for jobs and income. That is why after
Palestinian–Israeli consultation, large-scale industrial zones have
been planned at revealing locations (see the triangles on the map).
Projected to be established – with European financial assistance –
in the shade of sizeable Jewish settlements (below Ofarim,
Modi'in-Makkabim and Betar), these locations are highly indica-
tive of the unlikely prospects for indigenous Palestinian economic
rehabilitation in this set-up. Instead of industrial schemes being
primarily concentrated near the potential Palestinian metropolitan gateways (East Jerusalem and Gaza) and the adjacent cities, the
envisaged zones tie most of the Palestinian labour force in a
subordinated position to Israel's metropolitan core. In addition,
the targeted industrial zones are largely beyond Palestinian
control, rendering little public revenue, and appear not least to be
designed to enable perpetuation of the Israeli-imposed closure of
the Palestinian Territories.[15]

In addition to spatial and economic marginalisation, the
Metropolitan Plan may be interpreted as a scheme for demographic marginalisation of the Palestinian community. With
regard to the area's population build-up it is important not just to
consider it according to the traditional administrative division

along the Green Line but also to the anticipated division into
Palestinian and Israeli-administered domains resulting from the
Oslo process (the first in grey, the second white). The map
pictures Palestinian and Jewish urban habitation according to the
proposed and suggested Israeli planning schemes. The natural
increase in the district's Palestinian community is expected to
double the current number within the next 15 years to more than
one million within the depicted cantonal clusters, and to around
100,000 in the autonomous villages within the anticipated domain
under Israeli administration.

The settlement planning schemes shown on Map 5.6 could
accommodate, after a first round of construction, an extra influx of
approximately half a million immigrating Jewish settlers. Including the already settled residents, the scheme may bring the total
Jewish population in the district by the year 2010 to 800,000.

The demographic balance between the area's Palestinian and
Jewish communities for that year can be viewed in two ways.
From the perspective of the West Bank it would reduce the
Palestinian population to 60 per cent of the district's total
population, most likely to be contained in only 30 per cent of its
area as a self-ruled Palestinian domain.

The other perspective would be to approach the demographic
balance according to the anticipated domain separation pictured
on the map and no longer to what will be a derelict Green Line.
This would shift the spatial terms of the equation and include the
projected population weight of the 'seam' locations of Bet
Shemesh, Modi'in and Rosh Ha'ayin and not least also of West
Jerusalem itself. Accordingly it would double the above number of
800,000 Jewish inhabitants and bring the total number to 1.6
million. This would then reverse the demographic balance in the
opposite direction resulting in a 60 per cent Jewish majority in the
area of Map 5.6, controlling 70 per cent of the erstwhile district.

The City of Jerusalem

The last map in this overview (Map 5.7) is focused on the hotbed
of the Palestine–Israel conflict: the City of Jerusalem itself. This is
on the basis of two assumptions: first, that a peaceful settlement

Map 5.7
Metropolitan and Greater Jerusalem

will largely depend on what will be reached for Jerusalem, and second that Jerusalem serves as a cornerstone for both Israel and the Palestinians to realise their sovereign aspirations. Between the two is a cardinal difference that needs to be emphasised in this context. Israel's policy is aimed at retaining exclusive sovereignty in all of the country, as well as Jerusalem. The Palestinian claim, however, is inclusive in its readiness to share sovereignty with Israel, encompassing only the restoration of Arab sovereignty of the Palestinian Territories occupied in 1967, including East Jerusalem.

Nothing less than a complete hold over all of Jerusalem can ensure Israel of exclusive sovereignty, both in a political and in a geographical sense. Were East Jerusalem to be directly connected in those spheres to the city's Arab hinterland, in Palestine or in the neighbouring states, a restoration of the sovereignty lost in 1967 would become inevitable. This is already only on account of the dramatically increasing demographic weight of the Palestinian sector. Even a formula for Israeli sovereignty over the Palestinian surroundings based upon the situation more or less as it is today (see Map 5.1) would probably in the long run fall short of withstanding a restoration of Arab sovereignty.

That is why Israel aims to integrate Jerusalem within the country's geographic core, by means of establishing Jewish satellite cities around the capital, which socio-economically will be linked to Israel. The enormous costs of this operation are meant to be recovered when the emerging metropolis would gain access to the Arab markets after the expected normalisation resulting from the Oslo process.

For the Palestinians to recover and retain East Jerusalem as the Territories' crucial crossroads, economic hub and gateway to the Arab hinterland is, however, less a political option than an economic necessity. The main question in this context is whether Israel will be prepared to transfer a certain measure of Palestinian self-rule to Arab Jerusalem.

Map 5.7 is meant to provide a summarised but comprehensive overview of the decisive factors at play. In the previous map Jerusalem was approached from the perspective of the whole district named after the city. On this map Jerusalem will be scanned in a reverse sense, that is to say, beginning with the walled Old City (in the middle of the map), literally as the square kilometre standing central to the conflict, and from there to the metropolitan outskirts of the city.

First to distinguish within the Old City is the Haram-a Sharif (Arabic for 'the Noble Sanctuary') crowned by the Dome of the Rock (the minutely small open square with dot) next to the so-called Jewish Quarter (the adjacent small black square), separated from one another by the Western Wall, better known as the 'Wailing Wall'.

The next important feature to trace is the Green (cease-fire) Line of 1949. It distinguishes between Palestinian East Jerusalem (right) and Jewish West Jerusalem (left). Between 1949 and 1967, both were independent municipalities within two distinct sovereign areas, the first under Jordanian administration, the second under Israeli administration. The difference between the two municipalities was considerable. Despite its isolated marginal position West Jerusalem was pronounced the capital of Israel. East Jerusalem, however, declined in position and status to a remote provincial town in the shade of the Jordanian capital Amman. Whereas West Jerusalem as the seat of important governmental institutions was drastically expanded with new suburbs, urban development in East Jerusalem stagnated.

Only in the 1960s was the way cleared for its urgently needed revitalisation. This occurred when the Jordanian authorities endorsed the Kendall Town Scheme, introduced above (see the bold interrupted line around East Jerusalem on the map). This would enable a large-scale expansion of the Arab city by linking all Palestinian residential areas between Ramallah and Bethlehem within one connected Plan area. It would open up space for industrial and commercial areas and thousands of dwellings, characterised earlier as a fundamental condition for the rehabilitation of the Palestinian Territories as well.

This prospect was, however, aborted by the Israeli occupation of the West Bank and Gaza in 1967. First, the area of West Jerusalem was tripled by unilaterally dissolving the municipality of East Jerusalem and incorporating its area and that of adjacent Palestinian villages into the Israeli capital. This was officially justified as the long-awaited 'reunification' of the divided city. But in fact it merely added a new line of division right through the Arab City, because Israel excluded half of the Kendall Town Area, with important suburbs like Abu Dis and A Ram from Jerusalem under the motto 'A maximum of Arab Land with a minimum of Arab Citizens' (follow the extended municipal limits cutting through the Kendall Scheme Area).

Secondly, more than one-third of the incorporated area was expropriated in order to establish Jewish suburban settlements such as Ramot and Gilo. This was at the expense of thousands of dwellings projected there for Palestinian habitation according to the Kendall Scheme. Most of the remaining area has, moreover, been designated as 'open green zones', leaving only 15 per cent of incorporated East Jerusalem for the housing needs of the Palestinian citizens. This is dramatically inadequate in light of a shortage conservatively estimated more than a decade ago on behalf of the Jerusalem municipality at 20,000 dwellings.[16] Nowadays that figure should be realistically adjusted to 40,000, in view of the demographic age composition of the city's Arab neighbourhoods, taking account of the expected growth for the next 15 years.[17] Tensions are rising now that one open green area after the other is being rezoned for further Jewish habitation, scheduled to add another 20–30,000 dwellings to the nearly 60,000 already constructed in that category since 1967, while the number of permitted Palestinian dwellings in East Jerusalem is limited to 8,500 by Israel, far below the assessed requirements.[18]

On the whole this problematic issue is, however, overshadowed by the overall adverse effect of Jewish suburban settlements and roads upon the Arab city. Instead of the strongly needed solidification of Palestinian neighbourhoods as one integrated city, Arab Jerusalem has been dissolved into a sprawl of scattered, separated and constricted neighbourhoods, which are increasingly being drained of their natural population increase. Meanwhile, the Jewish suburban settlements initially established throughout the far corners of incorporated East Jerusalem are being mutually joined with further dwellings, institutions, public gardens and thoroughfares to become an inextricable part of West Jerusalem. This dichotomy renders impossible conditions for the much-needed rehabilitation of the Arab City in another capacity than just a tourist attraction.

This brings us to the current situation. Although a prominent physical reality, the accomplished Judaisation of East Jerusalem through roads and settlements leaves much to be desired for

Israel. This is for two basic reasons. While the established Jewish settlements intrude deep into the Arab City and have broken its cohesion, East Jerusalem still remains a part of the burgeoning Palestinian agglomeration between Ramallah and Bethlehem, with a demographic natural growth rate that may double its current population to about 800,000 within the next 15 years.

The possibilities for Jewish demographic counter-pressure – largely through immigration – within the municipal area are practically depleted. Mainly the southern section of East Jerusalem remains for a last round of settlement construction (see Har Homa). But there is more to consider. Not just demographically but also spatially, Israel's construction of 'eternal and undivided Jerusalem' is under increasing pressure. There are still possibilities for linking East Jerusalem, growing in the outlying suburbs, alongside the Western City to the adjacent Palestinian residential areas of the Arab agglomeration between Ramallah and Bethlehem. It is against the background of these two factors that Israel's Metropolitan Plan for Jerusalem should be analysed. Both are compelling Israel to take drastic measures in order to neutralise the expected Palestinian demographic predominance within metropolitan Jerusalem. That is the motive for the dramatic expansion of Jewish Jerusalem pictured on the map. Directly around the city, large-scale expansion of currently modest-sized Jewish settlements is projected, four to five times larger than their actual size. Which means that most of Jerusalem's Judaisation has yet to come. The map shows its primary locations (see the hatched areas). Clockwise from the northwest these are: Giv'at Ze'ev, in the East Ma'ale Adumim, and Betar and Efrata in the south. At those places Jewish 'Greater Jerusalem' is now arising in scaffolds, a reality largely ignored by the Palestinian leadership still viewing the city mainly in its current municipal dimensions. The outer ring of suburban settlements can accommodate in the next 15 years more than 200,000 new Jewish residents. Added to the number then expected to reside within East Jerusalem it may amount to half a million in and around Arab Jerusalem by the year 2010. Next, it is West Jerusalem, with an expected population of about 300,000, that is to throw the missing weight into the scale and neutralise the expected Palestinian population of 800,000 in the whole Arab agglomeration. Israel, however, aspires to more than just demographic neutralisation. Maintaining a population balance of 72 per cent Israeli Jews and 28 per cent Palestinians for the city, a cornerstone of Israel's Jerusalem policy, can only succeed by creating and somehow incorporating the outer ring of drastically expanded Jewish settlements. Once completed, it will be solid enough to keep Arab Jerusalem both administratively and functionally apart from the rest of the whole Arab agglomeration between Ramallah and Bethlehem and encapsulate it once and for all within the framework of Jewish Greater Jerusalem.

At that stage – the jurisdictional formation of a metropolitan council for Jewish Greater Jerusalem appears close at hand – conditions could become ripe for Israel to consider delegating Palestinian municipal self-rule to most of Arab East Jerusalem (darkest grey), except for the Jewish suburban settlements and the Old City. Although the current government is under little pressure to move in that direction, the advantages have been clearly recognised in consultation with Palestinian negotiators.[19] That is why this option has been pictured on the map.

To sum up: by truncating the emerging Palestinian metropolis, and twist its orientation away from its Arab hinterland toward that of Israel, a lasting Jewish domination of the rearranged and judaised metropolis appears ensured. In that way all factors will have crystallised to render the dismantling of Arab Jerusalem as a Palestinian indigenous city and metropolis irrevocable.

CONCLUSION

The Oslo Accord was overwhelmingly welcomed as a principal breakthrough in the conceived entrenched positions of the two parties in the Israeli–Palestinian conflict. At last both sides have committed themselves to reach a negotiated solution based on the principle 'Land for Peace'. In this article the viewpoints of both parties on how to achieve this have been reviewed, with an eye on the prospects for both populations to live equitably in peace and prosperity, in particular the Palestinian community, which has been deprived of those prospects for decades. What territorially still remains unresolved after the signing of the Oslo (II) Interim Agreement is currently, however, taking shape in the form of accelerated Israeli construction, laying firm foundations for what the process is to achieve in Israeli eyes. This principally concerns the separation of both populations each within distinctive administrative domains. According to that principle, Israel has been enabled to get rid of the densely populated areas, while reinforcing its hold over the developmental, infrastructural and strategic potential of the area beyond. Already at this stage it is possible to conclude from the proposed Israeli planning schemes what map of the territories will be held out to the Palestinians at the negotiating table as the envisaged exchange of land in return for peace. If the concerned planning schemes are not withdrawn and gradually materialise over the length of negotiations then a sobering conclusion seems inevitable. The Oslo Accord may in that case be considered as the preamble to those very schemes and accordingly as the document in which the future of the Palestinian people as an independent nation has been signed away.

NOTES

1. *Ma'ariv*, 25 October 1995.
2. *Al-Quds*, 16 December 1995.
3. The source for Map 5.1 is the annex with the so-called Interim Agreement, reprinted by JMCC, Jerusalem 1995.
4. Map 5.2 is based on the Topographic Map Series of Jordan (1966) and regarding the Kendall Town Scheme on the Regional Plan Proposal for Jerusalem (1964). The expected extension of Ramallah and Bethlehem is pictured on this map according to the projected urbanisation of the Kendall Town Scheme.
5. Sources for Map 5.3: the depicted state land according to the record of the Palestine Research and Information Centre (1993) and the permanently cultivated areas according to the Topographic Map Series of Jordan (1966).
6. Sources for the Israeli advanced territorial options pictured on Map 5.4A – The Allon Plan, from W. W. Harris, *Taking root; Israeli settlements in the West Bank, the Golan and Gaza–Sinai, 1967–1980* (New York: Research Studies Press, 1980). 5.4B – The Sharon Plan according to the most recent version reviewed in *Yediot Aharonot*, 7 August 1992, the Enclave Plan as reviewed in *Nativ* (Spring 1993). 5.4C – The proposal by the Jaffee Centre as publicised in *Settlements and borders* (Tel Aviv: The Jaffee Centre for Strategic Studies, 1995). See also the review in *Yediot Aharonot*, 2 December 1994. 5.4D – The 'Third Way' Proposal, from *A new hope for Israel's future* (Tel Aviv, 1995). N.B. Only the Allon and the Sharon proposals cover the area next to the West Bank and also the Gaza Strip. For the other proposals the Gaza Strip is depicted according to the situation after the Oslo I Agreement (1994).

7. A new Final Status Option is currently advanced by Ariel Sharon, stipulating a clustering of self-ruled Palestinian areas into three major 'cantons' altogether comprising around 40 per cent of the West Bank's area.
8. *A new hope for Israel's future* (Tel Aviv, 1995).
9. *A new hope for Israel's future.*
10. *A new hope for Israel's future.*
11. *Ha'aretz*, 21 December 1995.
12. *Ha'aretz*, 3 April 1996.
13. Sources for the bypass roads, Israeli cities and Jewish settlements on Maps 5.5, 5.6 and 5.7: Proposed Plan Schemes, Civil Administration Bet El and Municipal Archives Jerusalem, Regional Road Plan # 50 (1984) in combination with the 'Colors of Rainbow' bypass road scheme (1994). Sources for other map elements: 'Metropolitan Jerusalem Plan', Mazor Kahan (1995) and for the outline of Greater Jerusalem according to the suggestion of the Jerusalem Institute of Israel Studies as reviewed in *Kol Ha'ir*, 22 March 1996.
14. See: 'Capital's secret plan: new roads, new homes ...', *Jerusalem Post*, 4 November 1994.
15. See: 'Industrial Twilight Zones', *Jerusalem Post*, 6 December 1995.
16. According to the calculation in S. Kaminker, *Planning and Housing Issues in East Jerusalem* (Jerusalem: St. Yves Centre, 1994).
17. As can be gathered from the regularly appearing Statistical Yearbooks of Jerusalem, published by the Jerusalem Institute of Israel Studies.
18. According to the Information Bulletin of the Israeli Ministry of Foreign Affairs, March 1997.
19. See: J. de Jong, '"To save what can be saved"; Reading between the lines of Palestinian strategy on Jerusalem', *News from Within*, May 1996.

6 THE EFFECT OF THE OSLO AGREEMENT ON THE PALESTINIAN POLITICAL SYSTEM

Jamil Hilal

INTRODUCTION

The contention of this essay is that the Oslo Agreement has hurried, or has been manipulated to hasten, developments in the Palestinian political system toward what looks like a one-party system generating a neo-patrimonial-bureaucratic regime under the supreme authority of one leader.[1] Such a contention demands a look at the Oslo Agreement not simply as a text but also as a political tool fashioned at a specific historical conjuncture, a conjuncture defined by its regional and international context, which has specific socio-economic and institutional ramifications.

Such a comprehensive perspective is beyond the scope and mandate of this essay. Nevertheless, the essay will attempt to evaluate some of the political changes that have been instituted by the Oslo Agreement; in particular the general elections for a Palestinian legislative council in the West Bank and Gaza Strip and the election of the head of the Palestinian National Authority (PNA). Both events took place in January 1996.

PALESTINIAN LEGISLATIVE COUNCIL (PLC) ELECTIONS: THE BIRTH OF DEMOCRACY IN PALESTINE?

There are those who regard the holding of free general elections, by secret ballot, for the selection of members of PLC as heralding the birth of democracy in Palestine.[2] Such an

opinion is based on the fact that this is the first time that such
elections have been held, and that they have resulted in the
establishment of an independent legislative body separate from
an executive body.

The elected PLC obtains its legitimacy from the exercise of
popular will based on the universal adult franchise; it is formed
differently from the Palestinian National Council (PNC), which
operated on the basis of a different legitimacy. The PNC's
legitimacy was a revolutionary one embodied in the representation of all armed political groups in leading PLO institutions as
decision-making bodies, usually through a process of consensus
(at the top) rather than by majority vote, and an ideology
stressing the importance of national unity and armed struggle
with its centralist form of command. This legitimacy has
become, since the Oslo Agreement, formally defunct. Palestinians have known more or less free elections before but they
never went beyond municipalities (as happened in 1976 in the
West Bank and Gaza Strip) and student and professional
associations.

The significance, however, of the creation of the PLC for
Palestinian political life needs to be looked at within the political
and social composition of the historical context in which it was
created, and the role it is likely to play (separately or in
conjunction with other institutions) in shaping future Palestinian
political society.

It needs to be recalled that the Oslo Agreement was signed in
a regional and international situation characterised by rapid
changes in the relations of power. The Madrid peace conference
was started in the autumn of 1991, soon after the second Gulf
war, which marked a changing regional political order: a
divided Arab world; a militarily and economically shattered
Iraq; an isolated (regionally and internationally) and penalised
(financially and politically) PLO because of the position it took
in relation to the conflict in the Gulf, and mounting pressures
on the Palestinians in the Occupied Territories (closures by
Israel, much reduced remittances from relatives in the Gulf
states and from a financially starved PLO) and elsewhere,
especially in the Gulf states and Lebanon.

Internationally the Soviet Union, a traditional ally of the PLO, was in the process of disintegration, resulting, among many other things, in new waves of Jewish emigration to Israel, a flow that helped to expand settlement activity in the Occupied Territories. In contrast, the United States, a major ally of Israel, was strengthening its international dominance and enhancing its influence in the Middle East.

In short, the Madrid conference and the Oslo Agreement came as the balance of forces favouring the Palestinians was at its weakest. At the Palestinian level the Intifada, following three long years of intensive pressures and repression, was burning itself out. This new structured imbalance of forces was bound to take its toll and influence the contents of the Oslo Agreement.

But the PLC and presidential elections had their own specific context and ramifications. The most crucial are discussed below.

The Timing of the Elections

The elections came *after* the establishment of a Palestinian executive authority (self-ruling government). In other words, executive power (government), with its security, police, administrative and ideological structures and apparatuses, was established prior to the establishment of other state structures, especially the legislative and the judiciary. Prior to the elections the National Authority, as the acting government, was able to weaken the radical Islamic opposition when the latter tried to challenge its authority, and succeeded in establishing itself as the only central power. In this, the Palestinian Authority was aided by the Oslo Agreement and the international recognition it received, the financial aid and loans (though meagre by international standards) diverted to it by donors, and, most importantly, by the support of the major political faction of the PLO (that is, Fatah). In other words, the PNA had at its disposal both the growing semi-state bureaucracy (as a source of income and status) and police and security forces. It also drew on the support of a sizeable section of the population who saw in the establishment of a central Palestinian authority a source of security for themselves and their property, and a step towards the establishment of an independent state.

The World Bank

The growing influence of the World Bank on the direction of the Palestinian economy as a free-market economy, with emphasis on the private sector under the ethos of 'structural adjustment' is a factor of some importance. The philosophy of 'economic liberalisation' advocated by international organisations, the United States and the European Union, given the de-developed condition of the Palestinian economy inherited by the PNA after three decades of Israeli occupation, could only widen socio-economic and class inequalities. The advocacy of 'political liberalisation' and democratisation – in conditions of widening social inequalities, increasing poverty and deprivation – is not likely to fall on fertile ground. Those with increasing wealth as a result of 'economic liberalisation' find it in their interest to exercise more control on those who feel that such policies, coupled with Israeli policies of closure and restrictions, are producing unemployment, lower wages and more difficult living conditions.[3]

Premature Power

The establishment of a government prior to a state – with all its structures – was bound to affect the course of later political developments. Israel, supported by the United States, found the strengthening of the executive functions of the PNA convenient as 'security concerns', including the control of the Palestinian opposition represented by political groups that rejected the Oslo accords and advocated the continuation of armed struggle. This explains why the size of security forces established by the PNA was reported to have reached a level that exceeded by far, without serious objections by Israel or the United States, what was originally agreed upon between the two parties. In fact Israel raised the issue only after the armed confrontation of September 1996 in which the Palestinian police fought the Israel army in defence of civilians. Similarly, neither Israel nor the United States raised any objections to the formation of military courts (called state security courts) by the PNA, a step directed and used against the Palestinian opposition, particularly the Islamic radical groups and the Popular Front for the Liberation of Palestine.

In short, a centralised system of power was established before a necessary system of checks and balances was put in place. This established an *a priori* position of strength for the executive branch in relation to the legislature, the judiciary and non-governmental organisations, or what is referred to as 'civil society'. Some argue that this situation, enhanced by the absence of a basic law (or a constitution) regulating the powers of the government, with the backdrop of paralysis afflicting existing national institutions (represented by the PLO), has greatly encouraged officious, individualistic and autocratic styles of government which have begun to encroach – in the form of top-down regulations – into autonomous spheres of civil life. The fact that the head of the PNA (termed *al-rais* in the Oslo II agreement) combines this position with the long-standing positions of chairman of the Executive Committee of the PLO and leader of the major Palestinian political faction (that is, Fatah), has meant the accumulation of too much power in the hands of one man.

The Legacy of Occupation

It should be recalled that the PNA was established on a Palestinian territory that had been subjected to a long military and colonial occupation which penalised and repressed political organisations and obstructed the development of mass, professional and civil organisations and associations. The de-development of the economy of the West Bank and Gaza Strip, and the generation of its dependency on the more powerful Israeli economy, facilitated neither the growth of a strong workers' trade union movement nor the growth of a significant resident class of productive bourgeoisie with a strong interest in a democratic system of government.

The growth of Palestinian universities in the occupied West Bank and Gaza Strip has helped in building a strong student movement with a commitment to a democratic system of government, as exemplified in the clashes with security forces and in the regular democratic election that are held in universities for student councils.

Uncertain Financial Capital

Palestinian financial capital in the diaspora has no unifying or
formal links with the PNA and has not succeeded in creating a
'lobby' for itself *vis-à-vis* the PNA. It has refrained so far from any
substantive investments in the Palestinian economy, adopting a
wait-and-see attitude. The ambiguity surrounding the final settlement, the Israeli closures, the underdeveloped material infrastructure of the economy in the West Bank and Gaza Strip are all
factors that have persuaded Palestinian capital in the diaspora to
adopt a cautious attitude towards the PNA. It is important,
however, to recall at this point that Palestinian capital in the
diaspora has no particular commitment to democracy as such.
This capital, if one excludes the part that was made and is invested
in North America and Western Europe, was formed and operates
in economies with mostly undemocratic systems of government
(the Gulf states, Jordan, Syria, etc.). In so far as it is interested in
political democracy, this interest is confined to the rules and
regulations that protect the interest of private capital and its
freedom of movement.

Degrees of Independence

The timing of the elections for a Palestinian Legislative
Council, its size, functions and powers, were issues of
negotiation between the PLO and Israel (Oslo II). That is, the
process of democratisation (in terms of form, pace and content)
of the Palestinian political system was not left solely to the
Palestinians to decide. Calls for the democratisation of the PLO
institutions had become more frequent and intense many years
before the Madrid peace conference. Israel interfered in
negotiating the form and power of the elections in order to
circumvent the exercise of Palestinian sovereignty. In other
words, Israel's dominant concern in the negotiations was to
prevent and obstruct in every possible way the establishment of
an independent Palestinian state. Hence Israel used all its
weight to circumscribe the powers of the legislative council as it
bounded the powers of the executive authority of the PNA.

The fact that the election of the legislative council came within the framework of the Oslo Agreement was the main argument that was used by the Palestinian opposition to boycott the elections. It was thought that participation in the election would give legitimacy to the Oslo accords. This attitude of the opposition is not politically sagacious, but it does indicate that Palestinian elections came at a highly divisive political moment as far as Palestinian political society was concerned.

The Opposition's Boycott

The call by the Palestinian opposition to boycott the PLC elections had the consequence of accentuating the dominance of one political group, that is Fatah, as we will illustrate later. Furthermore the boycott of the elections (which took the form of a boycott of the whole election process and not simply the voting procedure) helped to no small extent to depoliticise the election campaign. But more significantly, the boycott marked a failure on the part of the opposition to seize an opportunity to legitimise its role as an opposition at the official and popular levels, as well as at the regional and international levels. The opposition could have presented itself to the electorate as a necessary and responsible component of a new Palestinian political system that was passing through a formative stage. This failure took place at a moment when the whole future of the Palestinian political system was being negotiated internally and externally.

Public opinions polls conducted prior to the January 1996 elections indicated a strong commitment by the electorate to taking part in the first general and free political elections that involved universal direct suffrage for everybody over the age of 18 in the West Bank and Gaza Strip. Just over two-thirds (69 per cent) of the electorate, according to one public opinion poll conducted by CPRS (Centre for Palestine Research and Studies) in Nablus in October 1995, thought that the election of the PLC would promote democracy in Palestinian society, and would generally bring changes for the better. A significant minority (37 per cent) thought, however, that the election would provide legitimacy to the Oslo Agreement, which they considered unsatisfactory. In another public opinion poll conducted by JMCC (Jerusalem Media and Communication Centre) in public opinion poll no. 11, December 1995, a month prior to the elections, some 82 per cent of the electorate strongly or moderately agreed that they had a civic responsibility to take part in the elections.

The indifference of the Palestinian opposition parties to the political attitudes of Palestinians in the Occupied Territories, as illustrated by their opposing the election and participation in the election process, could not pass without repercussions. One such repercussion was to marginalise and weaken the standing of the opposition parties among the populace of the Palestinian territories. An average of 73.5 per cent turned out to vote in the West Bank districts and some 88 per cent in the Gaza Strip. The turnout would have been higher in the West Bank had it not been obstructed by Israeli measures, as happened in East Jerusalem, where the turnout did not exceed 40.4 per cent.

It is beyond the framework of this paper to discuss these repercussions, which are not confined to the conduct of the opposition parties alone but need to be looked at within the whole political environment. By adopting 'rejectionist' policies rather than critical political programmatic alternatives, the opposition paved the way for Fatah to win an outstanding victory in the elections. This 'rejectionist' posturing came at a time when political and ideological pluralism, which has characterised much of the PLO's history, was under stress and the PLO national institutions were hardly functioning. This was used by the leadership of the dominant Palestinian political faction to weaken further and ultimately pre-empt Palestinian national institutions.

The occasion of electing a Palestinian Legislative Council in the West Bank and Gaza Strip provided an opportunity to stress the need for a new political forum and institutional structure for Palestinian government. It further called for the rethinking of the role and structure of the PLO institutions and the PLO's relationship to the PLC and the Palestinian Authority. This was necessary as the election involved only Palestinians living in the Occupied Territories and the returnees. The larger portion of the Palestinians were unable to participate in the election of their representatives or their government. A need for an all-embracing national institution representing the national interests of Palestin-

ians in Palestine and the diaspora remained. The old structures of
the PLO needed radical reform and a new impetus.

The Palestinian struggle for self-determination has entered,
with the Oslo Agreement, a new era demanding seemingly
opposed involvements; one stipulating the continuation of the
struggle for national rights and the other designating the need to
get on with the task of building the institutions of a modern state.
It involved a need to restructure the relationships between the
various Palestinian communities: those in the West Bank and
Gaza Strip, those in Israel, and those communities living in the
diaspora, especially in Lebanon, Syria and Jordan.

'Inside' vs. 'Outside' Palestinians

The elections of the PLC and the head of the National Authority
involved only one section of the Palestinian people, those residing in
the West Bank, including East Jerusalem, and the Gaza Strip, as well
as those allowed to return by the time of the Oslo Agreement (mostly
those who made up the PLO institutions). This indicated two significant things: the final transfer of the centre of gravity of Palestinian political activity and decision making from centres outside Palestine, where it has been for decades, to the Occupied Palestinian
Territories; and the marginalisation of at least half of the Palestinian
people who live outside Palestine. Palestinians outside the West
Bank and Gaza Strip were excluded from their innate right to participate in general elections which would inevitably affect their political future; and they were excluded, as communities, from taking
part in the negotiations concerning as vital an issue as the right to
return, which was left to the 'final status' stage of the negotiations.
The fact that the PLO, represented by the Palestine National Council (PNC) and the Central Council, was no longer active or effective
made Palestinian communities in the diaspora feel that their interests and aspirations had no venue or forum. This explains why there
has been so much opposition among these communities to the Oslo
Accord. The fact that the election of the PLC was tied to the Oslo
accords left these communities feeling excluded, frustrated and de-
jected. Nor can the effect of the Oslo accords on the politics of the
Palestinian minority in Israel be ignored.

The highlighting of a division between the Palestinians of the 'inside' and those of the 'outside' is an aspect of the PLC and presidential elections which – regardless of their importance and significance to any democratic transformation in Palestine – cannot be ignored in any discourse on future political developments among the Palestinians.

THE LEGISLATIVE COUNCIL AND THE NEW POLITICAL REGIME

Given the political moment that underpinned the elections of the PLC, the election laws that governed the election process, the boycott of the elections by the opposition political parties,[4] and the general popularity among the people of the West Bank and Gaza Strip of the idea of choosing their own representatives, the results of the elections are not surprising. It is worth remembering that the elections took place shortly after Israeli withdrawals from most of the Gaza Strip and all the towns in the West Bank, except for Hebron, which was scheduled for later. This induced in large numbers of Palestinians in the Occupied Territories an optimistic outlook on the progress of the negotiations and boosted confidence in the peace process and the PNA.

But democratic elections do not necessarily lead to empowering institutional democratic arrangements. The record of the PLC in the first year since its election does not leave much room for optimism. During that period the Council held 34 sessions and passed some 135 resolutions, none of which was implemented. During that year only one law (concerning local authority elections) was ratified by the head of the National Authority. Some of the leading members of the Council, such as Haidar Abdul-Shafi, felt that it had been marginalised by the executive authority or rather by the head of that authority. Some commentators believe that the PNA looks at the PLC not in terms of an embodiment of the separation of powers but in terms of its role in the national struggle for independence. They believe that the record of the government in this sphere justifies the popularity it has over the Legislative Council. They point out that public opinion polls give the performance of the presidency office a higher evaluation than the government and give the government a higher evaluation than the Legislative Council. In fact, the latter, a year after its birth, is allotted a lower rating than the security and police forces.[5]

One major reason for this is the political and social composition of the PLC, a composition that has strengthened a hierarchical power structure with one centre of power.

THE POLITICAL COMPOSITION OF THE PLC

Fatah competed for the Legislative Council seats with lists officially approved by the Fatah leadership, and also with candidates who put themselves forward for election without official approval. The resulting political composition of the 88 seats of the PLC was as follows:

- Fatah: 68 seats or 77 per cent of the total

- Secular (nationalist) non-affiliated candidates: 12 seats or 13.6 per cent of the total

- Political Islam-oriented non-affiliated candidates: 7 seats or 8 per cent of the total

- Others (a small secular party): 1 seat.

Of the 68 Fatah members who gained seats in the PLC, 47 members or 69 per cent came from officially approved lists (which totalled some 77 candidates). On the other hand, only some of the 21 non-official Fatah candidates (classified as 'independents' by the Central Election Committee) who gained seats to the PLC entered the elections because they opposed the politics of their leadership. In fact, just over 60 per cent supported the Oslo Agreement. Some of the non-official Fatah candidates put themselves forward for election hoping to improve their standing in their local communities, and others because they disapproved of the selection procedures. Still others disapproved of the policies followed by the PNA.

Similarly, not all non-Fatah candidates who gained seats were opposed to the Oslo accords or necessarily critical of the policies of the leadership. Some, however, most probably gained their seats because they had a clearly critical stance.

What the results of the PLC elections amounted to can be summarised as follows: Fatah gained just over three-quarters of the PLC seats. It is true that not all Fatah PLC members can be counted on to support the government (the executive authority); nevertheless, the government can be sure of a clear majority through Fatah support and the support of some of the independent members. Some of the members of the PLC had not been affiliated to any political party or group and are for that reason probably not highly politicised or carriers of strong ideologies. As such some will find in Fatah the group they can easily identify with since it has the least formulated ideology, demands least of its members, has the most to offer in terms of privileges, and remains acceptable regionally and internationally. On the other hand, some 14 members of the Council are, or were, affiliated or connected to currently active political groups that did not contest the elections.

The overwhelming numerical domination of the PNC by one political party could have been minimised, to some degree at least, had the opposition (both Islamic and nationalist-secular) organised its forces and contested the elections. It is difficult to estimate the composition of the PLC if this had happened. But there are indications that some change would have taken place. The success of candidates who lean towards political Islam in constituencies of the Gaza Strip where at the last minute the local leadership of Hamas called on its supporters to vote for them is an indication.

Another indication is the success in both the West Bank and Gaza Strip of independent candidates who were critical of Fatah policies and institution-building in the areas under Palestinian control. Some of these candidates, such as Haidar Abdul-Shafi (Gaza city constituency) and Abed al-Jawad Saleh received significantly higher votes than Fatah candidates. Other non-Fatah candidates affiliated to small political parties somewhat critical of the leadership of the PNA (e.g. the Palestinian People's Party and the Palestinian Democratic Union) gained a significant share of the vote in their constituencies. This suggests that a decision by the opposition to take part in the election in a unified block, or two blocks, would have lowered the Fatah majority in the PLC appreciably.

The overwhelming majority attained by Fatah in the PLC has to be attributed also to the election law that was adopted, favouring the larger political parties and movements. Election by a simple majority system tends to inflate the strength of larger political parties and deflate that of smaller ones. Some of the smaller parties' candidates who contested the elections and failed to gain seats had more than 5 per cent of the votes cast in their electoral districts.[6] A proportional representation system would have ensured a different political composition of the PLC as smaller parties and non-affiliated candidates would have been represented. Such a system, according to public opinion polls, had more support than the simple majority system.[7] As it happened, none of the smaller parties succeeded in gaining seats. The Palestinian Democratic Union (Feda) candidate who gained a seat in the Ramallah district, did so by contesting the election on an official Fatah list, and Haidar Abdul-Shafi gained his seat as a well-known public figure and not as the leader of the Movement of Democratic Construction. Others who are affiliated to or supporters of opposition political parties (particularly Hamas and the Popular Front) gained seats not as representatives of such parties since they contested the elections as independents. It is probable that the fact that they challenged their parties' decision to boycott the election helped to gain them votes.

The existing political composition of the PLC, irrespective of the conditions and factors that shaped it, raises the question whether the emerging political system in the Palestinian territories is a *one-party regime* (such as exists in Syria, Iraq, Tunisia, or until recently in Algeria). This question has to be raised not simply because Fatah and its supporters have an overwhelming majority in the PLC, but because they also dominate the executive branches of the PNA (ministries, agencies and apparatuses), as well as the PLO institutions (the Palestine National Council and its leading bodies) and its diplomatic missions. A majority of the ministers (15 out of 28) in the PNA government are Fatah members, as well as the overwhelming majority of the under-secretaries and their deputies.[8] All the top positions in the security forces are taken up by Fatah members. Most if not all of the Muhafivs (district governors) are affiliated to Fatah. The elected Speaker of the PLC is a member of the Fatah Central Committee

and one of the main Oslo accords negotiators. The directly elected
head of the PNA is the leader of Fatah, a position he combines
with the chairmanship of the Executive Committee of the PNC. It
is no accident that joint meetings of the PNA Ministerial Council
and the Executive Committee have become the norm. The
rationale behind this is that such meetings allow for decisions of
Palestinian national issues (basically negotiations with Israel) and
issues that concern specifically the West Bank and Gaza Strip.

THE WEAKNESS OF ORGANISED OPPOSITION

The weakness of organised opposition is a phenomenon that
extends, at the present, to groups inside the PLC and to political
groups in political society at large. It extends to mass organisations and is being extended to civil institutions.

Opposition inside the PLC

The composition of PLC members who are not affiliated to Fatah is
not favourable to the emergence of an organised opposition. Opposition has formed around specific issues but its composition has varied
according to the issue concerned. This is not surprising considering
the political diversity of members who are not affiliated to Fatah.
Three of this group belong to the Popular Front for the Liberation of
Palestine, six come from an Islamic background (five from a radical
background). Two were from a left-wing background not affiliated
to any of the existing political groups, three had differing affiliations
to PLO groups, and five have no previous or present political affiliation. With such a mixture of different political and ideological backgrounds it is difficult to envisage the formation of a parliamentary
bloc. Opposition stances have taken place on some issues but these
involved members from a variety of political tendencies, including
Fatah. In other words, the opposition in the PLC has no defined
political boundaries, hence the real difficulty of turning itself into a
unified bloc or a lobby.

The difficulty facing any attempt to form a parliamentary
opposition bloc can be illustrated by looking at the affiliations of

the 23 members in the PLC who clearly opposed the Oslo Agreement. Twelve of these members are affiliated to Fatah (two-thirds are candidates who were not on the official Fatah election list). The other half are composed of seven independent nationalists (secular leanings) and four independents from the Islamic camp. Similar figures are obtained regarding the 24 members who opposed amending the Palestinian National Covenant. Twelve are Fatah members, nine are independent nationalist and three are from the Islamic camp.

It is interesting to note that 24 members of the PLC gave a vote of no confidence in the new government that was formed in June 1996. Of these, thirteen were Fatah, six were from the independent nationalist (secular) camp, and five were independent but from the Islamic camp. It is still worth remembering that there were also persons in the last two camps who took positions supportive of the executive authority. Concerning the last issue, for example, four members from the secular camp gave a vote of confidence to the new government, whilst one abstained, and one absented himself. Of the Islamic camp, one member voted for the government and one abstained.[9]

In terms of its socio-economic composition, the PLC is heavily tilted towards the middle class. Three-quarters of the members of the PLC come from the towns of the West Bank and Gaza Strip; only one-eighth come from villages, and one-ninth from refugee camps. This does not reflect the actual distribution of the Palestinian population according to the three types of settlements. Moreover, women are grossly under-represented – they comprise not more than 6 per cent of the total membership of the PLC.[10] Similarly, workers or workers' trade unions are not present in the Council. This, coupled with the inconspicuous presence of the Palestinian left in the legislative institution, stresses the absence of those who can represent the interests of the working class and other disadvantaged groups. Nearly half (45 per cent) the members of the PLC are technocrats, the overwhelming majority being residents of the West Bank and Gaza Strip, and some 14 per cent worked as functionaries in PLO institutions, being returnees.

In other words, technocrats and bureaucrats comprise over 60 per cent of the membership of the PLC. Businesspeople formed 8 per cent of the Council, and those in private institutions some 6 per cent. The rest (a quarter of the PLC) are individuals who were active in the Intifada and in the national movement.

Over half of the members of the Council had a declared net income exceeding the equivalent of US$1400 per month and over three-quarters had a declared net income exceeding US$840 per month. In comparison, only a quarter of the Palestinian employed labour force has a net income exceeding US$620 per month.

The privileged position of the PLC members is reflected in the high degree of education that they enjoy; some 83 per cent of the Council members are university graduates, and nearly a quarter hold post-graduate degrees. The local bourgeoisie are directly represented in the Council only marginally. However, it can be assumed, despite its populist leanings, that Fatah represents the interests of the Palestinian wealthy strata. It is relevant in this context to mention that the landed and trading families in the West Bank and Gaza are present, although not strongly, in the Council.

The PLC remains, in many ways, a product of the Palestinian national movement and its transformation. Nearly three-quarters of the Council members are also members of leading political bodies of Palestinian groups (e.g., central committees, polit-bureaux, executive bureaux or their equivalent such as the Revolutionary Council in Fatah). These bodies have, however, become more heavily tilted towards the traditional local bourgeoisie and the middle classes, reflecting the changed balance of class forces resulting from the decline in the influence of the left organisations and the downturn in grass-roots activities and the size of mass organisations, particularly the trade union movement and the women's movement.

The Decline of Political Radicalism

A number of factors have combined to weaken political party affiliation within Palestinian communities in the years that followed the Intifada and the establishment of PNA. This decline is, however, more pronounced among the radical parties, Islamic and secular, being clearest among the latter. It is not the intention here to review and discuss all these developments. Some factors, however, are of particular importance: the changes in the international and regional situation and in the Palestinian socio-economic and political situation, the inability of the radical groups to mobilise large sections of the population for their anti-Oslo programme and to initiate the organisational changes necessary to deal with new developments, the result of the Oslo Agreement and the shift of the centre of Palestinian political and organisational activity to the West Bank and Gaza Strip.

It is the last factor which commands the other factors because it demanded a new style of organisation, a new programme and a new type of leadership more attuned to the changes taking place. These changes demand creative methods of achieving two tasks: the completion of national liberation and the imperatives of building new national institutions that can mobilise and direct efforts and resources for constructing an independent state and meet the needs of the people.

This is why the group of ten organisations formed in Damascus in opposition to the Oslo Agreement made no tangible impact on the course of events and produced no noticeable impact on public opinion in the Occupied Territories.[11] As a group, they retained their old structures and programmes and partisan postures. They failed to gain adequate support among Palestinians in the Occupied Territories to exert substantial pressure on the Palestinian leadership engaged in the negotiations to change its policies. The coalition, which united groups as ideologically and programmatically different as Hamas and the Popular Front for the Liberation of Palestine, could not be sustained for a long period. The fact that the coalition had its headquarters in Damascus proved a hindrance at a juncture when the central arena of political activity had firmly established itself in the West Bank and Gaza Strip. Many of the organisations of the coalition are tiny in the support they command, and most had no influence whatsoever in the Occupied Territories. The decision by the opposition parties which had influence in the PNA area to boycott the general elections did not help to improve their standing among Palestinians in this area. Their ineffectual role in a PNC meeting held in April 1996 to discuss amending the Palestinian National Charter did not help either.

Almost all the Palestinian political groups have in recent years faced internal discontent and division. This was witnessed within

the Fatah movement, with members putting themselves forward
for elections against the decision of the movement's leadership. It
was witnessed in the Hamas movement, with the local leadership
asking members, at the last minute, to go out to vote. It was
witnessed in the Popular Front, with candidates putting themselves forward for election and members exercising their right to
vote. It was witnessed in other groups as well. Many political
formations showed signs of internal conflict and strain between
the leadership of the 'outside' and the leadership of the Palestinian
territories. Nevertheless, none of the new political parties established after Oslo managed to gain seats or establish a noticeable
base. Almost all were very small splinter groups from older
political formations.[12]

The following table shows the rating given to the major
political groups in public opinion polls between December 1994
and December 1996.

Table 6.1

Major Political Affiliations of Palestinians in the West Bank and
Gaza Strip between December 1994 and December 1996 (%)

Affiliation	Dec 1994	Dec 1995	Mar 1996	June 1996	Dec 1996
Fatah	43.1%	55.3%	47.5%	43.3%	45.4%
Hamas	16.6%	9.7%	5.8%	7.8%	10.1%
Islamic Jihad	2.6%	2.0%	1.0%	1.9%	2.0%
Hamas & Islamic Jihad	19.2%	11.7%	6.8%	9.7%	12.1%
Popular Front	6.7%	3.8%	2.1%	4.0%	3.3%
Democratic Front	1.4%	1.5%	1.1%	0.8%	0.9%
Pop. & Dem. Fronts	8.1%	5.3%	3.2%	4.8%	4.2%
PPP & FIDA	1.6%	2.2%	1.9%	3.1%	1.7%
No affiliation to any of the existing parties	11.7%	13.8%	25.0%	28.1%	26.5%
Other parties	7.7%	4.8%	5.3%	2.9%	3.5%

(Source: calculated from results of opinion polls conducted by CPRS)

The figures shown in the table indicate that while Fatah maintained its size of support during the period between December 1994 and December 1996, both the secular and Islamic opposition lost a significant portion of their support.[13] Hamas and Islamic Jihad lost more than a third of their support, while the Popular Front and the Democratic Front, representing the secular opposition, lost nearly half of their support. Secular parties which supported, although not without criticism, the Oslo Agreement, retained their earlier strength but remained marginal. The table also shows that the parties that boycotted the legislative elections witnessed a sharp drop in their support after these elections. The opposition parties, apart from celebrations of certain occasions and seasonal protests and political statements, have not made any impact on the person in the street. They have not utilised the change in their status from underground organisations to publicly operating political parties. Nor has an impact been felt after the return of the leadership and experienced cadres of these political parties from the diaspora.

The table indicates a steady growth in the size of the electorate which does not support any of the existing parties, and a sharp drop in the size of those supporting 'other parties'. The relative size of those who did not support any of the existing political parties more than doubled between December 1994 and December 1996. This indicates a disillusionment with the existing party system. It is also indicated by the fact that the size of Fatah has not been growing despite the material and other resources it enjoys as the party in power. The withdrawal of Israel from the cities of the West Bank and from most of the Gaza Strip and the continuation of the peace process despite the many obstacles, particularly after the ascent of the right-wing Likud party to power in Israel, helped to maintain a relatively high level of support for Fatah. The popularity enjoyed by Arafat is an additional factor.[14] The support given to Fatah, however, could become shaky with any noticeable increase in corruption in government circles and if violations of human rights continue, since Fatah is – and is perceived as – the party in power. The support accorded to the ruling party could erode if the economic situation deteriorates further and/or the peace process reaches a dead end.

The Retreat of Mass Organisations

The post-Oslo period has witnessed a further decline in the role of mass organisations, particularly the women's and trade union movements. The exception to this is the student movement, which continues to be periodically active, although not to the level of the previous decade. It remains fragmented, however, and almost entirely confined to the level of each of the universities in the West Bank and Gaza Strip. Of relevance here is the change in the status of the PLO from a banned terrorist organisation to a recognised peace partner by Israel. Such a change had an effect on many of the mass and professional organisations, trade unions and associations, particularly those working in the Occupied Territories. This is because these bodies acted typically as 'fronts' for the underground political parties active in the West Bank and Gaza Strip, and thus their priority was resistance to the Israeli occupation. The general decline of party affiliation and the change of their status from underground to open activity have demanded a new role from these professional and mass organisations.

In the case of the trade union movement in the West Bank and Gaza Strip, additional problems presented themselves because of the colonial peripheral economy created in these areas. The dominant mode of production was formed around small family-type enterprises and day migrant labour employed in Israel. This migrant labour formed, up to the early 1990s, nearly 40 per cent of the Palestinian labour force in these areas. More permanent migrant workers found employment up to the mid-1980s in the oil-producing Arab states. This situation, combined with the territorial fragmentation of the Palestinian areas (that is, the West Bank, the Gaza Strip, East Jerusalem), made the unionisation of labour not an easy task. High rates of unemployment among manual workers, affected by Israeli closures of Palestinian territories, adds to the difficulties of unionising workers.

For the same reason, attempts to unify women, workers and student organisations failed as each of the main political groups chose to maintain control on its own mass or professional organisation, which adopted its political and social programme. The situation was further complicated by the fact that the headquarters of these organisations were situated outside Palestine. In most countries of the Palestinian diaspora, political and socio-economic conditions were different, and the PLO and its constituent factions could operate openly. After Oslo many of the leaders of mass and professional organisations were appointed to various positions within the PNA structures of authority, creating a conflict of interest. The change in the Palestinian political situation, however, has not as yet led to restructuring of their organisations, including the holding of elections, applying stricter rules for membership and formulating more relevant programmes. Such reforms, lacking for so many years, have become crucial since Oslo.

The importance of active mass organisations, professional associations and trade union movements to the distribution of power, and thus to democratisation, cannot be overstated. A strong and autonomous trade union movement has an interest in the formation and maintenance of a democratic state, since this gives workers a better collective-bargaining position. It also produces governments and employers more responsive to workers' rights. Similarly, a strong women's movement has an interest in democracy as it provides a suitable milieu for equality and attention to women's rights and needs.

The current weakness and fragmentation of both the trade union and women's movement is of no comfort to those seeking or hoping for the development of a constitutional government and a democratic state in Palestine. Nor is it for those hoping to prevent the emergence of another one-party state with autocratic forms of government. The paralysis of the existing political parties, and the absence of a single major popular party in opposition, are both factors that do not make for the development of democracy in Palestine. Hamas, which remains at the moment and probably for some time to come the largest party in opposition, is not a political formation that has the defence of human rights and the principle of equality as an utmost priority. It is a party, despite the transformations it has gone through and is likely to go through, that is dominated by an exclusivist, moralistic and organic conception of society. It perceives the sources of its socio-economic programme and values as sacred and thus unquestionable. This does not exclude attempts to co-opt it or sections of it by the PNA.

CONCLUSION

An analysis of the distribution of power in the existing Palestinian political system, the class structure, the paucity of resources available, the economic dependency, the specific process of state formation and the PNA position in the regional and international structures of dependency all lead to the following conclusion: formally, the emerging government in the Palestinian territories takes the form of a one-party state, but functions as a neo-patrimonial-bureaucratic regime where political power is being monopolised by a 'historical' personality. The party structure has been merged (through appointments of its cadres and many of its rank and file) into the administrative structure of the PNA and its security and police apparatus. This process could lead to the depoliticisation of the political party, which would again strengthen the regime. With the opposition and other political parties a process of political repression and co-optation has been used with some success.

The election of a Legislative Council has introduced a new form of legitimacy based on free and democratic elections and accountability. This form of legitimacy is coming into conflict with the older PLO 'revolutionary' legitimacy that has been routinised and personalised, but which continues to rely on the transitional situation of the Occupied Palestinian Territories and the conflict with Israel to renew its legitimacy. This contradiction is represented by the conflict between the executive authority of the PNA, represented by the presidency office, and the Legislative Council. The fact that the latter institution is dominated by the ruling party leads one to expect a form of compromise that is more relevant to the distribution of power within Fatah than a compromise promoting significantly the transfer to democracy.

The fact that Arafat led the nationalist struggle for three decades and has succeeded in establishing a national authority over a part of Palestine, albeit a very small part, has given him a popularity no other existing Palestinian leader enjoys. The fact that the struggle for political independence and against settlements, annexation and economic blockade continues, gives additional importance to this dimension. Public opinion polls conducted in the West Bank and Gaza Strip persistently give very high priority to democratic values, including political pluralism, freedom of speech, separation of powers, protection of minority rights, and free, regular and fair general elections.[15] Nevertheless, the transitional situation in which Palestinians find themselves seems to dictate the priority of the national over other dimensions.

We have seen similar developments take place in Algeria, Tunisia, Syria and in many Third World countries. In the case of Palestine, the head of the PNA was directly elected in democratic elections. He also holds the office of the Chairman of the Executive Committee of the PLO. More significant, however, is his direct control over the security and police forces and over all appointments to all top government positions, his control, through the manipulation of various administrative and other mechanisms, of the resources of the PNA, and his powers to delay and obstruct legislation so as to maintain and entrench his neo-patrimonial system of authority. All this points to a personalised system of authority, a system which does not rely on or allow the functioning of national institutions, and which limits the role of public administration to the management of the ruler's directives.

NOTES

1. Patrimonialism and neo-patrimonialism are used here in the Weberian sense (Max Weber, *The Theory of Social and Economic Organization* (New York: Oxford University Press, 1947)). These are systems of political authority based on 'personal' and bureaucratic powers exerted by a ruler. Patrimonialism involves a system of patron–client relationships. In the Palestinian case the party (Fatah) provides the system whereby top positions in the existing 'proto-state' are filled on the basis of loyalty to the leader. Hence the blurring of boundaries between public office and private interest, a situation which lends itself to corruption and *wasta*, or the use of connections to gain access to resources. The concept of neo-patrimonialism is preferred here to that of patrimonialism because the process is taking place in the context of creating the bureaucracies of a modern state. For an attempt to apply the concept of 'patrimonialism' to the Palestinian situation, see Rex Brynen, 'The neopatrimonial dimension of Palestinian politics', *Journal of Palestine Studies*, Vol. XXV, No. 1 (Autumn 1995) pp. 23–36.

2. The first general Palestinian elections, for a unicameral Legislative Council of 88 members on a multi-member constituency basis took place on 20 January 1996 in the West Bank (including Jerusalem) and Gaza Strip. The head of the PNA was also directly elected on the basis of the whole Palestinian territories forming one constituency. The West Bank was divided into eleven electoral districts and the Gaza Strip into five districts. The number of candidates to be elected followed roughly the size of the population of the district. Some 676 candidates put themselves forward for elections to the PNC, and two for the office of head (president) of the PNA (Yasser Arafat and Samiha Khalil). Ac-

cording to the Central Election Committee, over 73 per cent of the registered electorate participated in the election in the West Bank and more than 88 per cent in the Gaza Strip.

3. According to figures published by the Palestinian Central Bureau of Statistics (PCBS), unemployment in the Palestinian areas averaged during the period August to October 1996 some 21.8 per cent (18.5 per cent in the West Bank and 30.8 per cent in the Gaza Strip), while underemployment averaged 11.9 per cent (12.7 per cent in the West Bank and 9.8 per cent in the Gaza Strip). PCBS, Survey of Labour Force, August–October 1996, press release, 30/12/1996. See also, *The Economic Intelligence Unit Country Report*, Fourth quarter 1996, 'The Occupied Territories'.

4. The political parties that boycotted the elections included Hamas, Islamic Jihad, the Popular Front for the Liberation of Palestine and the Democratic Front for the Liberation of Palestine. The first two are 'fundamentalists' (political Islam groups), while the other two are left-wing secular groups.

5. In a public opinion poll taken in the last week of December 1996, the percentage of those who evaluated the performance of the 'presidency office' as good and very good totalled 75.5 per cent (39.7 per cent as very good, and 35.8 per cent as good), compared to 72.7 per cent who gave the same evaluation to the government (18.6 per cent as very good, and 44.1 per cent as good), and to the rating of 71.9 per cent given to the security and police forces (28 per cent as very good and 43.9 per cent as good), while the Legislative Council received a rating of 49.8 per cent (10.7 per cent as very good and 39.1 per cent as good). See: 'Results of Palestinian Public Opinion Poll No. 25', Centre for Palestine Research & Studies (CPRS), Nablus.

6. For example: Zahera Kemal (Feda) obtained 10.6 per cent of the votes in the Jerusalem constituency, and Rena Nashashibi (PPP) obtained 6.6 per cent of all votes in the same constituency. Both failed to gain a seat in the PLC while Ahmed al-Zughair (Fatah) who obtained 10.9 per cent of the votes gained a seat. In the Ramallah constituency Mustafa Barghuthi (Palestinian People's Party) obtained 5.9 per cent of the votes but failed to gain a seat while Marwan Baghouthi (Fatah) who gained 6.5 per cent of the votes gained a seat. In the Jenin constituency Saleh Ra'fet (Feda) obtained 5.4 per cent of the votes but failed to gain a seat while the candidate (Fatah) who obtained 6.5 per cent of the votes gained a seat.

7. One such poll, taken in mid-November 1995, showed 51 per cent support for the proportional system as against a 40 per cent support for the simple majority system; some 9 per cent had no opinion (Public opinion poll, 13–15 October 1995, Survey Research Unit, Centre for Palestine Research & Studies (CPRS), Nablus.

8. In June 1996, 34 out of the 39 (87 per cent) under-secretaries or deputy under-secretaries (where the post of the under-secretary is not filled) were Fatah members (usually members of the Revolutionary Council in Fatah). In all cases where the minister was not affiliated to Fatah, the under-secretary was.

9. The size of the political opposition within the PLC was, on the three major political issues mentioned above, between 23 and 33 members if those who abstained are counted. However, there was only a core of ten members opposing the government on all three issues. And this oppositional 'core' is not a group that is unified politically or ideologically: four are Fatah, three are from the Islamic camp, and three are from the independent secular camp.

10. United Nations figures (see Human Development Report for 1995) give an average of 10 per cent as the participation rate of women in the parliaments of Third World countries (United Nations, *Human Development Report* (New York: United Nations, 1995)).

11. Months after the Israeli Likud party won power in May 1996, a survey revealed that some 79 per cent of the adults in the West Bank and Gaza Strip supported the 'peace process'; the percent was 87 in the Gaza Strip and 75 in the West Bank (CPRS, Public opinion poll No. 215, December 1996). Similar results were obtained by another institute for October 1996: some 77.5 per cent of the public said they supported the 'peace process'; some 85 per cent in the Gaza Strip, and 72 per cent in the West Bank (JMCC, Public opinion poll, October 1996). One should be careful, however, in interpreting these results as in any way reflecting the acceptance of any settlement with Israel. In the CPRS survey mentioned above some 39.5 per cent of those interviewed supported armed attacks against Israeli targets while 48 per cent opposed them and 12 per cent had no opinion. A public opinion poll conducted by JMCC in December 1996 showed that 19.7 per cent of the sample 'strongly supported' the Oslo Agreement and a further 55.2% 'cautiously supported' it; that is, a total of 75% supported the agreement with differing degrees of support (*Palestine Report*, 3 January 1997). The same poll indicated that some 48 per cent (42 per cent in the West Bank and 59 per cent in the Gaza Strip) of those surveyed said that their economic situation and standard of living worsened after the Oslo Agreement against 9 per cent (8.7 per cent in the West Bank and 9.6 per cent in the Gaza Strip) who said that it improved.

12. In a survey conducted by CPRS in December 1995, only 3.5 per cent of those interviewed said they supported any of the new political parties announced after the Oslo Agreement.

13. The decline of the radical parties' support among youth and intellectuals is less than among the rest of the population. This explains why radical groups show significantly better results in university student elections than in public opinion polls. In Najah University student council elections that were held in December 1996, the Islamic Block (pro-Hamas) gained 39 seats, the Shabiba Movement (pro-Fatah) 36 seats and the secular opposition (pro-Popular and Democratic Fronts) 7 seats.

14. Public opinion polls continue to show high levels of popularity for Arafat, significantly higher than those registered for the Legislative Council. In a poll conducted over 26–28 December 1996 (three weeks before the withdrawal of Israeli troops from Hebron), some 75.5 per cent of those interviewed evaluated the performance of the presidency as good or very good compared to 49.8 per cent for the Legislative Council (CPRS, Poll No. 25). In another survey, 41.2 per cent of those asked said that Arafat is the personality trusted most, compared to 4.8 per cent who named Ahmed Yassin (the Islamic leader imprisoned by Israel) and 4.2 per cent who mentioned Haidar Abdul-Shafi. It is noticeable that 19.5 per cent said they did not trust anyone (survey conducted by JMCC, between 13–14 December 1996).

15. See *A Survey of Political and Social Attitudes among Palestinians in the West Bank and Gaza Strip*, August 1995, CPRS, Nablus.

7 THE POLITICS OF INTERNAL SECURITY: THE PALESTINIAN AUTHORITY'S NEW SECURITY SERVICES

Graham Usher

With the signing of the Israeli–Palestinian interim agreement on the West Bank and Gaza in September 1995,[1] it has become clear that future realisation of a peace settlement between Israel and the Palestinians no longer hinges on international legality.[2] Rather, it rests on a definition of peace that translates as unconditional security for the Israelis and conditional security for the Palestinians.

The interim agreement (or Oslo II) governs Israel's military redeployment in, and extends to the Palestinian Authority (PA) 'broadening' security and civil jurisdiction over, the West Bank. It mandates to the PA responsibility for the 'internal security arrangements' in Gaza and the other Palestinian autonomous areas for the duration of Oslo's three-year interim period. These 'arrangements' mark a depth of collaboration between Israeli and PA military forces far greater than anything experienced in the Oslo Agreement's Gaza and Jericho preamble, ranging from 'joint security coordination and cooperation committees' at the district level to 'joint patrols' at the local.

With Oslo II, PA security services are obliged to 'act systematically against all expressions of [Palestinian] violence and terror', 'arrest and prosecute [Palestinian] individuals suspected of perpetuating acts of violence and terror', and 'cooperate in the exchange of information as well as coordinate policies and activities' with Israel's security services. But they are not, 'in any circumstances', allowed to arrest or detain Israelis, despite the latter's 'right of movement' throughout the West Bank and Gaza, including inside the autonomous areas.[3] Should an Israeli be questioned by a police officer in these areas, it is the 'Israeli side' of the joint patrol that does the talking.

The arrangements are also operative. They not only set the pace of the PA's broadening self-rule during the interim phase but, very likely, will determine its eventual geopolitical shape. In the interim agreement, the PA is granted initial powers over civic services and public order in 448 Palestinian villages, covering around 23 per cent of all West Bank territory. But it has limited territorial and security jurisdiction in just 3 per cent of the territory – the seven main Palestinian cities of Jenin, Tulkarm, Qalqilya, Nablus, Bethlehem, Ramallah and (partially) Hebron.[4] Coupled with Gaza, this means the interim agreement authorises PA governance over around 65 per cent of the Occupied Territories' 2.6 million Palestinians.[5]

Three more transfers of territory are allowed for in the agreement, at the end of which the Israeli army should be out of everywhere in the West Bank except for Jerusalem (undefined), the borderzone (undefined), Jewish settlements (undefined) and 'specified military locations' (undefined).[6] But these further redeployments are conditional on the PA meeting Israel's security needs and can be suspended should Israel detect any 'infringement'.[7] The extent of PA's eventual territorial base in Oslo's interim phase is thus directly related to the degree that it protects the security of Israel, including the 'personal security' of the 145,000 Jewish settlers that now live in the West Bank and Gaza.[8]

In its scope, powers and infrastructure,[9] the interim agreement ensures Israel's security hegemony in the West Bank and Gaza until the resolution of these territories' final status, due, according to Oslo, in May 1999. The hegemony is grounded neither on international law nor on recognition of Israel and the Palestinians' 'mutual legitimate and political rights', as expressed in the original Oslo Agreement. It reflects rather older Israeli formulas of 'supremacy and subordination',[10] and is determined by the massively imbalanced distribution of military and territorial resources Israel holds over the PA in the West Bank and Gaza.

It follows – textually, at least – that any political and territorial movement towards Palestinians' historic goals of statehood and self-determination can occur only within the confines of this hegemony. For Arafat and the PA, the Palestinians' strategic

political alliance for the interim period is cast: it is going to be
security-led and with Israel.

The arrangements became tangible in the months following the
interim agreement's signing. Between November and December
1996, Palestinians in the six newly autonomous West Bank cities [11]
witnessed the prisons and 'civil' administration blocks of the Israeli
occupation become the barracks and police stations of Palestinian
self-rule. In each area, the 'guard' which ceremoniously led the
change were battalions of the PA's green-uniformed 'Palestinian
police', whose brief, stipulated under Oslo, is 'public order'. But they
were preceded and followed by several thousand more plainclothes
PA 'intelligence' operatives whose remit, unstipulated in Oslo, is
'internal security'.

THE PALESTINIAN AUTHORITY'S SECURITY FORCES

The establishment of a 'strong police force' is one of the few
unequivocal powers the PA is granted in the original Oslo
Agreement.[12] In the May 1994 Cairo Agreement, the number of
security personnel the PA is permitted to recruit for Gaza and
Jericho is 9,000. In the interim agreement, the number for the
West Bank is 12,000. In all agreements, it is stated that the
Palestinian police will 'constitute the only Palestinian security
force' and will have four operational divisions – civil, public
security, emergency and intelligence.

These prescriptions, however, are on paper, with neither the PA
nor Israel nor the international sponsors of the Oslo process in
any way bound by them. In November 1995, the PA's chief of
police in Gaza, Nasser Yusuf, stated before the UN's Local Aid
Coordinating Committee – one of whose tasks is to 'coordinate'
the assignment of donor money for police salaries – that, with the
move to the West Bank, the number of PA police would swell to
30,000. At around the same time, the PA's head of civic police in
Gaza, Ghazi Jabali, anticipated that the PA would eventually
require a police force of 'about 40,000' for the autonomy.

The main beneficiary of this inflation has been the PA's
intelligence division or, more precisely, divisions. According to
Khalid Bitrawi – a lawyer with the Palestinian human rights

organisation, Al Haq – at the time of Israel's 1995 West Bank redeployment there were 'seven, eight or nine' PA intelligence forces operating in the Occupied Territories.[13]

They work under a variety of titles: General Intelligence Service (GIS), Preventive Security Force (PSF), Presidential Guard, Force 17 and Special Security Forces (SSF). There are also smaller 'specialist' forces such as the PA's Coastal Police, Military Intelligence, Disciplinary Police and Universities' Security Guards. It is unclear whether these constitute separate forces, with their own command and structure, or whether they are subsumed under larger intelligence forces such as the GIS and PSF. There is also Fatah and its military wing in the Occupied Territories, the Fatah Hawks, which, in November 1994, was publicly reactivated by Arafat to 'work with the forces of the PA ... to protect this land'.[14]

TASKS

The worrisome aspect of these forces is not just their number, but their amorphous nature. 'There are no terms of reference for any of the security services,' says Bitrawi, which makes it impossible to define their different duties. It is a difficulty shared by their various commanders. In December 1994, PSF chief in Gaza, Mohammed Dahlan, defined his service tautologically as 'an organ of the PA which deals with preventive security issues pertaining to the PA'.[15] But the PSF's West Bank chief, Jibril Rajoub, has repeatedly described the PSF as 'an extension of Fatah' in the West Bank and Gaza 'in accordance with the new reality of the PA'.[16]

These two functions are not the same. Fatah is a political movement that draws its legitimacy from the PLO. The PSF is a quasi-state body empowered by the PA to maintain 'security'. No other Palestinian definition of the PSF's role exists, however. Nor are the intelligence forces specified in any of the Oslo agreements or decrees enacted by the PA, despite being armed by the latter, tacitly recognised by Israel and at least partially paid for by the donor countries under the international umbrellas of the UN and World Bank. In a precise legal sense, the forces are beyond the law in both the Occupied Territories and autonomous areas.

They exist, however, on the Palestinian street. In Gaza and throughout the West Bank, their operatives work alongside the official PA police as well as in those Palestinian areas where the police are currently prohibited, such as East Jerusalem. Their exact personnel strength is unknown, although, at the close of 1995, Dahlan admitted that he commanded a force of '12,000 men' in the Gaza Strip. Rajoub has at least an equivalent personnel in the West Bank, and this is for just one of the intelligence forces.

Taken together, the forces appear to have three main tasks. First, they are police forces. From the moment the Oslo accords were signed, PSF operatives especially have assumed the role of *de facto* police officers throughout the Occupied Territories. Their job has been to fill the 'law and order' vacuum left by the occupation as well as that anticipated after Israel's military redeployment.[17] Palestinian and Israeli human rights monitors[18] – as well as eyewitness testimony – have amassed scores of cases where PSF agents or Fatah activists (or Fatah activists claiming to be PSF agents) have intervened in Palestinian communities to fight crime, solve clan or family disputes and mete out punishments to those accused of 'moral offences' such as drug dealing and prostitution. In the autonomous areas, these interventions occur in the shadow of the PA's jurisdiction; elsewhere in the Occupied Territories, in the name of Fatah. But in all cases the intelligence forces are operating illegally and beyond the reach of any judicial scrutiny.

Second, the forces have been politically deployed to domesticate Palestinian opinion to the 'new reality' of the PA. The clearest instance of this has been the censorious stance taken by the intelligence forces against what had been, pre-Oslo, a relatively pluralist Palestinian press.

On 28 July 1994 – less than a month after Arafat returned to Gaza and Jericho – PA police banned distribution of the *An-Nahar* newspaper.[19] The ostensible reason was that the paper lacked a licence, a spurious charge given that it is published in Jerusalem and so outside the PA's jurisdiction. The real cause, in the words of a PA communiqué, was that the newspaper advocated 'a line that contradicts the national interests of the Palestinian people', a reference to *An-Nahar*'s pro-Jordanian editorialising.

One year later, the other main Palestinian broadsheet, *Al-Quds*, was suspended for a day 'by order of the President' (that is,

Arafat). It was about to run a piece by the dissident PLO executive member, Farouk Qaddumi, castigating the Oslo process as 'a surrender of Palestinian rights'. Sources say the paper's owner and chief editor, Mahmoud Abu Zuluf, had received a visit from the PSF warning him not to publish Qaddumi's statement. He ignored them; he did not ignore the President.

Al-Quds and *An-Nahar* are broadly loyalist in their politics. The oppositional press has fared worse. In 1995, the Gaza-based Islamist newspaper, *Al-Watan*, was shut down on two occasions – and its chief and deputy editors imprisoned – for publishing what the PA Attorney-General called 'inciteful material against the interests of the Palestinian people' (*Al-Watan* had published a story alleging the PA was using torture against Hamas detainees in its prisons).[20] In March 1995, the Jerusalem offices of the PFLP-aligned weekly, *Al-Umma*, were torched, after threats, say the editors, from the PSF that the magazine should drop its 'hostile coverage' of the PA.

Such actions have had an intimidatory effect. When *An-Nahar* returned to the news-stands on 5 September 1994, its editorial swore fealty to 'our brother, leader and symbol Abu Ammar' (Arafat). *Al-Quds* gave increasingly uncritical support to the PA, while reducing its coverage of the Palestinian opposition. In the wake of *An-Nahar*'s closure, the PSF's Moral Guidance Division laid down the terms of the new Palestinian ethos. It warned Palestinians not to be taken in by 'Western schools of thought ... which justify antagonistic policies toward the Third World by bringing up freedom of opinion, democracy and human rights. This is a futile attempt to strike at the national authority'.[21]

A more insidious effect of the new line has been to restrict the terms of what is permissible political discourse in the autonomy. On his return to Gaza, Arafat gave notice to an assembly of Palestinian journalists that, while he would respect 'freedom of the press', he would not tolerate publications that carried 'imported' or 'foreign' ideas. In July 1995, the PA's Information and Culture Minister, Yasser Abed Rabbo, promulgated a media law which empowers his ministries to ban any Palestinian publication that 'jeopardises national unity'.[22] It is left to Arafat and Abed Rabbo to define what is 'foreign' or what comprises 'disunity'. But it has been the pervasive fact of the PA's intelligence forces that has enabled them to enforce it.

THE ROME UNDERSTANDING

All of the intelligence forces – as well as the PA official police –
are implicated in these abuses. But the critical agency appears to
be the PSF. This is not just due to its size, but more its political
and social composition. Recruited almost exclusively from the
Occupied Territories, the force is made up of young Fatah
activists who won their political and military spurs in the Intifada
as prison leaders, youth cadres or 'fighters' in Fatah's militias.
Dahlan and Rajoub themselves not only lead but typify the
constituency.

Dahlan, the former leader of Fatah's youth movement in Gaza,
was expelled by Israel in 1986. Rajoub spent 16 years in Israeli
prisons and was one of Fatah's original leaders in the West Bank
wing of the Intifada's Unified National Leadership of the Uprising (UNLU) before he, too, was expelled in 1988. Both exude
enormous street credibility, and not only among Fatah activists.
Unlike the 'outside' PLO cadres, they know Israel and the Israelis,
and Palestinians from inside the Occupied Territories extremely
well. For certain sectors of Israel's security establishment, this is
their principal asset.

In January 1994, Dahlan and Rajoub met in Rome with the
then head of Israel's General Security Service (GSS), Ya'acov Peri,
and the Israeli Defence Force's then deputy (now full) Chief of
Staff, Amnon Shahak. The meeting was to sort out their complementary roles in the autonomy. The Rome meeting did not issue
any formal accord but rather 'an understanding'.[23]

In return for intelligence on the Palestinian opposition and particularly the Islamist Hamas movement, the GSS and IDF agreed to
grant the PSF a free hand to ensure 'order' in the West Bank and
Gaza, both before and after Israel's redeployment in these areas.
Under Oslo, the 'Rome Agreement' (like the PA's intelligence
forces) does not technically exist. But it is operational, a fact tacitly
admitted by the late Israeli Prime Minister, Yitzhak Rabin.

On 18 September 1994 – a full year before Israel's West Bank
redeployment commenced – Rabin was asked at an Israeli cabinet
meeting about the 'illegal' presence of PSF operatives in various
West Bank cities. PA security personnel operate throughout the

West Bank, answered Rabin, 'with Israel's knowledge and in cooperation with Israel's security forces to safeguard Israel's security interests'. The red line was that this would not be tolerated in 'sovereign' East Jerusalem.[24]

There is disagreement within and between Israel's security forces as to the precise role the PA's intelligence forces should have in the autonomy. But there is no dispute that, since Oslo, there has been a growing 'coordination of intelligence' between them.

On 11 October 1994, Hamas guerrillas announced that they had abducted an Israeli army conscript, Nachshon Wachsman, as ransom for the release of 200 Palestinian and Arab prisoners interned in Israeli jails. Three days later, Wachsman and three of his kidnappers were killed after a botched rescue mission by the army in the West Bank village of Beit Naballa, where the soldier had been held hostage. It was, say Israeli and Palestinian sources, largely information passed by the PA's intelligence forces to the GSS that led the army to its quarry.[25]

In September 1995, the GSS informed the PSF that two PFLP members, Yusuf and Shahar Ra'i, were 'wanted' in connection with the killing of two Israelis in the West Bank and were hiding out in Jericho. Within 48 hours, the two had been picked up by the PA police and sentenced to twelve years' imprisonment for 'incitement against the peace process'.

The GSS viewed this last liaison as 'effective cooperation', mindful that it would not look good on the Palestinian street for the PA and PSF to go public on such collaboration. But the IDF and Israeli Border Police wanted just this – the overt 'extradition' by the PA of Palestinian suspects into Israeli custody. Dahlan refused, stating in an Israeli newspaper that 'under no circumstances would the PA ever hand over Palestinians to Israel'. In retaliation, the Israeli army sealed off Jericho.

After a week the siege was lifted, with the Ra'i brothers staying put (and imprisoned) in Jericho. In this turf war, the GSS's post-Oslo policy of 'internal security' won out over the IDF's pre-Oslo advocacy of military might. Its essence was summed up by one of the GSS's closest allies in the Rabin government, Environment Minister and leader of the Meretz bloc, Yossi Sarid. 'After all,' he said after the Jericho debacle, 'as long as Palestinian killers sit in jail for 12 years, it is not so important which jail'.[26]

A MILITARIST AUTHORITY

Israel's insistence on 'internal security' imbues all of the various
Oslo agreements. A strong and massive PA intelligence force is
not so much tolerated by Israel as the precondition for any
Palestinian movement towards self-rule. Creating 'a reality
whereby internal Palestinian security will be in Palestinians'
hands'[27] was, after all, Rabin's main motive for backing the Oslo
formula in the first place.

'The Palestinians will be better at it than we were,' he said in
September 1993,

> because they will allow no appeals to the Supreme Court and will
> prevent the Israeli Association of Civil Rights from criticising the
> conditions there by denying it access to the area. They will rule by
> their own methods, freeing, and this is most important, the Israeli
> army soldiers from having to do what they will do.[28]

But that there should be a multiplicity of PA intelligence services
rather than a single unitary force relates less to Israeli prescriptions than to the 'factionalist' and patrimonial dynamics of PLO
politics. More precisely, it relates to the way Arafat has reconsti-
tuted the military structures of the PLO in and through the 'new
reality' of the PA. For this task, the PLO leader has required a
proliferation rather than concentration of forces.

A myriad of forces gives Arafat enormous scope for political and
financial patronage. Since Fatah's 'inside' Hawk and Black Panther
militias were formally disbanded with the signing of Oslo in 1993,
their cadres have been steadily absorbed into the PSF and GIS, making for an increasingly nominal distinction between Fatah's old
military structures and the PA's new intelligence forces. This served
a political need. Had these cadres felt excluded from the spoils of
self-rule, they might have formed an armed opposition to it.[29] Their
incorporation into the PA's intelligence forces thus not only pays
them a wage, it also affords them a political and social status com-
mensurate with their former role as fighters.

But, more importantly, 'a strong Palestinian police force' has
empowered Arafat to set up a military command to serve as his

primary arm of rule in the West Bank and Gaza. This command, essentially, is the transposition to the Occupied Territories of the PLO's old military structures formed in exile.

In the Cairo agreement, it was agreed that up to 7,000 of the PA's allotment of 9,000 police could be recruited from abroad, mostly from Palestinian Liberation Army (PLA) units stationed in Algeria, Egypt, Iraq, Jordan, Sudan and Yemen. In the interim agreement, 5,000 of the 12,000 new recruits are returnees, with nearly half coming from what remains of Arafat's loyalist Fatah constituency in Lebanon.[30]

These cadres have been deployed to form a PA military order which, with Israel's redeployment, was swiftly mobilised to parallel, overtake and then suborn the existing and emerging political and civilian orders in the West Bank and Gaza. In each of the current eight self-rule areas, there is at least one PLA battalion (that is, the 'official' Palestinian police), whose job it is to maintain 'public order'. The PLA's overall commanders are Nassir Yusuf in Gaza and Haj Ismail Jaber in the West Bank. These men are accountable only to the Supreme Commander of the PLO's military forces, both inside the Territories and out – that is, to Yasser Arafat.

Immediately after the West Bank redeployment, Arafat also appointed 'governors' for each of the PA's self-declared 'governorates' in the West Bank and Gaza. These 'civilian' leaders – Mustafa Liftawi in Ramallah, Mahmoud Aloul in Nablus, Izzadin el-Sharif in Tulkarm and Jamil Nasser in Jerusalem – were all formerly members of the PLO's old Western Sector (WS) wing. Prior to Oslo, the WS's task was to authorise and resource Fatah's political and military actions in the Occupied Territories.

The district governors' task now is broadly the same but 'in accordance with the new reality of the PA'. They look after civilian affairs and coordinate the PA's various security forces in their respective governorates,[31] largely through Fatah personnel appointed to these new governmental positions. The governors have no remit from or over the PLA or Palestinian police since this, under Oslo, is the PA's 'National' Security Force. They are answerable to the PA's Interior Minister, whose head is Yasser Arafat. No other PA or PLO body – whether appointed, elected or judicial – has power or purview over them.[32]

By such means, Arafat has amassed under his command a military force capable of quelling any domestic Palestinian opposition to Oslo. This, too, has served a political purpose. Had these military cadres been left in the diaspora, they would almost certainly have opposed Oslo (and therefore Arafat), risking a probably irreparable schism in the PLO between its inside and outside wings. The schism was avoided because, through the conduit of a 'strong Palestinian police force', the 'outside' has been brought 'inside', and with Israel's permission.

The various military apparatuses do not resemble an army, with a clear chain of command. They are rather horizontal forces, of indeterminate strength, with no hierarchy. They operate as quasi-independent militias rather than as parts of an overall structure. This is almost certainly deliberate on Arafat's part. It rehearses one of his most characteristic traits of rule, tried and tested in the PLO's former domains of Jordan and especially Lebanon. The method has been described by one (Israeli) journalist as 'one boss but a thousand franchises'.[33]

Because there is no hierarchy, the various military and intelligence forces compete and conflict with each other for the spoils of political, social and economic power. In the run-up to Israel's redeployment in the northern West Bank areas, there were intermittent turf wars between Fatah cadres belonging to the largely diasporal Presidential Guard (PG) and those allied with the PSF. These became especially nasty in Nablus, with the PG generally defending the interests of the city's more affluent residents and the PSF being stronger in the refugee camps, villages and poorer districts such as the Casbah.[34]

In Gaza, the fault line appears to be between the old 'inside' Fatah leadership – represented by Gaza's deputy PSF head, Rashid Shback, and Presidential Guard leader, Sami Samhandana – and 'outsider' PLA officers like Ghazi Jabali. These tensions also sometimes turn violent, especially over what many Gazans see as Jabali's zealous efforts to arrest Fatah activists wanted by Israel for extradition.[35]

In all disputes, the final arbiter is Arafat. This, too, serves a political need. By allowing tensions to simmer between the various forces, he fragments them and forestalls any alternative centres of power from coalescing against him. This is important not just because of the dissensions Oslo threw up in Fatah inside the Territories and out. More importantly, such divide-and-rule tactics weld together the divergent class, regional and generational constituencies out of which Fatah's 'non-ideological' brand of nationalism has evolved. If Fatah is to keep its hegemonic role in the self-rule regions, these different constituencies must somehow be kept under at least a loose form of unitary command. That command is Arafat. In fighting over the 'franchise', the PLO leader ensures that his forces – and the constituencies they represent – are not fighting over the 'boss', or over the political direction and interests he may at any time espouse.

CONCLUSION

Such means of rule demonstrate Arafat's prowess as a faction leader. Whether these are the qualities required to marshal the resources of Palestinians behind the task of building a state is another matter. For many observers, the PA's concentration of political and military power in the hands of one man and one faction bodes ill for Palestinians' democratic, economic and legal aspirations in the autonomy. In the longer term, they may prove mortal to their national goal of self-determination.

First, there is the economic cost of Arafat's militarist style of rule. At the time of the Cairo Agreement in 1994, the World Bank calculated the PA's annual budget for a 9,000-strong police force to be $180 million.[36] A police force three times this size would therefore cost over $500 million a year. Combined with a PA public sector of around 27,000 employees, the idea that the PA can financially cover such a bureaucracy from locally generated revenue and run much-needed social services is imaginary. The PA was not able to do so in Gaza and Jericho and has not been able to do so in the West Bank. What such an inflated public sector (in which 70 per cent of all jobs are security related) actually portends is an interim period every bit as economically dependent on and politically conditioned by donor money as was its Gaza-Jericho prelude.[37] Very simply, the PA does not require a 30–40,000-strong police force to facilitate the economic, social and political development of its 2.6 million people. A police force of this size is required only to keep the lid on a people in the absence of such development.

Second, there is the legal cost to Palestinians' civil, political and human rights under autonomy. The attitude of the PA's various military forces to these rights has been *ad hoc* at best and abusive at worst, and in all cases ungoverned by the semblance of due process. Between October 1994 and February 1995, PA police in Gaza undertook no less than five mass arrest sweeps, rounding up hundreds of Palestinians on 'suspicion' of belonging to the Islamist or PLO opposition, but 'without judicial warrant or sanction and contrary to the rule of law'.[38] In February 1995, Arafat authorised the setting up of 'special state security courts'. These supersede any independent judicial system, allow secret evidence, brook no appeal procedures and are tried by PLO military officers appointed by the PA. Verdicts are the prerogative of Arafat, who, according to the PA's attorney general, has sole power to 'confirm, ease or stiffen' any sentence passed by the courts.[39] By June 1995, 33 Palestinians had been tried and sentenced in them.[40]

The political violations are amplified by civic ones, as the PA security forces have aggressively asserted their own brand of rule in the Occupied Territories. In a report published in August 1995,[41] the Israeli human rights organisation B'tselem gathered testimony from 13 Palestinians who accused the PSF of 'illegal abduction', 'arrest without warrant', 'detention for lengthy periods without judicial scrutiny', 'refusing legal representation', 'refusing family visits', and the use of 'harsh torture techniques such as beatings, tying-up, threats, humiliation, sleep deprivation and the withholding of medical treatment'.

This was in the West Bank, before the 'official' extension of the PA's rule, and is a record of violations by just one of the PA's intelligence forces. In Gaza, there are now 17 PA prisons and detention centres run by either the police or one or other of the intelligence forces.[42] At any one time it is unclear how many detainees they hold because, says Al Haq, legal access to the prisons is 'not regular' and, in some centres, non-existent.

Yet it is the effect of such militarisation on the political and moral content of Palestinian nationalism which, in the long run, may exert the gravest toll. The PA's martial mode of governance has contributed to a process of de-politicisation of Palestinian society, in which many of its ablest members (in the Occupied Territories and outside) have 'collectively withdrawn' from the national struggle, reverting to individualistic or clan-based solutions to their needs and aspirations. This is not only regressive in itself, but is erosive of the essentially modern national identity the PLO – through its political structures and for all their faults – had brought into being.[43] It is also fatal for any future Palestinian strategy of resistance and independence, especially for the majority of Palestinians still adrift in the diaspora.

For these Palestinians, what the PA's ruthless adoption of Israel's internal security agenda actually signifies is a culture of defeat. It not only coincides with a political process which appears to be steadily reducing Palestinian national claims to an archipelago of the West Bank and Gaza. More corrosively, it has transformed notions of 'national interest' and 'national unity' (once their ideological trappings are removed) into a rationale for the practical implementation of Israel's territorial and security ambitions in the Occupied Territories.

NOTES

1. Israeli–Palestinian Interim Agreement on the West Bank and Gaza Strip, Washington, 28 September 1995, Israel's Ministry of Foreign Affairs, Jerusalem (October 1995). All citations from the agreement are from this text.
2. In particular, UN Resolutions 242 and 338 which emphasised the 'inadmissibility of territorial acquisition by force' and called for 'the withdrawal of Israeli armed forces from territories occupied in the recent [1967] conflict' have been practically superseded. On the abandonment of international legality entailed by Oslo, see Naseer Aruri, 'Challenges facing Palestinian society', *Middle East International*, 25 August 1995.
3. Interim Agreement, Annex I, Article II, pp. 33–4.
4. On 7 March 1997, the Israeli government transferred a further 7 per cent of the West Bank to the PA's civil and security jurisdiction and 2 per cent to its civil jurisdiction. The PA thus now commands civil and security governance over around 10 per cent of the West Bank.
5. Israel's further redeployment in March 1997 (see above) placed another 200,000 West Bank Palestinians under the PA's security control.
6. The territorial definitions of Jerusalem, settlements and borders are to be resolved during Oslo's final status negotiations. The territory covered by 'specified military locations' is to be determined by Israel alone – a point 'clarified' by the US following the Palestinian–Israeli Hebron agreement of 15 January 1997.

7. After a series of Islamist suicide attacks in Israel in February/March 1996, Israel reoccupied Palestinian villages in the West Bank. This is permitted under the interim agreement because most villages are located in the West Bank's Area B, where Israel retains 'overall responsibility' for security. See Graham Usher, 'Closures, Cantons and the Palestinian Covenant', *Middle East Report* (April–June 1996).

8. Interim Agreement, Annex I, Article II, pp. 33–4.

9. To implement redeployment, Israel established 62 new military bases in the West Bank and built 30 settler/military bypass roads. The total length of the roads is 212 kilometres; their land area comprises 30 square kilometres. Interview with Palestinian geographer, Khalil Tafakji, February 1997.

10. The phrase is Khalil Shakaki's, policy director of the Nablus-based Centre of Palestine Research and Studies. See his comments in Naomi Weinberger, 'The Palestinian National Security Debate', *Journal of Palestine Studies* (Spring 1995) p. 18.

11. The Israeli army did not 'partially redeploy' from Hebron until January 1997.

12. The Declaration of Principles on Interim Self Government Arrangements, Washington, 13 September 1993. Article VIII.

13. Interview with Khalid Bitrawi, September 1995. According to Amnesty International, by December 1996 there were twelve PA security forces. See Amnesty International, *Palestinian Authority: Prolonged political detention, torture and unfair trials* (London: Amnesty, December 1996).

14. Graham Usher, *Palestine in Crisis: the struggle for peace and political independence after Oslo* (London: Pluto Press and MERIP, 1995) p. 71.

15. Interview with Khalid Bitrawi.

16. Interview with Khalid Bitrawi. See also the interview with Rajoub in *Al-Quds*, 2 February 1995, in which he states that the PSF is the 'practical expression of Fatah since all its officers and personnel are Fatah members'.

17. On the law-and-order vacuum created by the Intifada, see Yizhar Be'er and Salah Abdel Jawad, *Collaborators in the occupied territories: Human rights abuses and violations* (Jerusalem: B'Tselem, 1994), pp. 13–14.

18. See B'Tselem, 'Neither Law nor Justice: extra-judicial punishment, abduction, unlawful arrest and torture of Palestinian residents of the West Bank by the Palestinian Preventive Security Service' (Jerusalem: B'Tselem, August 1995); and Amnesty International, *Palestinian Authority*.

19. *An-Nahar* ceased publication altogether in December 1996.

20. *Al-Watan* has also ceased publication. As well as cracking down on the opposition press, the PA has established three new Palestinian newspapers in the autonomous areas – *Al-Ayyam*, *Al-Hayat Jadida* and *Al-Bilad*. All three are loyalist.

21. Graham Usher, *Palestine in Crisis*, p. 68.

22. This includes the work of the respected Palestinian academic, Edward Said, whose books were banned from the autonomous areas in August 1996.

23. Israeli journalist Ehud Ya'ari summarised the 'understanding' as follows: 'Fatah-armed bands whose members were wanted by the Israeli security services, like the [Fatah] Hawks, will have special tasks. They will be charged with putting down any sign of opposition [to Oslo]; the intent is for them to administer show-punishments at the earliest possible stage, aimed at creating a proper respect for the new regime' ('Can Arafat govern?', *Jerusalem Report*, 13 January 1994).

24. See *Ha'aretz, Yediot Aharonot* and *Ma'ariv,* 19 September 1994.
25. This was certainly the view of Hamas, which issued a statement at the time warning the PA to 'cease supplying information on our mujahidin (holy fighters) ... to the Zionist intelligence and occupation authorities'. See Graham Usher, 'What kind of Nation? The Rise of Hamas in the Occupied Territories', *Race & Class* (October–December 1995) p. 77.
26. Graham Usher, 'Oslo 2: Frenzied Efforts Falter', *Middle East International,* 22 September 1996.
27. Rabin's statement to the Knesset, 30 August 1993.
28. *Yediot Aharonot,* 7 September 1993.
29. Following the suicide attacks in Israel in February/March 1996, the Fatah Hawks were outlawed by the PA as an independent militia. One of the reasons given by Dahlan was that the Hawks 'had grown too close to [the Hamas militia] Izzadin el-Qassam'. See Roni Shaked, 'The Hunt for Mohammed Deif', *Yediot Aharonot,* 12 April 1996.
30. PA sources estimate that around 50,000 Palestinians have returned to the West Bank and Gaza since the Oslo accords.
31. Interview with Tulkarm Governor, Izzadin el-Sharif, November 1995.
32. This includes the Palestinian Council, whose 88 members were elected in January 1996.
33. Ya'ari, 'Can Arafat Govern?'
34. Following Israel's redeployment from Nablus in December 1995, PA security forces arrested 25 members of the Fatah Hawks. In July 1996, one of these, Mahmoud Jamail, was tortured to death in a PA prison in Nablus. See Graham Usher, 'West Bank Towns under Arafat's Control', *Middle East International,* 5 January 1996 and 'Has Arafat Gone Too Far?', *Middle East International,* 16 August 1996.
35. Shback was a leader of the Fatah Hawks in Gaza, and Samhandana was for a brief period head of the PLO's Gaza office, post-Oslo but before the arrival of the PA.
36. Yezid Sayigh, 'Sovereignty and Security of the Palestinian State', *Journal of Palestine Studies* (Summer 1995).
37. Director of the Gaza-based Palestinian Centre for Human Rights, Raji Sourani, says that with 20,000 security personnel for about one million people, Gaza's police to population ratio works out to 1:50, 'among the highest in the world' (Interview, June 1995).
38. Gaza Centre for Rights and Law, 'Mass Arrest Campaign', Press Statement (9 February 1995).
39. Gaza Centre for Rights and Law, 'Appeal to Chairman Arafat to Reverse the Decree Establishing a State Security Court', Press Statement (12 February 1995).
40. Amnesty International, *Palestinian Authority.*
41. B'Tselem, 'Neither Law nor Justice'.
42. Bitrawi, Interview.
43. Jamil Hilal, 'PLO: Crisis in Legitimacy' and Azmi Bishara, 'Bantustanisation or Bi-nationalism?', *Race & Class* (October–December 1995).

8 VISION AND REALITY DIVERGING: PALESTINIAN SURVIVAL STRATEGIES IN THE POST-OSLO ERA

Dag Jørund Lønning

INTRODUCTION

In 1993, before the disclosure of the Oslo Agreement, I did anthropological fieldwork in Israel/Palestine on inter-ethnic dialogue-groups working for total Israeli withdrawal from the Occupied Territories of 1967 and a lasting peace between the two peoples.[1] Just after Oslo and the signing of the Declaration of Principles (DOP) in Washington, I talked to some of the Israeli dialogue participants. Neither they nor I were particularly optimistic regarding the agreement. We were all deeply worried by the lack of a final vision in the DOP able to satisfy even minimum Palestinian demands – thus making the whole process highly dependent on the most powerful party – as well as about the lack of possibilities for international intervention in the case of violations.

And yet, during the same period I received several letters from *Palestinian* friends stating their optimism for the near future, for the establishment of a Palestinian state, for the disappearance of the settlers, for their capital in Jerusalem. During my meetings with these people, who had lost almost everything, I had come to understand their strong belief in future victory, in eventual justice for some timeless tomorrow.

Subsequent trips to Palestine, in 1994 and 1995, however, as well as prolonged fieldwork in 1996, have been painful. My original hopeful research intention was to study the effects of a developing peace process on individual conceptualisations of the enemy 'other'. The reality I faced was a people trying to survive in the midst of economic deprivation,[2] closures and humiliation, as well as desperation and political frustration, all in the name of something their political negotiating partner, to some extent even their own leaders, as well as large parts of the international community called 'peace'.

Nevertheless, in the face of declining living standards, lack of freedom of movement, radical settlement expansions and continuous suffering in the post-Oslo era, all opinion polls and attitude surveys conducted in Palestine since 1993 have shown that a stable majority of between 70 and 80 per cent of the Palestinians have continued to support the peace process.[3] The same polls have also shown that a corresponding majority view the future optimistically.

This article addresses Palestinian confrontations with a reality which has turned out to be – at least until today – not what they thought, nor what they dreamt of or hoped for. Using ethnographic material, it relates to the individual Palestinian on the street and the interpretative frameworks and strategies utilised by him or her to conceptualise life-worlds and futures. This is a time when the Palestinian dream of real independence and justice stands in danger of being forever crushed by international power politics and a 'peace process' which might turn out to be the exact opposite. A special emphasis is put on two diverging responses to this political development, one being the cognitive transformation of it through optimism and hope, the other being a passive acceptance of powerlessness, leading to frustration and disillusion.

On the surface the strong Palestinian optimism towards the future and support for a process which has dealt serious blows to their dreams of an independent state and has led to a radical deterioration in their living conditions looks contradictory. I will try to deal with this contradiction, however, by promoting a thesis which may appear no less contradictory: vocalised support for the Oslo process may in fact be read as a form of 'resistance' towards it.

To defend such an argument, I will link Palestinian support for the Oslo Agreement to what I believe is the socially and politically very important and constitutive role of *hope* and *visions of the future* within the Palestinian tradition, culture and discourse of resistance. Palestinian political hopes are highly vocalised. Although often communicated in idiosyncratic ways, they nevertheless transcend the individual. They represent, first, existentialist reactions to feelings of powerlessness. In relation to power, however, their role is double. Ultimately they confer the dream of and belief in justice and independence, a collective Palestinian vision of an alternative society, thus constituting a powerful vocabulary of resistance.

I will try to demonstrate that hoping may be conceptualised as *one* form of survival strategy, and thus a kind of cognitive schemata utilised to read and map the social and political environment.[4] When this political environment seems unanimously hostile and a threat to the future, cognitive creative resistance – hope being one expression – takes the form of trying to penetrate the hostile surface and withdraw still latent possibilities and promises from within. It is a cognitive strategy of closing the gap between diverging vision and reality – or the actual unfolding of events. Through this form of creative resistance, processes, situations and events are cognitively remoulded, to gain a shape concomitant with the individual or collective's idea of the alternative society. Within such a scheme of interpretation, hope is lost only in so far as such a reservoir of potential promises has dried out.

And thus – a thesis supported by the same polls mentioned above – support for and hope in Oslo remains only as long as the process carries the promise of fulfilling the collective Palestinian vision of a just future.

DEALING WITH HOPE

The concept of hope, traditionally the property of theology and perhaps psychology, seems to be a difficult issue for the social sciences. Nevertheless, when hoping becomes narrativised collective strategy, transcending the individual mind, an interesting subject area for anthropology is defined. Palestinian political hopes may emerge from the individual and be communicated in idiosyncratic ways, but the hope itself is for an aim or a future vision which is more or less collectively shared. Thus it is impossible not to think of Obeyesekere and the concepts he calls *subjectification* and *subjective images*:

> ... cultural ideas are used to produce, and thereafter justify, innovative acts, meanings, or images that help express the personal needs and

fantasies of individuals. ... [S]ubjective images are consonant with the
culture and can be justified and legitimated culturally. Insofar as this
is the case, it is possible for subjective images to be later converted to
objective symbols.[5]

This discussion of relations and interrelations between personal
and collective symbols provides a theory of social integration – a
theory of the creation of cultural identity – and, in that sense, also
an interesting input to the linkages between individual hopes and
collective Palestinian political aspirations. Still, the definition
does not pre-empt the subject matter. Understanding the urgency
of the Palestinian predicament after Oslo, enables us to grasp the
role of hope within the society.

Hope is related to a near or distant future. One hopes for
someone to come, for something to happen, for some thing to
materialise, and so on. I might hope to get a new television for
Christmas, and I might, upon delivering my filled-out coupon,
hope to win a million in the national lottery. Our human world
is full of hopes, hoping being one of our most frequently used
cognitive capacities. It is, however, a difficult concept to use in
analytical terms, as it might cover both my egotistical
materialist aspirations, as well as the cries of a person whose
only hope is to be able to eat tomorrow, or for the soldiers to
stop beating him or the prison guards stop torturing him. The
first category of hope brings no catastrophe upon the person if
unfulfilled, the second is an existentialist kind of cognitive
mechanism which is set in motion when one's life or future is
threatened. A further characteristic of a hope of the latter
category is that it cannot be qualified; for a person or a people
spending a life under continuous occupation and suppression,
experiencing misery and deprivation, there is *no* alternative to
hoping for better days. Hope for a better future, whether
individual or collective, becomes what makes it possible to
survive the current miserable state of affairs. As such, as a
survival strategy, hope might become *belief* – giving meaning to
life – even strong belief, belief in happiness around the corner,
belief in ultimate justice for the downtrodden. The absence of
hope, perhaps best characterised as *loss* of hope, means
disillusionment, despair and possible mental illness.

HOPE AS RESISTANCE

Before the Intifada, the more popular version of the Palestinian
struggle for independence was in many ways characterised by the
Arabic word *sumud*, meaning steadfastness.[6] The concept conveys
a principle of standing firm, of being patient, of hoping and
believing in ultimate victory. I will try to show that particularly
the latter properties of the principle have developed strong roots
within Palestinian society and culture. Hoping and believing has
become a Palestinian popular and public strategy of conceptualising both present and future, of evaluating and assessing macro-
political events and processes, thus creating manageable images
out of powerlessness. Through narrativised hope and belief in
ultimate justice existing beyond all macro-political power matrix –
powers being outside the control of the individual Palestinian –
current misery and oppression is made transient and thus in one
way tolerable. Hoping becomes a creative kind of public cognitive
defence and resistance against frustration and resignation.

When you talk to Palestinians about their lives, all have stories
of suffering to tell. Suffering emanates from being Palestinian,
from living under occupation, from not being able to escape from
your identity – it's a collective experience. The 'confrontation
with the ethnic other' – the theory of ethnic/national identity
formation – is very apt in the Palestinian case.[7] The words may
differ, but the stories told convey the same meaning. The
individual body in a sense becomes a map to read the collective
identity and experience.

Yet, as suffering is collectively felt and individually embodied, so
is the hope for the reversal of today's order, conceptualised as the
Palestinian aim for independence and justice. This aim, in a way
resembling what anthropology would call a collective symbol, has
developed through many years of Palestinian public political debate
and struggle. Still, for the Palestinians living under occupation, it is
the form of the embodiment of the symbol which attracts attention.
In the conceptualisation of the future, collective symbolism/collec-
tive aims and individual existentialist hopes merge.

For most of the people you speak to, even the poorest of the poor,
even people who have been beaten or jailed and exposed to torture,

when you ask them how they see their future, their stories – highly
realistic in their descriptions of the contemporary tragic situation
both on the internal, regional and international front – generally end
with some vision of better days and justice ahead. Behind all the
oppression and misery there is a peculiar kind of optimism, in con-
versations often colliding with this anthropologist's far more pessi-
mistic images of the future.[8] Hope may be put on, for example, internal strength, on divine intervention, on Arab or European interference, or on a US change of policy. In short, virtually on anything.

The hopes for, and ideas about, implementation vary, but the
narratives about the 'glorious tomorrow' are strikingly similar
whether told by Abu Ali, the poor Hebronite street-vendor who
had to place his children in an orphanage when he lost wife and
job and whose brother was nearly tortured to death in an Israeli
prison or by Ghassan, who was almost tortured to death himself
and who repeatedly had his small Jerusalem shop destroyed by
settlers, or by Sa'id, who had to give up all plans of an education
and who, being without a permit to go to his capital, has
repeatedly been arrested, fined, and beaten severely by Israeli
soldiers on his risky daily trip to Jerusalem in search of casual
work to secure the survival of his big West Bank family.

Palestinian history, as well as the individual's interpretation of
it, is the narrative of the many lost hopes. The things people hope
for vary internally, and they change according to macro-political
developments and signals. Yet, as one hope is lost, a new one
always emerges.

Hopes may materialise from individual cognitive creativity,
from talking to friends and neighbours, from the media, and so
on. In daily street communication, hopes are communicated
loudly and clearly. Lively discussions are conducted about possible hope scenarios. From its point of origin, a new hope spreads
through widening social networks, sometimes even to become
collective and national. This was the case with (perhaps obviously
enough for a Westerner) the Oslo Agreement, or (not so obvious
for a more left-leaning Westerner) the widespread Palestinian
belief in US pressure on Israel materialising after the re-election of
Bill Clinton in November 1996.

Personally – being highly preoccupied with the Palestinian
struggle for independence – at the outset, I more or less

unconsciously attributed many hopes people communicated to me to some vulgar form of false consciousness, false beliefs detrimental to an individual's ability to stand up and fight for his or her rights. As I saw it, hoping for or believing in some international intervention which would never take place, created widespread passivity. For my first fieldwork period, addressing a different issue, I remember spending many evenings talking to Palestinians and trying to convince them that their hopes were highly 'unrealistic' in my view, that they had 'to realise the actual disastrous political development and do something about it'. As I look back upon it now, however, I see that I was a bad anthropologist. The hopes were simply too widespread and common for them to simply be resulting from 'lack of education' as even some members of the more educated, Westernised, higher echelons of Palestinian society claimed.

Grappling with these issues for later fieldwork, I only started to understand the real meaning of hope for my Palestinian friends upon realising the existentialist dimension, the lack of alternatives. Without these future visions of justice, the means of implementation being almost anything which it is possible to hope for, living through the current state of affairs becomes intolerable. Hope is what creates a space of life and future for Abu Ali, Ghassan, Sa'id, and so many other Palestinians. Through this cognitive creative act, it's as though, even for a flash of a second, the strong belief in a just and happy after-life in Islamic theology is made worldly; contemporary misery becomes merely transient, to be followed by days of glory for the Palestinian individual and people when the world will realise who were the sufferers and righteous ones, and who were the brutal occupiers.

Through the answers given, I also came to realise the stupidity in the question I asked some people: 'I can give you one thousand reasons why this will not happen [followed by me mentioning why for example the USA will never put pressure on Israel]. Tell me, do you *really* believe this?' The answer from several close friends came as follows: 'I *have to* believe it. What other alternatives do I have? Tell me!' I was not able to provide them.

Probing deeper, I discovered that these Palestinians *did* actually realise and grasp the factual situation, namely the near all-powerful and omnipresent Israeli occupation machinery, and their own lack of possibilities and capabilities to withstand it and fight it. For a Palestinian being randomly stopped and body-checked in Jerusalem, for another being stopped and beaten or left without water in the sun at a checkpoint for six hours, for a third having his house demolished, for a fourth having his farmland and future stolen by Israeli settlers in the Occupied Territories, there is nothing effective any of them can do to protest their treatment. With the growing distance between leaders and followers inside Palestinian society and the limited acceptance of dissent by Arafat's security apparatus, they further know that they have minimal, if any, influence on the political negotiations termed to settle their future. The only forms of resistance available to most Palestinians are emotional and psychological, creatively playing with feelings of hate and revenge, as well as hopes and beliefs.

Existentialist hope is the reaction to feelings of powerlessness. Often, in contemporary Palestinian society, the connection between the two is established through standardised oratorical techniques of closing arguments, so important in Arab society.[9] In Palestine in the shadow of Oslo, almost every day a person is arrested, another is killed or beaten up and settlers claim more lands, etc. Such events become narrativised and made the object of discussions among Palestinians wherever they meet. Listening to and getting involved in such discussions, I realised that the way they develop often follows standardised rules with prescribed and abrupt endings. Often, when a person exclaims 'But what can we do?' and another answers 'Nothing!', the conversation dies out, or the subject changes. Still, there is often a third way of closing the discussion. The following shortened transcript from my fieldnotes will exemplify:

A: The Jews arrested Jamil today. They raided the house, and they beat him and his cousin. They messed up everything. His mother was crying, she was afraid and hysterical, but they shouted at her and pushed her around. It was awful, no one understood why they took him!

B: Yes, I've heard about it. They treat us like animals. They're no more than fascists. They're no good people.

A: They do whatever they want. They don't want peace, that's for sure.

[pause]

A: But what can we do?
B: Nothing!
A: Absolutely nothing!
[long pause]
A: But one day ...
[end of conversation]

Power is out of reach, and hope for power rather than power itself becomes some kind of antithesis of powerlessness.

THE DISILLUSIONED

Still, as in any society, there are internal differences. Above, I wrote about the absence of hope leading to disillusionment. Disillusioned people are not hard to find on the Palestinian street. Some have given up altogether, preferring to discuss anything but politics, trying to live as good a life as the situation permits, pursuing money and romance.

I have yet to meet a supporter of Oslo – as it has been developing until today – who thinks it is a really good agreement for the Palestinians and a satisfactory answer to their national aspirations. Normally, people attach a wide range of conditions to their support, relating to Oslo's ability to implement the national vision. Ironically, however, among the least conditional and firmest 'supporters', one may find some of the most disillusioned Palestinians. Their rationale for support nevertheless pinpoints their frustration, and is often communicated as follows: 'I don't believe this peace is good for the Palestinians, but it was the best we could get. We stand alone with no supporters, and have to take what the powerful are willing to give us. Today we have nothing, but one little thing is still better.' The support thus consists in an acceptance of powerlessness, communicated in a tone of sadness and defeat. The only way they see the future becoming better than today's suffering is to accept the humiliating rules of the game of international politics, including the Oslo process. They have lost hope in any intervention outside what the negotiation process can give. Oslo was their last hope. At the outset they believed strongly in it, that it would satisfy the Palestinian dream. As time went by, frustration grew, but they kept on hoping.

The most remarkable differences between these people and those who still hoped were their eyes and the tone of their voices. Among the hopeful, the fire was still there, among the disillusioned it had burnt out. The first talked about the struggle and building their lives and future, the latter talked about closing their small businesses and leaving the country.

As a still hopful friend of mine told me: 'Without hope, you can't live.' Or, as another, a former supporter of Oslo, said when I asked him to reflect on the process:

> ... I have chosen to give peace a chance. Right now it doesn't deserve it. People have lost hope in peace, but deep inside they still believe. What else can they do? What is the other alternative for an integral human being? There simply is *no other alternative.*

HOPING AND LOSING HOPE: A TALE OF TWO BROTHERS

To me these two ways of conceptualising the post-Oslo era became especially vivid through my long-term friendship with the brothers Izzat and Ramsi. The two brothers, whom I got to know in 1993, are the two main breadwinners of a large West Bank family working in a small shop in East Jerusalem. After the closure imposed in March 1993, they had to go illegally to their capital, facing the danger of evading Israeli checkpoints in order to secure the means necessary for family survival.

Both Izzat and Ramsi were very active in the Intifada, and always strong supporters of the main PLO front, the Fatah, as well as of Yasser Arafat. But mainly, they were devout nationalists believing in their people and the struggle for justice and freedom. They were never fanatics. Israelis were welcome customers in their shop, and they did not believe in a Palestine 'from the river to the sea'. Rather, the two-state solution was the answer, with a Palestinian state being established according to what UN resolutions declare as occupied land: the West Bank, the Gaza Strip and East Jerusalem.

Four of the brothers' closest friends died for this idea, friends who were talked about as martyrs, losing their lives for the sacred aim of justice and a state.

The struggle was the brothers' lives, and they both lived by the cultural rules of the struggle: listening to nationalist music, being very polite to women and being devout teetotallers. Yet, religion was not communicated as the main reason: 'Drugs and alcohol destroy our people', they used to say, 'they work for the benefit of the Israelis, turning the people's mind away from the struggle.'

Their rejection of fanaticism, their fairness and their pride are some of the personal characteristics of Izzat and Ramsi which made me spend so many interesting moments in their shop.

When I met them again in 1994, the signs of a developing split between them in ways of conceptualising the recent developments could already be noticed, but I was nevertheless totally unprepared for the sight which appeared in front of my eyes at a crowded West Jerusalem night-club in October 1995. When I first entered the premises I had to stand quiet for a little while for my eyes to get used to the dim light, and to scan the crowd for familiar faces. However, the sight of a drunken Ramsi harassing women, was, to put it mildly, the last scenario I could have imagined.

When I gained my breath I managed to make my way through the crowd, and went up to him on the dance floor. He seemed at first a little embarrassed to see me, but we embraced, did the obligatory Palestinian male-to-male kissing, and went over to a quiet place in the corner. Here I sat with Ramsi for two hours listening to him telling his story while constantly drying his eyes with a worn-out handkerchief. Ultimately I was crying as well, as the depth of this personal tragedy became clearer to me.

On the surface, nothing really dramatic had happened to him during the last year. Two more of his friends had died, both of whom I had met. But in the past, such incidents had only strengthened his involvement in both the political and cultural parts of the struggle. However, his frame of reference for interpreting such incidents had gone through a radical change. In Ramsi's eyes, the backbone of his ideas and his whole life had fallen apart.

Crying, Ramsi argued that all he had believed in, all he had built his life and his pride around, had gone down the drain. Ramsi fought the struggle, he believed with all his heart in the struggle, it was his life. Following are a few fragments of what

Ramsi told me during our discussion, the emotional depths of which, however, can never be attached to a sheet of paper:

> Now, I have nothing any more. I have nothing to hope for. I have nothing to believe in. I am nothing. Six of my friends died in the struggle. For what? Nothing. All I used to believe in is crushed. We have a little autonomous piece of land here, and a couple of other pieces there. We have no state, and if we ever get one, it will not be the one we fought for. Our leaders have become dictators, the democratic ideals of the Intifada are crushed. The occupation continues, but nobody cares about us. Our nationalism is dead. All those ideals which used to guide my life do not exist any more ...
>
> I used to be proud. Now I am rude like everybody else. I never touched alcohol. Now I am drinking too much. It had nothing to do with religion. Like everything else it had to do with politics and the struggle. But how can I be what I used to be when the politics is dead and the struggle is dead? What is there for me to do now? Chasing girls is my new politics. When I am sober I feel dirty and ashamed. But why shouldn't I have fun like the others? Look at the people around you, this is *their* 'peace'. This is Israel's peace. We are left in misery, but they can continue to have fun. So why shouldn't I have fun. The girls here are almost like prostitutes, they go with many men. Palestinian girls are decent, very few of them go with men. But if this 'peace' does not give me the chance to live decently as a Palestinian, why shouldn't I reap the fruits of 'peace'? ...
>
> So I drink, I chase the girls. I live the life of 'peace'. I am dirty, I know it. There is only the skin left of the person who used to discuss with you. But, tell me, you have many years of education and everything, what shall I do?

Crying myself, I had to admit that, despite all my 'education', I could not provide my friend with an answer. In the end our conversation died. Ramsi withdrew into himself. So did I, thinking about this tragedy which had been revealed in front of my eyes and thinking about how far it was from the Norwegian media coverage – with the emphasis on Norway's diplomatic triumphs – about 'a new era for the Middle East' to the bench where Ramsi and I were sitting. Was Ramsi a product of a 'peace' which in reality is the strengthening of the strong and the weakening of the weak?

My stay in 1995 was short, and I did not have the opportunity
to sit down and talk properly with Ramsi's brother, Izzat. Yet,
upon returning for fieldwork in 1996, I spent a lot of time with
both of them. Ramsi was the same decent man he always used to
be, but his language had changed. If he was allowed to choose the
subject, it would be anything but politics. He had started working
part-time at a tourist restaurant, and talked a lot about his
experiences there. He also briefed me about the different pubs in
Jerusalem, as well as about his marriage plans. The energy and
happiness, however, had vanished from his face and speech, and
when I started talking about the political situation, he tried to
evade it, but told me several times that he had given up altogether
and tried his best to escape from reality. He had long ago lost faith
in the Palestinian leaders, the Arab world, and the international
community, but realised that he had no power to influence
anything. Several times he provided analysis of the current
developments, but the words and metaphors he chose belonged to
the language of a social scientist inspired by Machiavelli or Social
Darwinism. A vocabulary of cold and down-to-earth 'realism' had
taken the place of hope. The picture he painted was the same as
that evening I met him drunk one year before, one of defeat. With
Oslo, the Palestinians had lost the battle, he said, and the
challenge thus became to make the best of one's life accordingly.

The contrast with his brother Izzat is enormous. They have
grown up together and worked together for many years. They have
a sense of decency and love for their fellow human beings; they
are both generously hospitable. Yet, in their visions for the future,
they represent two contradicting approaches. Izzat remains the
eternal optimist, even in the face of the most violent and lethal
blows to the Palestinian people. Nor does personal suffering
remove his optimism, as when East Jerusalem settlers who have
occupied a house near the shop regularly come to throw their
garbage or their dirty water on the pavement outside. Even when
he is caught at an Israeli checkpoint, beaten and mistreated
severely by Israeli soldiers, he remains optimistic.

The latter happened during my last visit. Izzat and Ramsi were
both caught on their way to work. To be able to control the
situation entirely, however, the soldiers left Ramsi, and drove
away with Izzat in the army jeep. They took him to a remote area,

and started beating him. One told him that he would be hit in the head if he spoke, another said that the same would happen to him if he didn't speak. A third did the name-dropping, and both Izzat and his family were called dogs and donkeys. Izzat knew he couldn't do anything, but responded that if he was a donkey, why did they speak to him at all? This comment made the soldiers furious, and four clubs fell on Izzat's head, his back and his feet. When they finished with him and took him back inside the West Bank, he was barely able to walk.

Yet, working illegally in Jerusalem and without any social benefits, he had no choice but to walk the same long route around the checkpoint the day after. Three days after the incident I met him at his workplace in Jerusalem wearing a big cap to hide the bruises on his head. His body was aching severely, but he *had* to keep going through his ten-hour tough work-day.

Still, not one word of complaint came from his mouth. Instead he chose to talk about the prospects for peace in the Middle East, and the different scenarios which would make this happen. Izzat is certain that one day justice will be reinstalled, and the Palestinian state with Jerusalem as the capital will emerge. One thing has changed, though, in the way Izzat communicates his hopes: the Israelis are no longer part of them. Izzat was a strong supporter of Oslo at the outset, he no longer is. Oslo is in many ways a lost hope for him. He has also lost his hope in the peace forces in Israel, although he remains a firm supporter of the idea of two states for two peoples. Furthermore, he still believes that Israelis and Palestinians *can* live together in peace.

His current hopes, however, all focus on outside forces, as well as internal Palestinian strength, being able to force Israel to leave the Occupied Territories of 1967. After the clashes in September 1996, where Palestinian police intervened to prevent a total slaughter of Palestinian students, Izzat argued that the Palestinians would sooner or later be able to kick the Israelis out on their own. After relations between Israel and the neighbouring Arab states started to deteriorate, Izzat hoped for both Syrian and Egyptian military intervention. After the visit to Jerusalem and Ramallah of President Chirac of France, during which he severely criticised Israel, Izzat told me that now the Europeans had finally understood what was happening and would force Israel to make peace. Before the American elections, he argued that Clinton would definitely change his pro-Israel policies after being re-elected.

All these different hopes surfaced and then diminished in importance on the Palestinian street during the autumn of 1996.

One evening, some time after the American elections, I sat with Izzat for a long time. Clinton had publicly stated that he would not change in his strong support for Israel. I, being 'realistic', had told Izzat this before, and I wanted to hear his reactions to Clinton's statement. Following are Izzat's comments, and his new hope:

> Yes, you were right, we believed that something would happen after the American elections, but now it seems that Clinton doesn't have the courage to do anything at all. He just follows what Israel wants. We can't expect anything from him. He does not accept the UN resolutions which ask for Israeli withdrawal from the territories occupied in 1967. The Americans did it in Iraq, but they don't want to do it here. The fulfilment of those resolutions is the only thing that can lead to peace here. But the Americans don't want it, and the Israelis don't want it. They don't want peace.

I intervene, and return to my experiences with the settlements.[10] I ask him as I've asked so many others, if he still believes that the Israelis will leave the settlements and East Jerusalem. His answer, his new hope, comes as a total surprise to me:

> Yes, because it says so in the Koran. The Koran explains all about what will happen here in the future. It says that one day a huge army of Moslems will come here and liberate the country from the Jews. The Koran tells us that the Jews will gather in this country in huge numbers over a period of years. They will fight everyone, kick and hit everyone, wage war against everyone, rejecting any offer of peace. This will go on for many, many years. But then one day, Moslem armies will come from Africa, from the peninsula, from Iraq, from Iran, from Jordan and from Syria. The stones and the trees will speak, the wind will help. Together they will fight the Jews and drive them out or finish all of them to restore peace and justice. Then this place will become one of the most beautiful in the world.

I'm taken by surprise, but ask him if he, as a not very religious person, really believes this deep down:

You're right that I'm not religious, but still I'm Moslem, and I believe what is written in the Koran, the history and the prophesies. Regarding Israel and the place here, we have already seen that so many of the signs about which Mohammed told us have come true. And also, you know, you can't sit curled up like a baby with your arms over your head your entire life just taking humiliation after humiliation. After they hit you, rape your sister, kill your neighbour, put your cousin in jail, sooner or later you react. You can't live in humiliation your entire life, at least I can't. Hope is my weapon, without it I would be nothing here as the situation is. There is no way I can accept not getting my state and my capital. I believe this goes for most Palestinians; they will not accept such an Israeli solution. Then there will definitely be war. And, as I told you, even though I'm not very religious, I still believe in the Koran. And the holy book tells us everything that will happen. It will not happen now, you see what state the Arabs are in and you know how I look upon them, but at least some time in the near or distant future justice will come to us. The Arabs will unite, and once again become spiritually clean and militarily strong. God is just, and he will not sit and watch us being humiliated forever.

I intervene again, and remind him about what he said about the UN resolutions, that the fulfilment of those is the only thing that can bring peace. My question thus becomes: 'But what if the Israelis agree to withdrawing from the occupied territories, do you still believe that the Moslem armies will come and finish them off?' His answer comes quickly and without hesitation:

No, of course not. This is also in the Koran, it tells us clearly to live in peace with our neighbours. If they do what you say, we will not touch a hair upon their head, and we will live peacefully together with them. We do not *want* war, we want peace and justice. The whole commandment of Jihad is null and void if they agree to peace. But it doesn't seem like it. They don't want peace, they want to continue treating us like dogs and donkeys. But then they must face the consequences.

Later the same evening we turn to the question of leadership. Izzat, a new-born critic of Oslo, still supports Arafat, the main Palestinian architect. When I suggest that this to me looks like a contradiction in terms, he has an answer even to this one. A hidden hope is there, along with a conspiracy, resolving the 'contradiction':

> Yes, Arafat had problems in the beginning, but now, especially after the clashes, he has learned the game. He knows what he is doing, and how to play the cards. You know, we have a saying in Arabic: follow the liar to the end of the alley. This is what he's doing, following the Israeli liars to the end of the alley. When they come there, he will expose them. Just you wait and see.

I leave after this last hope has been presented. On my way back, I start thinking about how the Israelis can afford to make an enemy out of this man. He is always so friendly to them when they come to his shop, but all he receives is humiliation. Will he end up like his brother?

During my next meeting with Izzat, as if to reject my question, he presents me with the following scenario:

> Nowadays I follow the news very closely. I don't only watch parts of it, but the whole thing. And what I can see from this is that there will be a war between Israel and Syria soon. I believe also that soon, but not immediately [referring to my scepticism towards US policies in the Middle East], the USA will give the green light for the Arab states to take back Golan and the West Bank. I'm positive that this will happen, because the signals are there in how the news is presented.

His strong enthusiasm and belief in his cause are his buffers against disillusionment. His reality, both on the personal as well as on the collective political level, is very tough. Yet through his hopes it becomes merely transitory. The days of justice await around the corner.

Upon saying goodbye to Ramsi and Izzat for my return to Norway for Christmas, Izzat promises me that things will have changed for the better when I return.

HOPE AND 'REALISM': OSLO, THE LAST HOPE?

My Oxford Dictionary provides the following behavioural definition of 'realism': 'behaviour based on the facing of facts and disregard of sentiment and convention'.[11] I have already argued that this form of 'realism' – being an interpretative scheme – is employed by the few more or less unconditional Palestinian supporters of Oslo. They don't like the way it is turning, but still feel it's all the Palestinians will ever get.

Taking the Machiavellian-like New World Order into account, it is not difficult to understand their approach. Within such a paradigm of interpretation, Oslo is in many ways the last hope for the Palestinians. The leadership has taken part with all its prestige, arguing that there is no alternative or way back. Oslo is supposed to be the process whereby the conflict between Israelis and Palestinians will be settled forever. A final status agreement, signed by both parties will, at least in theory, be internationally binding, and the part which would break it would face severe international criticism and/or possible sanctions (still, taking current practice into account, only in theory).

With the negative political, social and economic development in Palestine after 1993, there would thus be ample reason to expect that most Palestinians would start rejecting Oslo. Yet, polls give us a different picture.[12] My Machiavellian version of realism, implanted on the Oslo Agreement, has however little explanatory power when we talk about this majority. Few Palestinians have ever read the agreement, and the ones outside the Palestinian Authority who have, many of them academics, do in general oppose it. Furthermore, the amazing results of an opinion poll published by *Palestine Report* (Vol. 1, No. 21, 1994) showed that 72.7 per cent of the Palestinians support the peace process, whilst at the same time 65.2 per cent still did not recognise Israel's right to exist. Taking into account what the Oslo process actually is about, this would be the prototype of a contradiction in terms.

Thus, to explain the support for Oslo, I believe we need to return to the concept of hope. Above, I argued that Palestinian ways of hoping represent creative cognitive acts of penetrating the hostile surface of the political environment and of searching for latent promises from within. Most Palestinians, analysing Oslo by the use of such an interpretative map, do not yet see the process's reservoir of promises as empty. It continues to be conceptualised as another hope which might lead to the implementation of the

ultimate vision of a just future. As such, however, the support is
by no means unconditional.

When you talk to Palestinians who argue that they favour the
peace process, the most important reason given for their support is
the need for peace. For so many years people have lived without
the possibility of leading normal lives. Palestinian youngsters, like
all youngsters of the modern world, want the opportunity to travel
freely, to get a job, an education, a future. They want the
opportunity to move without having to be alert all the time for
checkpoints and soldiers. People want to get rid of ever-present
anxiety for their loved ones, fear of death and arrests. Thus, Oslo,
screened through the filter of hope, is supported as long as it is
seen as an instrument capable of fulfilling these needs.

There are a few additional reasons for the support, however,
one being the role of leadership among the Palestinians, and
especially the role of Arafat. Traditionally, leadership, analytically
perhaps best conceptualised as clientism, has played a very
important role in Arab societies. People need patrons to gain
access to favours and goods, and leaders need followers to establish
power bases in the struggle for political influence. A hierarchy of
leaders thus forms the top echelons, with the all-powerful on the
top. In this model, politics in a sense becomes a leadership
prerogative.[13] The Palestine Liberation Organisation retained
aspects of this model of social organisation in its set-up, yet it can
be seen even more clearly in the construction of the Palestinian
Authority established after Oslo.[14] Nowadays, people told me, if
you don't have some contacts inside the PA, you *are* nothing and
can achieve nothing.

Talking to people, one finds partly social, partly cultural
attitudes to strong leadership as a necessary evil to make society
work (PR opinion polls will provide evidence). A Palestinian
woman I know who worked on an education programme on
democracy before the Palestinian elections told me that she found
it more or less impossible to divert people's interest from form and
faces to content and party programmes. Furthermore, the following extract from a conversation with a friend, a former top figure
in Fatah who withdrew from politics after Oslo protesting the
human rights violations of the PA, represents a fairly general
Palestinian approach to the current situation:

Well, as I told you, Palestinian leaders have become more and more remote from the people as they sit behind closed office doors surrounded by security guards. But people still need leaders. We have a saying in Arabic, that if you find three men walking together towards a junction, they would all choose different directions if one of them failed to assume leadership. This saying, I believe, reflects human nature.

Even though there is a lot of criticism against many of the 'big-shots' within the PA, Arafat himself has so far retained a remarkable popularity on the street.[15] In one sense he's a mythic figure, the father of the nation, the symbol of the Palestinian struggle for so many years. Both on the international level as well as among the Palestinians, there is no other side to Arafat than the struggle. It has been his life and thus he has a lot of trust among the majority of the Palestinians. Returning to Oslo, when Arafat says that this is a process which will in the end lead to a Palestinian state with Jerusalem as its capital, people believe him, or perhaps feel – in the face of contradictory developments – that they have to believe him. Furthermore, Arafat is not only shielded from criticism by the official Palestinian media – probably to a large extent due to political pressure from the PA security – but so many people I talked to chose to direct their criticism towards Arafat's aides and deputies instead. This part of a conversation with another Palestinian friend, a former supporter of Oslo, will exemplify:

I trust the chairman, but not the people surrounding him, people like Nabil Sha'th, Abu Mazen, Abu Ala. They made the Oslo agreement and the other agreements, and created all our problems now. Who are they? They were never in jail, they were never stopped at checkpoints.[16] They have VIP status and don't know what suffering is. The chairman *wants* a Palestinian state, he wants what's best for the Palestinians. He knows everything, including the content of the secret papers under the table. I trust him, but Oslo was a mistake. We can't do anything but trust him and continue with our lives. There's nothing we can do, absolutely nothing.

My friend introduces another issue into the picture, the idea of secrecy and under-the-table deals, an idea which is closely connected to leadership. This conceptualisation emerges from a long Middle Eastern tradition of making politics and political agreements. When leaders meet, be they Arab or Israeli, there are always lots of discussions and speculations on the Palestinian street about what kind of conspiracy or secret will be revealed next. This is based on an understanding that there is always more to the subject matter than what is currently publicly known.[17] My friend's support for Arafat thus centres around his trust in the chairman, and the belief that sooner or later a revelation will show that what at the moment seems like contradictory behaviour on the part of the leader is in the long term to the benefit of the Palestinians.

Thus, there are many different and complementary reasons why people state their support for the Oslo process. Yet, as if to emphasise that the support is conditional, if you ask the same persons if they would continue to support it even if it fails to remove the settlers, fails to deal with the refugees, and fails to return the Occupied Territories of 1967 and secure an agreement on Jerusalem, the answers are loud and clear: 'Of course not, that is not peace!'[18] The hope is there only in so far as it provides a means to implement the collective future vision. Oslo is the last hope only for the disillusioned 'realists'.

In the Palestine of 1996, three years after the signing of the DOP, more and more critical voices are heard. As the Oslo process has brought only more misery to the masses, and the Israelis – now under a new right-wing leadership – have continued their occupation policies of land confiscation and detentions, so many are starting to lose hope in Oslo. 'There is no peace', is a current saying on the street, along with a renaming of Oslo from 'peace process' to 'piss process'.

Oslo has been communicated in leadership rhetoric as well as on the street in the value-laden language of hope. Yet, as reality sinks in, the process stands on the verge of losing its anchoring in this Palestinian way of conceptualising the future. With the present Israeli policies, as well as with the PA's even worsening record when it comes to human rights and internal democracy,[19] Oslo is about to become another of the many lost hopes of which Palestinian history consists. The language of war is once more dominating Middle Eastern political discourse, and below the surface the Palestinian street is boiling.

One outburst was the semi-war between Palestinian civilians and soldiers and Israeli soldiers in late September 1996, leading to nearly a hundred deaths and probably more than a thousand wounded. Continuing Israeli occupation and territorial confiscation, lack of Palestinian strength in the negotiations as well as lack of internal democracy, had created extreme frustration among the Palestinians. The Israeli opening of the tunnel near Al-Aqsa Mosque provided the spark that lit the fire. The uproar itself started when Palestinian students from Bir Zeit University and different schools in the Ramallah area marched towards an Israeli checkpoint to protest the 'lack of peace'. Talking to some of the people who took part and barely survived the clashes, their stated most important reason for participating was their feeling of betrayal relating to the dichotomy Oslo as hope / Oslo as reality. 'We heard withdrawal, we got redeployment' was one of the comments. 'We heard that the settlements would disappear, but in reality they grew' was another.

However, these students did not talk in the language of defeat and resignation. A new hope had surfaced, conceptualised as the power of the people, the determinacy of the people never to give up until their rights were secured. As one student said: 'We have lost hope in the peace process, and partly in our own leaders, but the Palestinian people will never give up. We *will* have our rights one day.'

In the eyes of these students as well as in the eyes of so many Palestinians I talked to, Oslo is just another hope. The struggle continues, and beyond Oslo there are new hopes.

CONCLUSION

In this article I have tried to show that there is a clear connection between having or getting a vision of a just future and the ability to maintain or fabricate hope. This thesis is supported by substantive anthropological research on so-called millenarian movements,[20] as well as on recent ethnic/national revivalism.[21]

Georg Henriksen has worked among the Naskapi Indians in Canada for nearly thirty years, with a major focus on the Indians' meeting with the white man's world.[22] The Indians (or *Innu*) had no knowledge of and few possibilities to influence the market economy which flooded their small village in Davis Inlet in Labrador. Thus, from being proud hunters in the Canadian inland, the small community fell prey to alcoholism and serious frustration. Hope for the future was lost among the inhabitants, as they were both unable to identify their enemies as well as to master or understand the ideas of capitalism or visualise a role for their own little society within this new and complicated economic structure.

In many ways this would be a picture which could be used to describe the fate of not only many indigenous peoples around the world, but also as a general input to lives under external influence and occupation. And yet, regarding many indigenous groups, globalisation of ideas of ethnic self-determination and cultural rights might seem to have somewhat reversed the trend. As these new ideas and visions reached Davis Inlet, hope gradually returned to the inhabitants as a language had been discovered which could be used in their dealings with Canadian authorities. A difficult and slow, but yet noticeable, rehabilitation of the society has thus started.[23]

When it comes to the Palestinian situation, the similarities are striking, but so are the contrasts, giving us a further clue to the important role of hope in the struggle. First, Palestinians are perfectly aware of and knowledgeable about their enemies and their strategies. Second, Palestinians have had their collective vision for a long time. They have had UN resolutions supporting their claims, and at least vocal support from vast parts of the world. Their hopes thus have a secure anchoring in an established and fairly well-articulated idea about a future, just, society. At the same time, as I have argued, they have an existentialist character, functioning as responses to powerlessness and deprivation, enabling the individual to maintain his or her integrity and stability in a situation of severe physical and psychological stress.

I have rejected the concept of 'realism' as a viable analytical tool in an attempt to conceptualise the seemingly contradictory Palestinian support for a process which thus far has brought them little but continuous suffering. First, concepts like 'reality', 'realism', 'the real', are at best analytically problematic. Second, hoping extends all of them. In the same way as human beings shape reality through their constructions of it,[24] so may visionary and/or existentialist hopes – be they subjective images or collective symbols[25] – create or fabricate a reality which is no less real than the 'realist' analysis of the social scientist or the journalist.

This is also the message of Desroche in an eye-opening work about hope.[26] With a metaphoric twist, he likens hope to a rope and further to the concept of miracle. Consider the following introduction to his work:

> In this rite, the officiant – fakir, shaman ... or juggler – throws a rope like a lasso 'in the air'. It should fall down. But the officiant assures us that it has mysteriously anchored itself somewhere, and to prove it, he or his disciple climbs up the rope. The rope does not give way. *It holds.* And it carries the weight of the man as he climbs.[27]

Yet, Desroche strongly emphasises the word *miracle* and not fake magic. A 'realist' interpretation does not pre-empt the subject matter:

> I confess: perhaps, impressed by the very abundance of these phenomena, one becomes sceptical about the validity of the axiom, according to which these *representations* – oneiric, liturgical, cultural, utopian, ideological, in short, *imaginary* in one way or the other – are explicable 'in the last analysis' *by* and, all things considered, reducible *to, situations* of social, economic, technological or demographic *reality*. Certainly, as we can see, these situations weave a system of restraints which determines these representations, but this social determinism is just that gravity which the grace of the imaginary 'underdetermines', as it were, giving freedom and setting free. Forces of *pressure* pose and define a question. But it is the forces of aspirations which formulate and offer an answer. It is as though human beings – personalities and/or collectivities – who are burdened by the weight of necessities, found something *like the rope* to be a message, an announcement, a 'revelation', a gospel. Whether they believe this rope to have come from elsewhere, or whether they think it came from within themselves is of no consequence. In both cases it is a rope that they throw in the air, in other words, into space, into the clouds, into the sky. To the observer, it seems like there is nothing to keep it up, except for the impalpable and inconsistent worlds of fantasy, wanderings and absurdity. And yet this rope is anchored. *It holds.* And when humans grab hold of it and pull themselves up, it *takes the strain*, it maintains its rigidity, even if, believing that they are bringing heaven

down to the earth, they are only moving their ancient lands up towards new heavens ... If an imagination is thus *constituted*, it is no less a *constitutive imagination*, the constructor of a social reality. It is not without hazards and pitfalls. For if hope is identified with this constitutive imagination, it cannot be so without sharing in both the characteristic *fullness* and *emptiness* of the imaginary.[28]

I fully share Desroche's reservations. An imagination is always on one level – some would say 'in the last instance' – empty. And yet it is the sheer strength of the hope which carries the promise of a more decent future for the Palestinians. Hopes are not false consciousness and detrimental to the fighting spirit of the individual. On the contrary, only the hopeful person has something to fight for. The solid anchoring of the vision – the rope leading to glory – in the Palestinian imagination, creates, as Desroche argues, a reality. It creates a power of the people which can penetrate time and all occupation and suppression barriers. The strength of these hopes, seemingly surviving all political blows to the Palestinian people, should demonstrate to all parties to the Oslo process that without a political solution that can meet the individual aspirations no peace will prevail in Palestine.

The Oslo process has so far done little to give real content to the imagination. And yet, first, with the image of Palestinian students marching forwards towards checkpoints amidst live bullets and fallen comrades imprinted on my mind, and, second, upon hearing them and many other Palestinians talk about their willingness to give their lives for the cause of justice, I firmly believe that sooner or later the people, if not aided by the international community, will do it themselves. Hopes and visions not only cognitively remould social processes, they may also – as shown above – be transformed into political action.

NOTES

1. Dag Jørund Lønning, *Bridge Over Troubled Water: Inter-ethnic Dialogue in Israel-Palestine* (Bergen: Norse Publications, 1995).
2. Current unemployment rates are set at 38 per cent in the West Bank and 51 per cent in Gaza. Since Oslo per capita income has declined from $2000 to $950 in the West Bank, and from $1200 to $600 in Gaza. The GDP has dropped 25 per cent (interview with Mohammed Shtayyeh, director of Palestinian Economic

Council for Development and Reconstruction, *Jerusalem Post Money Magazine*, 9 October 1996).

3. These numbers relate to the period from Autumn 1993 to Spring 1997. With the extremely expansive settlement policies of Israeli Prime Minister Netanyahu, as well as with increasing public critique of the whole Oslo process from the Palestinian leadership, the numbers have dropped throughout 1997. See polls series from Center for Palestine Research and Studies and Jerusalem Media and Communication Center.

4. See Dorothy Holland and Naomi Quinn (eds), *Cultural Models in Language & Thought* (Cambridge: Cambridge University Press, 1987). See also Roy D'Andrade and Claudia Strauss (eds), *Human Motives and Cultural Models* (Cambridge: Cambridge University Press, 1992).

5. Gananath Obeyesekere, *Medusa's Hair. An Essay on Personal Symbols and Religious Experience* (Chicago: The University of Chicago Press, 1984) p. 137.

6. See for example Christopher Hitchens, 'Foreword' in Edward Said, *Peace and Its Discontents. Gaza–Jericho 1993–1995* (London: Vintage, 1995); Ted Swedenburg, 'The Palestinian Peasant as National Signifier', *Anthropological Quarterly*, Vol. 63, No. 1 (1990) pp. 18–30.

7. See for example Lønning, *Bridge Over Troubled Water*; Ali H. Qleibo, *Before the Mountains Disappear. An Ethnographic Chronicle of the Modern Palestinians* (Jerusalem: Kloreus, 1992); George M. Scott Jr, 'A resynthesis of the primordial and circumstantial approaches to ethnic group solidarity: towards an explanatory model', *Ethnic and Racial Studies*, Vol. 13, No. 2 (1992) pp. 147–71.

8. An opinion poll from *Palestine Report*, Vol. 2, No. 29 (1997) shows that although the vast majority of Palestinians are highly critical of the way the Oslo process has developed, when asked about the Palestinian future, 12.4 per cent nevertheless say they are 'optimistic', and another 62.2 per cent say they are 'somewhat optimistic'. However, the first figure represents a decline of 6.6 per cent since October 1996.

9. See for example Smadar Lavie, *The Poetics of Military Occupation. Mzeina Allegories of Bedouin Identity Under Israeli and Egyptian Rule* (Berkeley/Los Angeles/Oxford: University of California Press, 1990).

10. On 10 November 1996, settlers came in to take a vast piece of land belonging to several villages outside Ramallah. When the inhabitants asked to stage a peaceful 30-minute protest, the Israeli soldiers started shooting. One person was killed and twelve seriously wounded. I was in the vicinity of the area when this happened and witnessed parts of it.

11. A. S. Hornby with A. P. Cowie and A. C. Gimson, *Oxford Advanced Learner's Dictionary of Current English* (Oxford: Oxford University Press, 1974).

12. Regarding the Oslo Agreement, 19.7 per cent say they 'strongly support', 55.2 per cent say they 'cautiously support', 19.1 per cent 'do not support' and 6.0 per cent have 'no opinion'. Yet 78 per cent say they support the peace process in general (*Palestine Report*, Vol. 2, No. 29 (1997)).

13. Fredrik Barth, *Political Leadership Among Swat Pathans* (London: The Athlone Press, 1965); Michael Johnson, 'Political Bosses and their Gangs; Zu'ama and Qabadayat in the Sunni Moslem Quarters of Beirut' in Ernest Gellner and John Waterbury (eds), *Patrons and Clients in Mediterranean Societies* (London: Duckworth, 1977); Lawrence Rosen, *Bargaining for Reality. The Construction of*

Social Relations in a Muslim Community (Chicago: The University of Chicago Press, 1984).

14. *Jerusalem Report* writes: 'The multiheaded creature of the Palestinian Authority's security system is designed to create ambiguity. Arafat, Gazans say, is the only one who knows everything' (17 October 1996).

15. During the summer of 1996 there were signs of widespread criticism of Arafat as the people's frustration over the stalled 'peace process' grew, and more and more reports came out about the use of torture in Palestinian jails. Yet, with the Palestinian police forces' participation in the clashes in September 1996, and Arafat's tougher positions towards the new right-wing Israeli administration, his popularity rose tremendously.

16. The political prisoners are extremely important to the Palestinians, and having spent time in an Israeli jail is often taken as proof of a national consciousness.

17. This aspect of Palestinian politics is discussed in an interesting way by Tore Bjørgo in NUPI-Rapport No. 111, *Conspiracy Rhetoric in Arab Politics: The Palestinian Case* (Oslo: NUPI, 1987). Nevertheless, by attributing conspiracy rhetoric to another kind of 'false consciousness', Bjørgo does not take into consideration, first, that conspiracies happen frequently, and, second, that trying to disclose and preparing oneself for possible conspiracies has been a major form of political interpretation in the Middle East for hundreds of years.

18. See opinion poll in *Palestine Report*, Vol. 2, No. 29 (1997).

19. See for example Roni Ben Efrat, 'No Bagatz and No B'tselem: The Palestinian Authority and the Use of Torture', *Challenge*, Vol. 8, No. 1 (1997). See also Amnesty International's reports from 1996 especially *Palestinian Authority: Prolonged Political Detention, Torture, and Unfair Trials* (London: Amnesty, December 1996).

20. See for example J. Mooney, *The Ghost Dance Religion*, Bureau of American Ethnology, Annual Report No. 14 (Washington DC.: US Government Printing Office, 1896); P. Worsley, *The Trumpet Shall Sound: A Study of 'Cargo' Cults in Melanesia* (London: MacGibbon and Kee, 1957). See also Roger M. Keesing, *Cultural Anthropology. A Contemporary Perspective* (New York: Holt, Rinehart and Winston, 1981).

21. The literature here is vast. For a summary, see Thomas Hylland Eriksen, *Ethnicity & Nationalism. Anthropological Perspective* (London: Pluto Press, 1993).

22. See Georg Henriksen, *Hunters in the Barrens. The Naskapi on the Edge of the White Man's World* (St. John's: ISER, Memorial University of Newfoundland, 1973).

23. Personal communication from Georg Henriksen. See also G. Henriksen, *Life and Death among the Mushuau Innu of Northern Labrador* (St. John's: ISER Research and Policy, 1993).

24. This is another theme which has been extensively debated within all the human sciences. Within anthropology, Clifford Geertz's *The Interpretation of Cultures* (New York: Basic Books, 1973) has been especially influential. For a contribution by the author, see D. J. Lønning, '"Are we friends or enemies?" The management of enemy images in a new political situation in Israel-Palestine', Ph. D. project description, University of Bergen (1995).

25. Obeyesekere, *Medusa's Hair*.

26. Henri Desroche, *The Sociology of Hope* (London: Routledge & Kegan Paul, 1979).

27. Desroche, *The Sociology of Hope*, p. 1. Emphasis in original.

28. Desroche, *The Sociology of Hope*, p. 3. Emphases in original.

9 THE 'VOICE OF PALESTINE' AND THE PEACE PROCESS: PARADOXES IN MEDIA DISCOURSE AFTER OSLO[1]

Lena Jayyusi

Broadcasting media have had a significant role to play, historically, in the life process of the modern territorial nation state. In the Third World, the establishment and development of broadcasting has gone hand-in-hand with the formation of the post-colonial nation state on the one hand (including the crystallisation of a centralised discourse of national identity), and with the emergence and consolidation of particular regimes on the other. In this trajectory, the relationships between identity, sovereignty and legitimacy have been problematic, and have often given rise to countervailing dynamics. The media in the transition to a post neo-colonial order may thus become one of the major sites where contradictions arise or become evident. In the Palestinian case, after Oslo, this is distinctively so. Given the development, not of a formally sovereign state, but of a national authority (a proto-state), which is still obliged to negotiate over issues of jurisdiction, access, land, water, markets (all the issues vital to sovereignty) with the colonial power that remains effectively *in situ*, the new Palestinian broadcast media are put in a particularly paradoxical position. This paper explores just how this paradoxical position is evidenced within the discourse of the Palestinian broadcast media specifically around two critical issues: the problematic of legitimacy, and the meaning and status of the peace process itself. The focus here is on radio broadcasting for reasons indicated below.

NEW MEDIA, PARADOXICAL ORDER

The development of the Palestinian electronic media was grounded in the Oslo agreements, and the process that emerged from them. For the very first time, a Palestinian radio service was instituted intra-territorially and, moreover, linked to the setting-up of an intra-territorial jurisdiction of sorts, the Palestinian National Authority (PA). For the very first time, a Palestinian television service was established – a centralised audio-visual channel of mass communication that transmitted signals, images and messages, publicly and intra-territorially.

Two dimensions are immediately apparent in these developments, which have a bearing on the character of both the transmission and the reception of these media in the newly constituted Palestinian autonomy areas. First of all, the media offered an index of the accomplishment of Oslo: of the fact that Palestinians could, for the first time, speak for themselves and represent themselves. Here, the issue is not only one of actually 'saying' or visually representing and narrating something, but of the 'legitimacy' of doing so within public space without sanction of any kind, notably those traditionally encountered: censorship by the occupation authorities or censorship (formal and informal) by Arab states or Western institutions in the diaspora. It was not only the ability to broadcast, but the international (and US/Israeli in particular) acknowledgement of the right to do so that seemed to index the importance of the birth of Palestinian electronic media in the West Bank and Gaza. In other words, what was evidenced and embodied in the establishment of the new electronic media, and their caretaker institution, the Palestine Broadcasting Corporation, was a transformation in the 'space' allowed Palestinians by the hegemonic global order. And what that made possible was the new ability to give voice freely, not only to a collective discourse of struggle, and not only within limited channels, monitored adversarially by various parties the world over (and therefore constricted, or subject to attempts at delegitimisation), but to give voice to the variegated needs, concerns, dreams and opinions of Palestinians conversing with each other in view of the world without interference; conversing over both collective and more personal levels, in many of the mundane ways that people converse. A conversation, in other words, not simply about crisis, and not only one engaged in moral legitimisation and political persuasion, as the pre-Oslo public discourse of Palestinians so often was, but one whose main currency could be ordinary civic, social life. This, after all, is what radio, at least, has especially come to be identified with in the routines of peoples elsewhere.[2] In other words, the electronic media suggested the possibility of Palestinian self-production, and self constitution. Through them, a Palestinian world could be depicted, transmitted and rebuilt.

At the same time, the other dimension that was embedded in the birth of the electronic media in Palestine was the emergence of a means of not only nation-building but state-building: the building of the legitimacy of the PA itself as an institution. Here were channels by which the PA could itself communicate with the populace, and attempt to refashion the imagery and self-image of the people in such a way as fitted in with the (national) agenda of the moment, and its requisites as conceived.

Immediately, the significance of the electronic media as modes of transmission, and the significance of the modality of their reception, becomes apparent. On the one hand there is what might be described as the populist conception, with an emphasis on self-representation and self-production, for example, the electronic media's declared importance as tools for building national civic institutions, the 'space' afforded the ordinary citizen through the call-in programmes. On the other hand, there is what might be called the political, even the statist conception, with its focus on state-building and state legitimation. A set of potential contradictions between these two conceptions comes into focus here; these contradictions are inherent in the very project of state building itself, a project that can come about not only through a process of institutionalisation, consolidations and crystallisation, but also by a process of multiple silencing, and the deployment of procedures of delimitation and control, which must extend to the regulation of media institutions.[3] Moreover, given the conditions in which these media were founded, indeed, the condition in which the PA itself began to function and operate, as an 'authority' emplaced within a continued girdle of occupation that, as it turned out, grew more constricting with time, was it possible for these two conceptions, the populist and the political, to be seamlessly fitted together? After all, the legitimacy of the modern state is embedded in its claims to represent the rights and interests of a territorially located nation. What contradictions and paradoxes in the conditions of media production and reception were inherent in, or contingent on, this double dynamic that was embedded in the situation of the Palestinians as a whole after Oslo? Do these problems become visible in the discourse of the electronic media themselves?

What is at issue here is the paradox between the discourse that represents the 'achievements' of self-representation, as evident in the birth of the electronic media themselves, (the accomplishment of Oslo), and the severely partial and limited character of that self-representation, that achievement of Oslo, given the insertion of the PA within the structure of occupation. That 'insertion' is a functionally double-edged, paradoxical configuration. But that, after all, is the issue of Oslo itself: partial, limited, but opening up a space. The question at the heart of Palestinian discourse after Oslo has been: what kind of space? Is this a space that carries within it the dynamic of expansion of genuine Palestinian self-governance, and of the ultimate achievement of national goals, or is it a space of entrapment, a space for the consolidation of various forms of Israeli control over Palestinian lives and territory; indeed a space for the insertion of a mediating system of control that works synergistically with the Israeli occupation? Was this to become an arrangement for a bantustan, or was it really just the beginning for the fully independent national state?[4] This is, of course, the paradox of all such interim and partial conditions. It is here that the tension between the discourse of 'liberation' and the discourse of 'occupation' surfaces. For the defining feature of the Palestinian condition after Oslo is the simultaneous double horizon that shapes it: the 'space' (real and imagined) afforded for the projects of nation-building and of state-building (the sub-text of the Oslo Agreement for Palestinians), and the limits and confines, the radical contingency of that space, imposed by a still active project of occupation that it encounters.

It is in this context that the two problematics identified earlier are significant, and can reveal the developments within Palestinian discourse itself: how does the issue of legitimacy emerge? And how is the 'peace process' addressed within the frame of the Palestinian national imaginary? The two questions are closely connected, given that the Oslo accords were signed in an atmosphere that saw far from unconditional support being given it by various Palestinian parties and constituencies. In addressing these questions, however, it is important to keep in mind the distinction between public discourse generally and media discourse more specifically. The relationship is methodologically problematic. One way of treating it is through asking to what extent the media functions as a public sphere,[5] and to what extent its discourse is embedded in, and productive of, an organisation of institutional and state directed objectives and concerns. We will keep this in mind as we address the two questions above. The analysis here will deal specifically with radio broadcasting, rather than television broadcasting (or both), for two primary reasons: first, there are significant differences between the kind of work that radio, as an auditory medium, and television, as a medium of visuality, can do, which must remain beyond the scope of the present paper. Second, radio is a technology and a medium that is more ubiquitous in its reach and its ability to be incorporated into people's everyday routines. In Palestine, moreover, the ability of radio transmission to cover almost the entire region of the West Bank and Gaza (and even beyond), for most of the day, was achieved early on. Television, on the other hand, remains relatively constrained in its outreach, not least because of the political problem of securing appropriate frequencies and wavelengths in negotiations with Israel.

THE DISCOURSE OF PEACE: EMPOWERMENT VERSUS DISEMPOWERMENT

The Peace Process as Elision

Oslo provided a framework within which the expectation of a phased implementation of its own provisions, and the phased resolution of various aspects of the Palestinian national problem, was embedded. As a framework, it had the mark of international

legitimacy: it had been developed, in the final instance, on a
public stage, enacted as a public ritual with an international
audience, and with the 'partnership' of the single remaining
superpower. In the context of the realities on the ground after
Oslo, such as the continued confiscation of land at a previously
unprecedented pace, the closure, the refusal for months to
implement the redeployment agreement from Hebron, the continued activity of settlers, and the attacks on Palestinians in Hebron
and elsewhere, the violations of human rights, this feature became
increasingly marked within the discourse that was broadcast over
the Palestinian media over the two years succeeding their
establishment. This was for a very good reason. The processual
unfolding of the trajectory envisioned by the PA, and at any rate
promoted publicly by it – that is, the eventual establishment of an
independent Palestinian state, with Jerusalem as its capital – was
clearly seen, and visible, as one that was (at the very least
potentially) not-in-the-making, in the policies and pronouncements of the Israeli government. This visibility was itself an
emergent visibility, that came more and more into focus with the
changeover to a Likud government. There were, of course, some
Palestinian voices during the Labour Party's tenure that drew
attention to this, and Labour's minimal policy in moving towards
Palestinian autonomy, and its maximal policy in setting new facts
on the ground in anticipation of the final phase negotiations,
asserting its hold over Jerusalem, and so on, was evident to many.
Yet, until the Likud government took power, it was possible for
voices within the PA to focus on 'talks', 'negotiations', the phased
character of the process, the garnering of all the symbols and
markers of international legitimacy on the way to statehood, the
issue of Hamas and the other Islamic groups, and thus Palestinian
threats to the peace process, the return, the various aspects of
reconstruction and so on. The year after Oslo had indeed seen
remarkable changes and developments, including the first ever
Palestinian national elections, and the return of many prominent
and politically active Palestinians, and if one were to focus on
these, then the 'development' of institutions, and the reconstruction of Palestinian society, could indeed be treated as phased
accomplishments with more to come. This becomes gradually
more and more difficult, beginning, perhaps, with the war in

Lebanon that the Labour Party government launched, leading
into the election of the Likud, and the trajectory following that
with regards especially to Hebron, the plans for integrating the
municipal infrastructure of East and West Jerusalem, the September tunnel events at Al-Aqsa Mosque, the continued closure and
so on, all of which received considerable and ongoing attention
over the Voice of Palestine (VOP) radio.

In this context, the legitimacy of the PA, as a party to an
unfolding process, and from its own side, as an enforcer of the
perceived requirements of that process (the campaign against
Islamic activists and their roundup following the bus bombings in
February/March 1996) stands challenged and even potentially
threatened by visible signs of an alternative process at work, that
of the consolidation of Israeli control, and the exercise of Israeli
power to intensify precisely what was supposed to diminish and
disappear as a consequence of the Oslo process: settlement
expansion, land confiscation, political disenfranchisement in
Jerusalem and civilian deprivation. It is in this context that the
repeated refrain within Western media that the conduct of Israeli
policy (in Hebron, over settlements, Jerusalem) puts Arafat under
pressure within his own population, makes sense. There are other
threats to perceived legitimacy, of course, namely, the conduct of
the PA *vis-à-vis* its own population. Nevertheless, Palestinian
discourse over the media came increasingly to focus explicitly on
the 'peace process' itself. Not only were reports on talks, negotiations, and so on a standard (and by any account a necessary)
component of news and discussions of public affairs, but the
'peace process' acquired a centrality in the way that matters were
formulated. Instead of constituting or describing Israeli policies
primarily as violations of fundamental rights, of national rights, or
of property rights (in the context of land confiscation), they came
to be refigured repeatedly as 'attacks on the peace process',
'violations of the peace process', 'obstacles to the peace process'.
Whereas in the Voice of Palestine (VOP) broadcasts during the
autumn of 1994, a lot of airtime was given (in newscasts and the
interviews which were then a regular feature of those) to items
that can be said to index and embody the *process* (negotiations,
meetings with the Israeli side, institutional formations, redeployments, the return of exiles), broadcasts during the autumn of 1996

devoted more and more airtime, across a range of programme
genres, to explicit mention of, and direct reference to, the peace
process as an *entity in itself*. In 1994 (and even the autumn of 1995)
talk of problems, violations and occupation practices was often
accompanied by an orientation to procedural redress, which kept
the Oslo process as a tacit background understanding, which
assumed at least some measure of mutual orientation to its
framework by the Israelis. By 1996 such matters were more and
more constituted as endangering the very framework of Oslo, now
brought into the foreground. For example, the following report,
about a demonstration by Jerusalem residents against the destruction of Palestinian homes by Israel (citing a lack of construction
permits), is typical of newscasts in the autumn of 1994:

> [The demonstrators] demanded of the Israeli government that it not
> take any measures that can affect the peace process and that it *speed up*
> *the operation of transfer of powers* to the Palestinian National Authority.
> They also demanded that the National Authority place the issue of the
> destruction of houses *at the top of the agenda of negotiations* with the
> Israeli side' (5:00 p.m. newscast, 10 September 1994, emphasis added).

And in an interview with Abu Al Adib, a member of the PNC, on
29 October 1995, speaking of the Israeli demands of that time that
the PNC Charter be speedily amended, he points to the delays on
the Israeli side, and declares that Israel's meeting its timely
obligations was a prerequisite for the convening of the PNC, but
says in this context: 'It means that *we want Israel to help us in*
arriving to all our rights, to see Palestinian sovereignty extend to all
parts of the West Bank, to see the withdrawals'. Compare this to
the political commentary on the programme 'A New Day' (7:00
a.m., 16 December 1996) where the commentator says: 'The
President says that Netanyahu's government *does not want peace*
and is *evading its obligations* towards the peace process, emphasising
that the agreements concluded between Israel and the National
Authority are not bilateral agreements but international ones', an
item repeated more than once in the course of the programme.
And 'Everyone in this world talks of the danger of settlement and
its dangers for the peace process in the region.' By this point in
time, discourse over the media, and in fact official discourse

generally, weaves between mention and delineation of violations, sometimes presenting them in terms of rights, and articulation of such violations *in terms of* the peace process. Indeed, although on many occasions the question of 'rights' comes up, it is also nevertheless itself routinely coupled with reference to the peace process and its sanctity. This 'larger than life' treatment of the peace process came to be dominant in the discourse.[6]

At many junctures, when violations and positions taken by the Israeli government could well be couched in straight political terms, or in moral-political terms, one is surprised by a formulation of the problem as endangering the peace process. This is both on the part of Palestinian officials, who are systematically reported and interviewed on the VOP, as well as VOP news, commentary and interviews, and by various others who appear on the programmes. For example, in the speech of PA President Yasser Arafat, given on 15 November 1996, the anniversary of the declaration of independence, he says:

> You hold fast to the peace, the peace of the brave, and the peace process, and you *sacrifice for its continuation* and its stabilisation, and you place yourselves in the face of the world in your true and radiant picture, for you are the fighters, the fighters for peace. And on this occasion, I salute President Husni Mubarak, and Egypt's leading role under his wise leadership, in supporting our people and their national authority along the track of its negotiations with *Israel which uses all its weapons in order to fatally hit the peace process*. As I salute the stances of his majesty King Hussein that are supportive of the Palestinian people, and also the Arab positions, and the Arab League and its Chairman who is taking a prominent role in uniting the Arab ranks around the entitlements of the peace process .... (emphases added)

In the aftermath of the decision to proceed with settlement activity on Jabal Abu Ghneim (called Har Homa by the Israelis), this kind of formulation of the problem became particularly pronounced. In his speech to the Palestinian Legislative Council, broadcast on the programme 'Events of the Day', at 2:00 p.m., 15 March 1997, Arafat talked of the settlement project as part of a 'plan aiming at the destruction of the peace process'. On 18 March, the day the bulldozers were expected to begin their work,

one of the persons interviewed on the 12:00 p.m. news pronounced in exemplary manner that 'we have to hold fast to the
peace process', a view repeated over and over by various others.
And on the 2:00 p.m. 'Events of the Day' of the same date, a
reporter's description of the situation was 'the predicament
through which the peace process is passing as a result of these
procedures'. Netanyahu's 'fundamental aim' was said to be 'the
destruction of the peace process'. And on the 12:00 p.m. newscast
on 30 March, it was said of Palestinian diplomatic initiatives that
their 'sole aim is the protection of the peace process'.

This is, incidentally, also a feature of the discourse within the
media and official circles of other Arab countries, most notably
Jordan and Egypt. Reports of the Palestinian stance there are also
routinely cast in such terms. For example, in the Jordanian paper
Al-Ra'i, on 28 March, Arafat was quoted as having said:

> we feel that the crime of the Israelis against Jerusalem ... (their editing)
> ... the judaisation of Jerusalem and the building of settlements ... is a
> genuine crime against the peace process and the agreements signed in
> the White House under the auspices of the US President Bill Clinton,
> and against the letter of assurances which we received in Madrid from
> the American administration, signed by the former Secretary of State
> James Baker, and also against international legality. (original editing)

By talking of the 'attack on the peace process' and the 'endangerment
of the peace process' in the context of reports on Israeli settlement
activity, or Israeli land confiscation, or other occupation-related
practices, an odd kind of shift is evidenced. What is implemented
here is a specific kind of elision,[7] a 'play of euphemism': what is
endangered directly, after all, with such activities, is Palestinian
rights, Palestinian livelihoods, Palestinian freedoms, Palestinian
lives. What is directly under attack is, indeed, Palestinian national,
civil and human rights, yet what is often described as being under
attack is the 'peace process'. The point, of course, is not that there is
no genuine fear or belief, that as a result of such policies the project to
resolve the conflict peacefully is endangered, and that this could
result in a breakout of violence of some kind, which could be to the
detriment of all concerned. The point, rather, is to ask what such an
elision accomplishes, as it shifts focus from the issue of the direct

consequences of the relevant actions and policies, to the 'peace process' as the casualty. One of Netanyahu's aims is, after all, as given in his own pronouncements and that of the Likud, the securing of permanent unchallenged Israeli hegemony over Jerusalem as a whole. The 'peace process' is, in some respects, beside the point here. The point is not that Netanyahu 'does not want peace', as frequently repeated, but that what is paramount for him is that he does not want a process that undermines or intervenes in Israeli Jewish hegemony. One has to ask, therefore, under what circumstances, and by dint of what relevances, does this kind of formulation come to be employed, and alternatively, at what kind of discursive points, and with what implications, is the focus on the direct outcomes and casualties of Israeli policy produced? How do the two modalities of public/media narration and discourse inflect each other and dovetail to jointly and mutually produce a specific politico-discursive landscape?

At least a couple of dimensions are involved here. There is the strategic sub-text evident in the elision between the direct objectives of Israel's policies (for example, settlements) and the peace process (a collapse of first-order and second-order consequences), and there is the politico-rhetorical dynamics such discourse is geared to produce, the interlocutors inscribed within it, and its mode of address. For in the weaving between the detail of occupation policy by Israel (as opposed to negotiation policy, talks and so on)[8] and direct references to the peace process, comes the detailing and specifying of the process itself, its obligations and standards, the precepts that apply to it, and the horizons and expectations embedded in it.

In the example of Arafat's words, reported above in the Jordanian *Al-Ra'i*, the specifics of the policies in Jerusalem, themselves described as 'crimes', are recast as crimes in terms of peace, not in terms of Palestinian national rights in the first instance.[9] In the extract from Arafat's speech on the anniversary of the Declaration of Independence – 'you hold fast to the peace ... and the peace process and you sacrifice for its continuation and its stabilisation' – the phrasing is clearly euphemistic. In describing Palestinians as making sacrifices not for their own futures or national objectives, but for the peace process, this formulation reduces the Palestinians' self-vision (for which sacrifice is made) to 'peace': an abstraction that has multiple and contestable

renderings and embodiments.[10] Such discourse could push into
the background injuries done to people directly, and to a
particular body politic, and set up 'peace' as the overriding
objective, thus submerging the objectives that had classically
provided the main framework of Palestinian national discourse:
justice, rights, freedom and independence in the homeland. These
objectives of the Palestinian struggle, which were, after all at issue
within the project of resolution that Oslo was supposedly about,
and which were explicitly enunciated in the Madrid address read
by Haidar Abdul-Shafi in October 1991, remain shadowy within a
discourse whose main framework is merely that of 'peace'.[11]

The discourse, however, is not one-dimensional, but multiplex,
and a constituent of its emphasis on peace is the emphasis on 'process' and 'peace as a process'. The above extract from Arafat's 15
November broadcast speech, for example, is also an affirmation that
emphasises (like much of the media discourse on 'endangering the
peace process' and the violations of the accords) the temporal,
phased, unfolding character of the peace and its accomplishments.
Indeed, reference to 'attacks on the peace process', assurances of
intent to 'protect' that process, and statements that Israel's primary
objective is the 'destruction' of that process, as evidenced in the
constant impediments and obstacles placed in the face of the implementation of the already 'signed agreements' (the *sine qua non* of the
entire operation), keeps the 'processual' aspect of Oslo as a dominant
framework, focusing on the necessarily deferred character of the
resolution, the unavoidably consequent, rather than immediate, entitlement to the final objective. An implicit functional/rhetorical
consequence here is that it deflects or undercuts the moral responsibility for the current condition of Palestinian life, the accountability
for it, from the Palestinian leadership who chose to enter into and
ratify Oslo, and thus *it maintains the legitimacy of Oslo as a framework*.

The Peace Process as a Trajectory of National Expectation

The emphasis on the processual character of the peace process
within the VOP, is, therefore, also an emphasis on continued
expectation, the continued challenge of negotiation, a continued
expansion of the space of Palestinian action. It is not, as is evident

in the Israeli or American discourse on the 'peace process', centred on the idea of 'peace', but rather on 'process'.[12] Already, within this emphasis lies the kernel of a focus on procedure and international law and legitimacy to which we shall return presently. This emphasis involves an affirmation of the condition and entitlement to collective national expectation, a constituent feature of the Palestinian national imaginary. In listening to (or reading through transcripts of) programmes, interviews and call-ins on the Voice of Palestine, one is repeatedly struck by the continued refrain of national expectation, of the imagining of a trajectory of national redemption and national accomplishment: the establishment of the independent Palestinian state with Jerusalem as its capital. The discourse marked by such phrases as 'revolution until victory', 'until total independence', the declared objective of establishing a state on 'any liberated "shibr" of the homeland',[13] an integral constituent of Palestinian discourse before Oslo, all express an orientation to the timed character of the Palestinian national project. The motifs of national goals and expectation, transformed after Oslo in terms of the means envisaged, but consistent in the ends publicly envisioned by the Palestinian leadership, are both evident in the editorials and commentaries by anchors and reporters (reflecting an official media stance) as well as by ordinary citizens of all ages and constituencies, who call in for various reasons and on different programmes.

Thus, the particular modality in which reference to the peace process is executed opens up a space for, and reaffirms the validity of, Palestinian expectations, and through that is an aspect of a legitimating practice designed to confirm, sustain and inscribe 'faith' in the Palestinian leadership, and in Oslo as initially projected. Secondly, and in the same breath, it makes its claim *vis-à-vis* the Israeli government itself; makes the demand implicitly that more is rightfully and legitimately expected. But this implied claim on the Israeli government is a promise addressed, and obligation implied, to the Palestinian population: more is forthcoming by right, more is demanded, more will be insisted on. On the one hand, the euphemistic description of developments as 'attacks' on the peace process carries the danger, if not intent, of inviting a politics of quietism. On the other hand, in the

unavoidable emphasis on process, on an unfolding trajectory still
unfinished, an emphasis necessary for the legitimisation of both
PA and Oslo, it continues to invite a fullness of expectation, a
continued allegiance to the 'Palestinian dream', an affirmation of
the national imaginary.[14] The emphasis on the 'processual' aspect
of the peace process, and the repeated refrain of hope that 'work'
(of whatever kind) will continue, until the building of the
Palestinian state with Jerusalem as its capital, is a platform that is
meant to carry the tension between the 'discourse of liberation'
and the 'discourse of occupation', resolve the paradoxical character
of the situation, and secure its legitimacy in the face of apparent
difficulties (the latter enumerated and described in terms of Israeli
obstacles, impediments or evasions). Thus, what runs through the
discourse is an orientation to a 'timeline' that is made to function
as both diagnosis and prognosis for the conditions and problems
encountered on the road to the ultimate objectives. This is evident
in particular in the programmes surrounding the eighth anniversary of the Declaration of Independence.[15]

In the speech of Arafat himself, broadcast over the Voice of
Palestine, and in the comments and editorials by members of the
VOP staff on the air, as well as in the thoughts and greetings
voiced by numerous callers to the call-in, direct broadcast
programmes, a double construction is encountered: the importance and historic significance and joy of the day was the
declaration and accomplishment of independence after years of
struggle, an occasion on which to pray for and look forward to the
independence of Palestine; the day marks Palestinian independence and is an occasion to dream of and struggle for an
independent state. Alternatively, the day's celebrations of the
Declaration of Independence are described as particularly joyful in
the context of the PA, often explicitly described as the 'Palestinian
state', and hope is expressed that eventually full independence will
be accomplished, or that the next anniversary will witness
Jerusalem as capital of this state. For example, one official calling
into 'Good Morning Palestine', on 15 November 1996, said: 'In
this glorious day, our Palestinian people declared its document of
independence, it declared its determination to establish its
independent Palestinian state ... the establishment by our people
of its national authority is a step on the way of accomplishing this

aim ...' And in response to a question addressed to a police official on duty at one of the street celebrations, the latter answers:

> We say in this Palestinian wedding for which we waited so long, joy to our people and this achievement had as its price enormous sacrifices from our people until we arrived at national independence, and we wish, God willing, that next year we will have accomplished our victory and Jerusalem will have returned as the capital of our independent Palestinian state.

In the programme 'Defenders of the Homeland', broadcast at 1:15 p.m. of that day, another caller says: 'We say on this occasion, which is dear to our hearts, and it is the occasion of the eighth declaration of independence, the independence of the state of Palestine on the land of Palestine, God willing in the very near future.' And on the 'Voice of Youth' at 5:10, a caller proclaims: 'This day is for us a great day in which the birth of the Palestinian state took place and this declaration was effectively the first nucleus for the establishment of our independent Palestinian state with Jerusalem as its capital.' What intervenes and carries the connection between the two terms, mostly implicitly (but at times made explicit) is the idea of a process of struggle, a trajectory of liberation with stations on the way, partial achievements on the road to the final dreamed-of and ultimate objective. But how can one talk of independence and hoped-for independence in one and the same breath? How can one talk of 'independence' in the context of closure? What kind of a political culture does it encourage, contribute to, presuppose? This is a question worth asking, and worthy of a thoughtful answer. The dangers inherent in this kind of discourse are very real, for at times it hovers on the edge of oxymoron, the 'timeline' almost collapsed. This is, however, perhaps itself reflective of that paradoxical condition of the Palestinians after Oslo, indicated earlier, a condition not lost on Palestinians themselves.[16] Moreover, in the talk of officials and others over the VOP, a genuine conception of progress is made available, a process in which word and act go together in a particular organisation, where the word is itself, much as the philosopher J. L. Austin proposed, a kind of act, and the declaration of independence embodies an act of independence,

which is a building block of the 'process' of struggle itself.[17] The
conception at work here is that affirmation is an aspect of the
struggle of Palestinians (long denied, censored and suppressed)
and a precondition for the achievement of recognition; that full
independence of a state institution, and of territorial independence, is to be accomplished through independent action, including
the declaration of independence, which becomes a rallying cry for
the national movement. In other words, the 'word act' establishes
the ground for other forms of action, and for material accomplishments. This kind of sensibility is not too distant from a liberation
movement which, despite its rhetoric, and the rhetoric of its
opponents and detractors, did not really place armed struggle at
the heart of its procedural agenda, but rather placed diplomacy
and the international quest for recognition at that heart.

In this discourse, and as part of the work of the VOP, details of
the manifold series of measures taken by Israel, all over the West
Bank and Gaza, and across a whole set of domains, are provided
daily in a number of news programmes, in addition to news
bulletins. In describing itself as 'the Voice of Palestine', radio
programming has to present such details, for they constitute the
fabric of everyday living conditions and experiences for Palestinians, and the indices and measuring rods of the progress towards
their dreams, aspirations and hopes, as articulated over and over
in various forms, and on the street, for decades. But such details
construct an implicit narrative which could be articulated around
a motif of suppression and oppression (and potentially of official
Palestinian failure). The discourse of the VOP (like the discourse
of the leadership and of Palestinian officials) therefore deals with
this narrative horizon in such multiple ways. On the one hand, the
very reality, and the continued intractability (and intractable
continuation) of such detail, of such activities and events, points
to *a policy*, and unavoidably raises the question of responsibility in
its two faces: the responsibility for authorship, and the responsibility for response. The persistent articulation of the problem as
attacks on the peace process, in part, addresses the first issue. And
it does so by implicitly reaffirming Oslo as a framework, securing
the legitimacy of expectation that was grounded in it, pinning the
problem on the freezing of the process, rather than the process
itself, and thus, on the decisions of specific actors on the Israeli

side. The discourse that continues to articulate Palestinian demands, also as a process and project, addresses the second. Thus the discourse on the peace process evinces a topography which incorporates a set of features; at the same time as the emphasis on 'process' and the 'timeline' inscribed within it, and as part of it, is the affirmation and legitimisation of popular Palestinian expectations. Together with that, mutually embedded in it, and embedding it, is the increased detailing of the Israeli policies that do injury to people and their lives, and to the problems, violations, disagreements and difficulties represented by these policies. It is in this discursive complex that two sets of practical-political upshots are accomplished: the parameters and obligations of the Oslo agreements, as understood and subscribed to by the Palestinians, are specified, and the Oslo accords are legitimised; and, by implication, the Palestinian leadership's initial and continued espousal of them is also legitimated. In other words, that the Oslo agreements, and the Oslo peace is a process in which eventually restitution (however envisioned) and resolution of the national predicament would or could come about is thus reaffirmed, and through that the legitimacy of the PA, and its policy, is also confirmed.

FROM MORAL NARRATIVE TO DUE PROCESS: A DISCOURSE OF INTERNATIONAL LAW AND LEGITIMACY

There is, however, another feature to the VOP (and official) discourse that is pervasive and striking, and works to 'secure' the specification of Oslo and the legitimacy of expectations embedded in it, and this is the emphasis on international legitimacy and legality. Together with the increasingly explicit reference to the 'peace process' comes an insistent emphasis on the international framework within which it was forged and within which the peace agreements were concluded.

The emphasis on both international legitimacy and legality has long been an aspect of Palestinian discourse in certain settings; and for good reason. In the context of a national liberation struggle which faced a globally mobilised political movement

(Zionism) and a state, both accorded 'moral' legitimacy by the powerful states of the West and indeed significantly dependent on that support politically and economically, the resolutions of the UN General Assembly (originally the body which first voted the 1947 partition resolution) become a significant matrix for a counter-narrative that accords legitimacy to the Palestinian side. This is acutely more so in the context of a liberation movement without the political and human means to wage an actual war of liberation on the ground, because of the effective removal of its population from the original site of its national being and self-image.

This emphasis on international legality, which is in fact an index, and an invocation and affirmation of legitimacy, becomes increasingly more pronounced after Oslo, and even more after the election of the Likud. Repeatedly, the reference to 'signed agreements' and to 'international legitimacy' is made when a question of Israeli action, response or statement is raised. This again implicitly reaffirms the Palestinian leadership's right to expect the process of Oslo to unfold with a positive trajectory, rather than the negative one visible from the position of the Palestinians. As a consequence, it further reaffirms the legitimacy of the faith in Oslo, of Oslo itself, and thus of the Palestinian leadership and its position, decisions and risk-taking. Above all, it undermines the radical critique of Oslo.

The question remains: what about the issue of human rights that has long been a central feature of Palestinian public discourse? How is it articulated within the context of the Israeli practices that are detailed and delineated within the public space of the media? The issue of human rights is repeatedly raised in the framework of international legitimacy and legality. In the week of 14 November, the very week during which Palestine witnessed widespread celebrations of the anniversary of the Declaration of Independence (15 November 1988), a number of events took place that helped refocus views and discourse around the issue of human rights, and their international and legal standing. One was the decision of the Israeli Supreme Court to allow the use of 'physical pressure' on prisoners to extract information (including the use of the *hazz* or 'shaking' method which had been known to cause brain injury and death). The other was the fining of four

Israeli soldiers one agorat each (equivalent to one-third of a US cent) for the killing of a Palestinian civilian at an impromptu checkpoint, by the Israeli military court. The third was the broadcast of a home video made by a Palestinian of two Israeli border guards at the Ram checkpoint on the way to Ramallah, beating, humiliating and abusing young Palestinian men. These three events garnered front page and editorial attention in the Palestinian press, and much airtime over Palestinian radio and television.

All three events were discussed and presented in terms of human rights principles, and the principles of international legitimacy simultaneously. One fundamental tacit understanding, produced by implication within the discourse, is that 'human rights' and the principles of international law have an essential connection with each other: international law here is produced as that which is congruent with the principles of morality and the acknowledged principles of human rights. In this case, Israel is seen and treated not only as an 'outlaw' in so far as these kinds of action are taken, but as being in violation of the fundamental precepts of moral law. Indeed, international legitimacy and legality here mean that Israeli law and legality (which sanction such behaviour and actions, or permit them, or leave space for them) are themselves suspect. In other words, again, what is produced here as problematic is not only and starkly the violation of human rights in itself. It is not a struggle for a politics of recognition (dominant in the pre-Oslo period) that informs and structures the discourse, but the violation of international human rights law, some of which Israel is a signatory to, including the document on the banning of torture. The primary issue raised is Israel's non-implementation of the internationally legitimated and recognised human rights principles and agreements, under inter-national moral law. What informs and structures the discourse here is thus the politics of implementation: it is a legalistic discourse. We may ask what is at stake here in the subtle shift from the politics of recognition to the politics of implementation? It is the appeal to the Western powers to intercede, to invest practically in their own commitments and recognition, to bring pressure to bear in order to assure the implementation of their own moral law. What may be detected here is the internationalisation of the framework that discursively constructs the issues: a set of global interlocutors are inscribed already within this discourse. Indeed it is by such subtle framings that one can locate the implied addressees, or at least some of them. What this simultaneously inscribes is, perhaps, a distinct set of global power arrangements within which Palestinian life is unavoidably located.

This is not to say that a straightforward discourse of moral outrage is never evident, nor that the violation of human rights involved in these three events which simultaneously became public, were never addressed in clearly moral terms. Indeed, the issue of the beating of the Palestinian men at the checkpoint was also addressed in terms of the nature of the occupation, and the conditions of possibility for such dehumanisation as was evident in this behaviour. The discussion took place at times strictly in moral terms.[18] What is notable, however, is that in any single programme, or any single newscast over the course of these two or three days (replicated on many other occasions with other events), the violation of human rights is couched in terms of a politics of implementation, a politics of obligation, a politics of international law and legitimacy. The underlying implication is that the struggle for 'recognition' has been accomplished, at least internationally. It is this deeply embedded premise that perhaps leads, in the aftermath of the events at Jabal Abu Ghneim in March 1997, to the description of Israel as having become 'isolated' on the world stage.

In conclusion, and to return to some of the earlier questions raised: Palestinian discourse, broadcast over the Voice of Palestine, has a dual character. On the one hand there is a discourse of political legitimation, directed towards the Palestinian interlocutor, the popular constituency. Indeed, it is precisely in the discourse that focuses on the 'peace process', in the ways that we have indicated, that a concern with legitimation is made evident. It is obvious, at least on this level, that the PA (and VOP) perceive and/or present themselves as expressive of, and answerable to, Palestinian popular national expectations. And in this it is reinforcing the very expectations of national accountability that will continue to constrain it and define the grounds of its legitimacy.

On the other hand, there is a discourse of implementation, of obligation, (the 'obligating agreements') that inscribes both the Israeli interlocutor, and more significantly the international interlocutors. To talk of the peace process in these ways, to redescribe human rights violations and practices that threaten national goals as well as the coherence and integrity of everyday life, in terms of the preservation of the peace process, is to claim the relevance and consequence of these actions to all parties concerned, and not only to Palestinians. It is to draw a wide circle of consequence for these policies, implicating various international parties as potentially affected, and to inscribe a regional/ global community of interest. It is in this that the 'globalisation' of the conflict, and its proposed resolution, is indexed. What is evident here is the overall shift from a discourse and politics of recognition, grounded in a moral narrative, to a discourse and politics of implementation (of compliance) grounded in a legal framework. Human rights issues are themselves recast within a legalised discourse. It may be said that in this, a politics of recognition is still at stake. And indeed, it is not possible to treat the two frameworks as completely discrete. But what is fundamentally at stake here, in part, is precisely the embedding of law in moral precepts on the one hand, and in political projects and power arrangements on the other (the latter itself amenable to moral assessment) that the problematic of post-Oslo Palestinian political life encounters.

NOTES

1. This paper draws on a larger research project funded by the Social Science Research Council (USA) and the Ford Foundation, and conducted while a Senior Research Fellow at Muwatin Palestinian Institute for the Study of Democracy. The project was originally begun under the auspices of the Annenberg Scholar's Programme at the University of Pennsylvania. All programme materials referenced in the paper are part of an individual collection made in the course of the project, with the help of the project's research assistant, Bassam Al Mohr.
2. Indeed, one of the striking discoveries for Palestinian radio personnel, quite early on, was the immediate and widespread popularity and success of live programmes, where ordinary people could voice their concerns, opinions and questions on a wide range of issues. As a result, this kind of programme became a staple in a number of time slots.
3. On this topic see, for example, Monroe Price, *Television, The Public Sphere and National Identity* (New York: Oxford University Press, 1995). His analysis

reflects the position that: 'For all the brave talk of separating press from the government, issues of state and media are deeply intertwined; and in that intertwining rest the most subtle questions of enhancing opportunities for speech without abridging fundamental freedoms' (p. 21).

4. See here, for example, the interview with Azmi Bishara, 'Bantustanization or bi-nationalism' in *Race and Class*, Vol. 37, No. 2 (October–December 1995) pp. 43–9.

5. See Jürgen Habermas, *The Structural Transformation of the Public Sphere* (Cambridge, MA.: MIT Press, 1989).

6. In Arabic, the 'peace process' is actually described as 'the peace operation': *amaliyyat al-salam*. The concept of 'operation' carries the same unfolding, temporal, processual connotations: beginning or onset, procedures and strategy, objectives, accomplishment at some deferred moment. As a term it is derivative from the concept of *amal* – which denotes both 'work' or 'deed', according to context.

7. For a philosophical treatment of 'elision' and its socio-moral consequences, see Eric D'Arcy's *Human Acts: An Essay on their Moral Evaluation* (Oxford: Clarendon Press, 1963), especially Chapter 1. See also Chapter 6 of Lena Jayyusi, *Categorization and the Moral Order* (London: Routledge and Kegan Paul, 1984).

8. In fact, a particular adjective to describe practices of occupation came into use over VOP broadcasts: *ihtilaliyah* (strictly: 'occupationist').

9. It is a significant feature of language use, and the practical and rhetorical strategies that may be employed within different narratives and discourses, that all actions can be, as the linguistic philosopher J. L. Austin demonstrates, redescribed in such a way as to bring in more or less of their perceived consequences into the description. See his *How To Do Things With Words* (J. O. Urmson, ed.) (New York: Oxford University Press, 1973).

10. Indeed, on the morning programme 'A New Day' on 7 April 1997, one interviewee distinguished between a 'military peace', and a 'civilisational peace'. And on 31 March, another interviewee talked of a 'Palestinian peace', distinguishing it from Netanyahu's rhetoric of peace.

11. In fact, the classical Israeli platform was always phrased in terms of 'peace', or later 'peace with security', to which the classical Palestinian (and Arab) response was 'peace with justice'.

12. Even in Israel and the US, the discourse of 'endangering the peace process' is often encountered. The point to keep in mind, however, beyond the superficial resemblance, and beyond the point of the standardisation of a 'hegemonic discourse', or 'idea', is that of the function of the discourse in the locations in which it is used and produced; of the 'political space' opened up by it. And this, it is obvious, may be different with different positions in the power relationships between the parties that deploy the same terms: indeed it is precisely this gap which represents the hegemonic dimension of a discourse.

13. *Shibr* is a non-standard unit of measurement – the distance between the thumb and the smallest finger when the hand is open with fingers fully extended.

14. At least, the dream as conceived in the Transitional Program, adopted by the PLO in 1973.

15. For the full text, see *Journal of Palestine Studies*, Vol. XVIII, No. 2 (Winter 1989) pp. 213–16.

16. In the words of Yusuf Al Qazaz, Director of Programming at the VOP, and

frequent anchor of various news programmes: 'Dear ones, Palestinian men and Palestinian women, mighty women and mighty men, let us celebrate to the utmost the anniversary of the Declaration of Independence by raising the flags, let us encircle our whole life with hope, despite what the occupation spreads forth of siege and gloom and closure; but this great duality in which the Palestinian people lives, this duality has become the story of our everyday lives ...' (Good Morning Palestine, 15 November 1996).

17. Austin, *How To Do Things With Words*.

18. A good example comes, in fact, from a programme on Palestinian television called 'Guest of the Day', broadcast at 9:00 a.m. on the morning of 19 November 1996. But these moral terms had other organisational features, and a specific pragmatics of their own, one of which seemed to be the discrimination of a range of Israeli actors/interlocutors.

10 REFLECTIONS ON THE REALITIES OF THE OSLO PROCESS

Azmi Bishara

The Israeli elections of 1996 brought to light the dilemma in Israeli–Palestinian relations – the imbalance of power and the inequality in the commitments on paper of the two parties. That is to say, in the final analysis and in the absence of mutually accepted principles like the right of self-determination or even the simple acknowledgement that the West Bank and Gaza are Occupied Territories, the Oslo Agreement depends on one party's commitment to it and the other party's interpretation of it. It is regulated mainly by the existing balance of power rather than by elements of relative justice derived from the above mentioned mutually accepted principles. To make matters worse, Oslo reverses the traditional relationship between means and ends. The objective has become the perpetuation of the peace process rather than the conclusion of a just peace. The 'process' has also bred the agents who have an interest in keeping it going.

In the absence of any agreement on the final objective, the whole process depends on the intentions of the Israeli government. If one chooses to ignore the historical injustices inherent in the agreement, this remains its basic difficulty. When the government of Israel changed, the reading of the agreement changed too. A new government came to power that was not committed to the objective that the Palestinians believed – or perhaps deluded themselves into believing – the agreement was leading to. The way the Palestinians threw themselves behind Labour during the elections, clinging to the hope of a Labour victory, demonstrates how they had become hostage to Israeli public opinion. This is a relationship of imbalance and dependency.

The tragedy is that, following the elections, the Palestinians became obsessed with one issue: making sure that the Likud would live up to the Oslo Agreement. They totally missed the point that the calamity could lie precisely in the Likud's adherence, not only to the agreement, but also to what was kept out of the agreement, and which depended on Labour's good will in the final status negotiations: settlements, refugees, Jerusalem, sovereignty and so on. In fact, it was clear that the Oslo Agreement would impose itself, in the formal sense, on the Likud as well, as the only game in town. But the Likud government is bound not to the spirit of the agreement, nor to the aspirations of the Palestinian side, nor the verbal promises made by the previous government, but rather to its own interpretations of the text of the agreement. All that was not put in the text, delayed until the 'final status negotiations', is not binding for the Likud government, which, since it came to office, has been involved in an effort aimed at dictating its version of the final status solution through the use of force, leaving the Palestinian side only two options: either to search for the components of their own power in this confrontation, or to accept the dictates of the Likud. The Likud is committed to maintaining the ring roads and the bypass roads that lay the infrastructure of future settlements; it is committed to expanding the settlements; it is committed to the absurd division of the West Bank into areas A, B, and C under Oslo II, a division which has severed the links binding the Palestinian population centres together.

For Netanyahu the Oslo Accord merely served as a mask to the above mentioned activities, which actually undermine all that remains from the agreements. He cannot openly abandon the process because of international and local considerations, including the fact that the commitment to Oslo was a major plank of his winning election programme.

In the negotiations that have taken place since the Likud returned to power, the Palestinians have concentrated on three issues in a way that shows they still cannot play the game like the Israelis. First, they made an issue of the redeployment of Israeli troops from Hebron. Of course, Palestinian insistence on what was agreed is crucial for the continuation of the peace process – we cannot just do what the Likud government wants – but the

redeployment, actually initially delayed by the Labour government and not by its successor, was bound to take place in any case
because of international and Arab pressures on Israel. Second, in
Jerusalem the Palestinians have insisted on keeping open the
Orient House – the unofficial Palestinian seat of government –
which is not part of any written agreement and which in all
likelihood would remain open in any event. While they were
insisting on preserving the Orient House, Jewish settlement in
Jerusalem continued unabated. Third, in the beginning the
Palestinians made an issue of Netanyahu meeting with Arafat,
which Netanyahu had deliberately avoided. Again, Netanyahu
could not have put off meeting with Arafat indefinitely, but
because of Palestinian insistence he succeeded in portraying the
meeting itself as an Israeli concession. Arafat learned later to play
by the same rules against Netanyahu, as a protest against Israeli
refusal to meet its previous commitments or against Israeli new
settlements in Jerusalem.

There are three new factors that could restore some semblance
of balance to the Israeli–Palestinian relationship. First, because of
provocative Israeli attitudes, including an agreement on military
cooperation with Turkey, which is directed against any Arab
cooperation in the future and revives memories of the Baghdad
Pact in the 1950s, the Arabs in general and the Egyptians in
particular are in the thick of things again. Historically, Egypt
always has had a role to play, but this time round it is bringing the
other Arab countries (especially Syria and Saudi Arabia) in with
it. This factor, together with the international solidarity which has
been absent since Oslo, and only lately reactivated in the form of
Resolution 134 of the General Assembly of the United Nations,
can only be invested in a confrontational strategy; it cannot affect
the negotiations in the narrower sense, because the only international player allowed in is the United States, which is also the host
of the whole process. This fact became clear after the crisis caused
by the Israeli settlement in Jabal Abu Ghneim, which was annexed
to Jerusalem. The efforts that were undertaken at the international
level, the meetings, conferences and declarations of the Islamic
conference, the Arab League, the Non-Aligned States, the European Union, made a lot of reverberations but, in the absence of a
clear strategy of escalation, could not themselves affect the

negotiations. The American delegate to the region remained the gavel of the 'process'.

Second, the recent confrontations especially during the clashes of September 1996 between the Palestinian Authority (PA) and the Likud government, showed the Israelis that they cannot govern the West Bank and Gaza the way they govern the self-proclaimed Security Zone in South Lebanon; they learned that Antoine Lahd cannot be the model for the PA.[1] So the meaning of the clashes of September 1996 is that Labour's expectation that it could create a quisling PA which it is entirely able to manipulate to suit its own purposes has collapsed. It is now clear to the Israelis that, even within the confines of its bantustan situation, the PA also has its own interests and purposes. The PA is neither historically nor culturally, and after all else is said, not even politically capable of playing the role of the South Lebanon quisling regime/security zone. This has opened up the possibility of a national Palestinian dialogue between the PA and the opposition Palestinian parties. The PA, however, has so far sought to use the dialogue only as an instrument to squeeze Israeli concessions. It does not see the genuine importance of a national dialogue to Palestinian society, because its internal policies, if they exist at all, are totally subordinated to the needs of the negotiations with Israel as the PA imagines them. The PA could not draw the appropriate conclusion from this: that in the confrontation with Israel, Palestinian civil society is its basic strategic asset. Since territorial sovereignty is lacking, sovereignty over institutions and through elected national institutions will have to take its place. In situations such as this, democracy becomes the requisite condition for actual sovereignty. Moreover, the outcome of the unbalanced negotiations with Israel can also be affected through winning some international respect for the Palestinian polity, but, for this to happen, the Palestinian polity needs to demonstrate through its actions that it is worthy of making the transition to statehood. This would increase the pressures on Israel very significantly. Of course, even this would not mean that liberation would be at hand or that a Palestinian state would be inevitable. It would merely create the possibility for such an outcome in the future. Democracy can save the PA from 'Lahdism', while the absence of democracy will turn its bantustan situation into the

final status. The PA still prefers to leave civil society to the control
of the different competing security apparatuses, who are gradually
extending their control and monopolising the whole of public
space.

Third, the right-wing religious government of Israel has
abandoned the basic concepts of Oslo, and at the same time its
room for manoeuvre became narrower due to internal political
crises. The crisis which has befallen the Israeli–Palestinian peace
process in the aftermath of the Israeli renewal of settlement
activities in Jerusalem in the first half of 1997 does not resemble
any of its predecessors. In the recent past, crises revolved around
issues concerning the implementation of the interim phase, the
jurisdiction of the PA, the extent of the withdrawal from Hebron,
the release of women prisoners, and so on. Compromise solutions
were reached either with respect to these issues themselves or
through concessions being made *vis-à-vis* other similar issues.

This crisis, however, involves the basic concept of the peace
process, and the distinction between interim agreements and the
permanent settlement insisted upon so firmly by Rabin and Peres,
and opposed by Palestinians who criticised Oslo. Nowadays, it is
the Israeli Likud government which has abandoned this distinction. In return for the implementation of its commitments under
Oslo, Israel is demanding Palestinian concessions on final status
issues. This is the significance of Jabal Abu Ghneim and
Netanyahu's declared determination to proceed with the expansion of the settlements in the West Bank.

The right-wing religious government is no longer capable of
implementing commitments made by Peres and Rabin independ-
ently from a final Palestinian–Israeli agreement that suits their
own conception. This was also the motivation behind the contacts
between Labour and Likud in early 1997 to form a national unity
government on the basis of an agreement on 'the Nos' which
should become the basis for an Israeli national consensus in the
final status negotiations with the PA, and which would allow the
Labour Party to provide an alibi internationally for justifying this
deviation from the principles of Oslo. An agreement was reached
between MPs Beilin (Labour) and Eitan (Likud) that included all
four 'Nos': to withdrawal to the borders of June 1967, to the
division of Jerusalem or sharing sovereignty over the city, to

dismantling the settlements, and to the return of the refugees. All that remains can be called a Palestinian state *à la* Labour, while the Likud keeps only the option of extending the powers of the PA, including granting them the title of a state, open for negotiations: 'You wanted a state, here have your state.' Practically, under the umbrella of the Israeli national consensus – 'the four Nos' – nothing remains open for negotiation in the final status talks except for a modification of the agreements already reached at the interim phase, that is more redeployments and more authority for the PA.

Due, however, to internal developments in Israel that have more to do with the conflict between old and new elites over the control of the Israeli establishment than with the negotiations, a conflict that culminated in a judicial, moral and political scandal, Netanyahu lost the option of forming a national unity government. As a consequence of this loss, he has also been deprived of his most important tool, one that kept the unity of his coalition while negotiating. With the assistance of such a prospect, he was able to threaten the more radical and smaller parties of his coalition; after the crisis he is more likely to be threatened by them. He has also lost the option that helped confuse the Labour opposition, and kept it waiting for such a possibility, while after this crisis the opposition is likely to become more prominent in Israeli politics. Netanyahu has become more vulnerable to international and local pressure that can export the crisis in the negotiations to Israel as an internal political crisis. There are more political and social circles in Israel that can accuse Netanyahu of bearing the responsibility for any price that Israel may be obliged to pay due to the impasse of the negotiations. This presupposes, however, that there is a party which has the interest and the power to make Israel pay the price, except that certain currents in the PA are apprehensive about the PA's ability politically to endure a long period of time without 'the process'.

Scepticism here does not concern the Palestinian population, whose living conditions have anyway deteriorated, in almost all respects, since Oslo: standards of living, employment, the economy in general, human rights, freedom of movement and freedom of expression. It concerns the Palestinian elites, the so-called VIPs who are connected to Israel through a network of needs and interests that cannot be satisfied unless the negotiations, and the mediating role played by them, proceed uninterrupted.

An authority that is obsessively engaged in the search for a source of power that is independent of, and external to, its own society, and seeks to monopolise economic activity and public space while sabotaging the process of institutionalisation of social and political spheres, cannot begin to conceive of the power of its own society except in the negative sense; that is, as a power that should be firmly suppressed before it turns into empowerment.

In this context the PA has woken up to the significance of representative elections only in this negative sense. The election of the Palestinian Legislative Council created an entirely new avenue for mobilising Palestinian civil society in the confrontation with Israel. It provided an opportunity to forge an authentic Palestinian political and legislative experience, and to unite civil society in support of a legislative council that shares power with the executive authority, sets up a system of checks and balances, and strengthens its hand in its dealings with Israel.

There could have been a parliamentary Palestinian opposition, just as there is an opposition in the Knesset. But the Palestinian opposition missed that opportunity by not fielding candidates in the elections, and, in so doing, it adopted a trivial and historically irresponsible role. A second opportunity to empower the Council is now being missed by the PA. The Palestinian delegation had fought hard during the negotiations with Israel to enlarge the membership of the Council and to grant it legislative authority, but now that the PA no longer sees the PLC as important to the confrontation with Israel, it is downgrading and marginalising it, instead of allowing it to play what could be a vital role in that struggle. Instead of Arafat and those around him taking on Israel on their own, there could have been a confrontation between the Palestinian people and Israel; not an Intifada, which today would simply lead to a Palestinian civil war, with Israel looking on from the outside. That was the whole point of the Oslo Agreement.

The point of Oslo was precisely to allow Israel to avoid dealing with a Palestinian popular uprising, making this instead the responsibility of the Palestinian police; otherwise, what did Israel stand to gain from Oslo? That was Labour's position, not just the Likud's. Given this situation, a new model for an Intifada of the Palestinian people, in their conflict with Israel, must be looked for. The basic strategy should be to mobilise Palestinian society, the Palestinian people and the Palestinian polity for the confrontation with Israel. This is what clearly took place in the fighting of September 1996, which began as a spontaneous uprising imposed on the PA by its own party Fatah, among others. Later, the PA utilised the events in the negotiations on the Hebron issue. Given Palestinian circumstances, however, there is a limit to how far escalation can be taken. Israel is applying counterpressures and the confrontation between the Palestinian people and Palestinian Authority on the one side and Israel on the other cannot achieve results in the absence of Palestinian democracy – this is where the Council comes in.

The tragedy is that while there is a large bloc of Council members who are trying to carve out a role for it, they have no real decision-making power or say in matters with real relevance to Palestinian political life. Their efforts at formulating basic laws, or at drafting a constitution, remain fruitless verbal exercises. The PLC also has no say in matters concerning relations with Israel, including the negotiations, the issue of the settlements and so on. The Council can protest. The purpose of legislative assemblies, however, is not to protest but to provide direction for the executive branch. In the Palestinian case, the order is reversed. The legislative branch should be the source of authority and the symbol of sovereignty, but here we find that neither the legislature nor even the executive authority embodies sovereignty. A single person, Yasser Arafat, does that, or thinks he does. Such a situation cannot contribute to a more balanced relationship with Israel.

In my opinion, the Palestinian ruling elite either does not understand, or does not want to understand, that the issue of empowering the Legislative Council is no longer a luxury but a dire necessity, as is the freedom of the press, political pluralism, the rejection of the use of torture against prisoners and orderly democratic life.

The Palestinian ruling elite will not have an indigenous power base unless these conditions are satisfied. They cannot resist Israeli pressures by saying that their hands are tied, that the people will not accept this or that, and so on, because both Israel and the United States are aware of how insignificant Palestinian public opinion is for the PA.

As a consequence, Palestinian society will not be mobilised as it could be for the confrontation with Israel for a long time to come. In any case, Palestinian youth does not seem eager to be instrumental-ised in the face-off with Israel, or driven to the checkpoints to face Israeli soldiers each time there is a crisis in the negotiations. In any case, the negotiations lack any transparency regarding how this sacrifice would be used – would the sacrifice be used for national purposes, or used instead for the promotion of elite interests? In the absence of democracy and with the deterioration of living conditions under a strangling closure, popular mobilisation could be deflected into a catastrophic confrontation with the Palestinian Authority instead of Israel. Recent events have shown that only a mobilised Palestinian society is capable of making an impact on the inter-national situation, or the Arab world or Israel; when activated, it becomes the basic strategic reserve for the Authority in its struggle with Israel.

THE NEW PALESTINIAN VIPs

A new Palestinian elite emerged from the womb of the 'process'. It is composed of individuals in Palestinian leadership circles who have become part of the fabric of Israeli–Palestinian relations, who approach matters that relate to the general interest from the narrow-est of perspectives – that of their own vested interests. Certain mat-ters rest in their hands, and their commitment to the Palestinian cause has become conditioned by their need for permits to pass through Israeli military checkpoints and by the commissions they get, thanks to their Israeli connections. Having good connections in Israel can make you rich. This group of co-opted individuals – which includes also some former militants and prisoners – has become, in a way, a clientelist network, and for them the main issue is how to keep the peace process alive under all circumstances. In the process itself their privileges can become a source of pressure on them; for exam-ple, after any 'terrorist' action or during Israeli holidays a hermetic closure in the Occupied Territories is imposed by Israel. During this closure all permits to pass the checkpoints are cancelled including those granted to the so-called VIPs. Only members of the exclusive status (VIP 1) – a new category invented by Israel – are allowed to keep the permits. Only Israel defines who is and who is not a VIP 1.

My estimate is that the hard core of the new elite consists of a few hundred individuals, but the circle of people who have ties with them, and who therefore benefit from the situation, number in the thousands. The group has a hierarchical structure, with several channels connecting them to Israel, from officials in the smallest ministry to those responsible for security, the economy or civilian coordination. The importance of any given individual varies according to Israeli calculations; one moment this individual is important, then, suddenly, someone else is.

This pyramid of VIPs is a new phenomenon for Palestinian society. We have had PLO militants and bureaucrats who controlled the purse strings for the disbursement of contributions to the resistance movement. There have always been those with ties to Jordan, or other Arab countries, and their agendas. But being a VIP is something new. Israel decides who is a VIP, who has freedom of movement and who has the power to make deals.

In August 1996, *Ha'aretz* quoted a former legal adviser to the Israeli Foreign Ministry just before he left office as saying something to the effect: 'We control electrical power, water resources, telecommunications and so on. We control everything. There are a number of natives who serve as middle men. What could suit our purpose better?' His advice to the Likud Cabinet was to read the Oslo Agreement carefully, and he added: 'If you read it, you not only will accept it, you will become its enthusiastic supporters. The power imbalance between us and the Palestinians never served our interests better in the past, not even before the Intifada.'

No doubt the old Israeli plan to create a co-opted Palestinian leadership has succeeded to a large extent. Tragically, the price of all this is that Palestinian society has been neutralised and is resentful. Palestinians cannot travel, they cannot satisfy their daily needs without the services of this elite group. Palestinian society has been penetrated from top to bottom by its clientelist network. Had the Legislative Council been effective, it would have supervised the activities of these VIPs. Montesquieu understood that the system of checks and balances characteristic of democracy worked not because of altruistic or even democratic motives but because of vested interests, because factions balanced each other out. It is possible to institute a system in which one branch of power acts as a watchdog over the other and serves as a counterweight to it, not for reasons of democracy, but because it is in the interest of one branch to limit the power and authority of the other.

The frustration accompanying the 'process' and the formation of its social, political and security agents contributes to the emergent character of a new Palestinian individual who is acquiring a dual personality: a private persona that is sceptical and derisive, and a public persona that is scared and sycophantic, much as in Eastern Europe, where this phenomenon allowed the communist regimes to last as long as they did there. This civic culture, which can be termed dualistic, accepts a schizophrenic split between the public sphere, as the sphere of authority, and the private sphere as the sphere of freedom; it allows undemocratic regimes to prosper. Such regimes can turn a blind eye to what goes on behind closed doors. In fact, they understand that hypocrisy in public life is a source of strength for them.

SEPARATION WITHOUT SOVEREIGNTY OR A BI-NATIONAL STATE?

There are no possible routes available for the development of a national option leading to sovereignty unless the indigenous Palestinian factor can be brought in through politicising civil society by making room for political pluralism, and a democratic system. Political pluralism means an active party system. The old Palestinian party system, which had taken the form of PLO factions, disappeared with the collapse of the PLO and of the leftist ideologies that had linked themselves to the socialist bloc. The Fatah organisation, which is supposedly the ruling party of the PA, discovered only recently that it is being marginalised by it, and that the PA has produced a new 'party', that of the VIPs. These are searching for an alignment with the security apparatuses, which have absorbed into their ranks many Fatah militants. Such an alignment, if it succeeds, would totally marginalise what is left of the party system, including Fatah which is beginning a fight for its political and institutional survival as a ruling party. Again, if it succeeds, this alignment, and not the Legislative

Council, will be the decision maker of the future, including in issues such as who will succeed Arafat.

Full national sovereignty was historically the precondition for the gradual development of democracy. But since democracy was institutionalised as a political system, the question of democracy presents itself wherever there is authority and power. Wherever there is political power, even if it is less than sovereign, there is a question of its misuse. Full national sovereignty is not a sufficient condition of democracy, as is commonly believed in the Third World, nor is sovereignty real, that is, the sovereignty of a people, unless it is expressed in a democratic system.

The view that delays raising the issue of democracy until full national sovereignty is achieved turns the historical process of the birth of democracy into a structural theory, while in the Palestinian case the opposite is true. There is need of an active public opinion, an active parliament, of political pluralism, that is, a party system, with the dynamism and power to effect change, and to create new Arab and international alignments. But if the current situation continues, if Israel continues to control the political game, there is only a dead end in sight. The current Palestinian leadership cannot, for historical and cultural reasons, sign an agreement embodying the kind of permanent settlement that Netanyahu wants. Without an active and politicised Palestinian public sphere to pressure the PA, this grim reality will not provoke the reaction, indeed the explosion, that it should.

The new government of Israel, which is unable and unwilling to find a common language with the prevailing Palestinian elites as Labour did, together with the anti-democratic activities of the PA, undermine slowly but surely the national option incorporated in the two-state solution. The most important factor in this context is the process of building and expanding settlements. As long as the national option remains viable and is sustained by people's yearning for national independence in a state, the settlements remain a colonial activity that impinges upon the sovereignty of one side. Settlements in this case are a kind of theft or even armed robbery; they cannot be tolerated, because sovereignty on land is indivisible.

When it becomes fully apparent that an independent and democratic state occupying every inch of the West Bank and Gaza

Strip free of Israeli settlements is not realisable, it will be time for
the Palestinians to re-examine their entire strategy. We will then
begin to discuss a bi-national state solution that will do away with
the system of apartheid that is anchored in the realities of Oslo.
Apartheid means separation without sovereignty. The coming
future awareness of an apartheid system in effect here will have to
produce new options and strategies for action. Awareness of the
reality counts even more than the reality of apartheid itself, and as
long as the consciousness of this is absent, so are the political
attitudes that it potentially will give rise to.

This could possibly mean that the Palestinians in the Occupied
Territories and the Palestinians in Israel will opt in the future for
a single political unit within a bi-national state. There could be,
for example, a Jewish-Israeli political unit and a Palestinian-Arab
political unit, which together will constitute a Jewish-Arab polity
with two separate legislative chambers as well as a common
parliament. I believe this could become a programme in the
future. I am not referring to a democratic secular state which is
supposed to be non-national, nor to an Arab secular democratic
state, but to a secular democratic state which is bi-national, a
federal or confederate system comprising two national communities. The South African project of building one multicultural
South African nation as their antithesis to apartheid is not viable
in our case, because here we already have two developed national
identities, and it is too late to dream about merging them into one
nation. Only in such a context will it be possible to resolve such
problems as the refugees and the settlements. Settlements will no
longer pose an insurmountable obstacle within the context of a
single bi-national state. If the Israelis should choose to settle in
the West Bank, then so be it; we Palestinians, too, will have the
right to set up residence in Tel Aviv for instance.

Until now the bi-national option has been a rhetorical exercise,
an argument against Israeli occupation of the West Bank and
Gaza. It merely stated that Israel should either annex the
Palestinians or give them independence, it cannot deny them both
citizenship and national independence. The bi-national option,
which is still only an idea for now, presupposes the impossibility
of a separation into two states. If the only alternative is an
independent Palestinian state which is fragmented and truncated,

then we should go for a bi-national state. Only under such circumstances, or if it becomes clear that there is no possibility of dismantling the settlements, will the bi-national option become a political possibility. Settlements cannot continue under the national option, that is, if there are two separate states; borders cannot be permeable in one direction only; that would constitute usurpation and theft.

The bi-national option is still not a political programme, but a project with cultural and intellectual aspects, opposed to the racist implications that accompany all national separatist projects. Notice, for example, the racist demographic arguments used by Labour to convince Israelis how important separation is. Among the peoples and the elites of both sides the bi-national approach is still not viable as a political programme, for the national option is not exhausted yet. It is also still less acceptable for the Israelis than for the Palestinian state. It has no political agents and no organisational expression. Actually it is still more of a political discourse than a political programme or even project. Nevertheless, it only indicates a shift from the national discourse which has dominated the political culture of both sides, the victims and the victimisers. The Palestinians refused to accept Israel as a fact, and later capitulated to it as a fact too. But between rejection and capitulation there was no room for recognising the nationality of the Israelis. Such a recognition can only be consistent with itself as bi-national if it refuses to accept the historical process that led to the formation of this Israeli nationality, because this would imply a Zionist re-reading of Palestinian history.

The struggle for such a vision in the future will require patterns of organisation probably more akin to the organisation and thinking of the African National Congress, than to that of the PLO. It would involve the restructuring of Palestinian political life, opening whole new avenues for struggle.

Between hard facts and absent consciousness, all we can do is turn back to rhetoric. Regardless of how strong Israel may be today, in the long run it has only two options; a national solution or a bi-national solution: that is, either an independent Palestinian state as part of a two-state solution involving separation, genuine sovereignty and territorial integrity, or a bi-national state requiring annexation. There is no viable third option. Of course,

the Likud's intention is to convince us that there is a third
solution – perpetuating or merely introducing cosmetic changes in
the status quo. That is the key to Netanyahu's rise to power.

NOTE

1 Antoine Lahd was leader of the Southern Lebanese Army which was
   established and continues to be maintained by Israel in occupied Southern
   Lebanon, designated 'the security zone' by the Israelis. Lahd is widely viewed
   by most Arabs as a collaborator and quisling.

BIBLIOGRAPHY

Abu-Lughod, I. and B. Abu-Laban (eds) (1974) *Settler Regimes in Africa and the Arab World* (Wilmette, Ill.: Medina University Press).

Abdul-Shafi, Haidar (1994) 'A political reading of the declaration of principles' in *Challenges Facing the Palestinian Society in the Interim Period* (Jerusalem: Jerusalem Media & Communication Centre).

Amnesty International (1996) *Palestinian Authority: Prolonged political detention, torture and unfair trials* (London: Amnesty International).

Anda, T. (1989) *Intifada – Opprør mot Israel* (Oslo: Universitetsforlaget; in Norwegian).

Artz, D. (1996) *Refugees into Citizens: Palestinians and the End of the Arab–Israeli Conflict* (New York: Council on Foreign Relations).

Aruri, Naseer (1995) 'Challenges facing Palestinian Society', *Middle East International*, 25 August.

Aruri, N. H. (1995) 'Early Empowerment: The Burden Not the Responsibility', *Journal of Palestine Studies*, Vol. XXIV, No. 2.

Austin, J. L. (1973) *How To Do Things With Words* (Oxford: Oxford University Press).

Barth, Fredrik (1965) *Political Leadership among Swat Pathans* (London: The Athlone Press).

Be'er, Yizhar and Salah Abdel Jawad (1994) *Collaborators in the occupied territories: Human rights abuses and violations* (Jerusalem: B'Tselem).

Ben Efrat, Roni (1997) 'No Bagatz and No B'tselem: The Palestinian Authority and the Use of Torture', *Challenge*, Vol. 8, No. 1.

Benvenisti, Meron (1984) *The West Bank Data Project: A Survey of Israel's Policies* (Washington/London: American Enterprise Institute for Public Policy Research).

Benvenisti, Meron (1989) *The Shepherds' Wars* (Jerusalem).

Bisan Centre (1991) *The Intifada and Some Women's Social Issues* (Ramallah: Bisan Centre; in Arabic).

228 AFTER OSLO

Bishara, Azmi (1995) 'Bantustanization or Bi-nationalism: An Interview', *Race and Class*, Vol. 37, No. 2.
Bishara, Azmi (1996) *A Contribution to the Critique of Civil Society* (Ramallah: Muwatin Publications; in Arabic).
Bjørgo, Tore (1987) *Conspiracy Rhetoric in Arab Politics: The Palestinian Case* (Oslo: NUPI).
Brand, Laurie (1988) *Palestinians in the Arab World* (New York: Columbia University Press).
Brynen, Rex (1995) 'The Neopatrimonial Dimension of Palestinian Politics', *Journal of Palestine Studies*, Vol. XXV, No. 1.
Brynen, Rex (1997) 'Imaging a Solution: Final Status Arrangements and Palestinian Refugees in Lebanon', *Journal of Palestine Studies*, Vol. XXVI, No. 2.
Butenschøn, Nils A. (1994) *The Oslo Agreement – Peace on Israel's Conditions* (Oslo: Gyldendal: in Norwegian).
Butenschøn, Nils A. and K. Vollan (eds) (1996) 'Interim Democracy: Report on the Palestinian Elections 1996', *Human Rights Report*, No. 6 (Oslo: Norwegian Institute of Human Rights).
Butenschøn, Nils A. (1997) 'The Oslo Agreement in Norwegian Foreign Policy', *CIMES Occasional Papers* (Durham: Centre for Islamic and Middle Eastern Studies).
Center for Palestine Research and Studies (1995) *A Survey of Political and Social Attitudes among Palestinians in the West Bank and Gaza Strip* (Nablus: CPRS).
Cobban, H. (1984) *The Palestinian Liberation Organisation: People, Power and Politics* (Cambridge: Cambridge University Press).
Cohen, J. and A. Arrato (1994) *Civil Society and Political Theory* (Cambridge, MA.: MIT Press).
Corbin, Jane (1994) *Gaza First – the Secret Norway Channel to Peace Between Israel and the PLO* (London: Bloomsbury Publishing).
D'Andrade, Roy and Claudia Strauss (eds) (1992) *Human Motives and Cultural Models* (Cambridge: Cambridge University Press).
D'Arcy, E. (1963) *Human Acts: An Essay on their Moral Evaluation* (Oxford: Clarendon Press).
Declaration of Palestinian Independence, II, 1988 (1989) *Journal of Palestine Studies*, Vol. XVIII, No. 2.
Desroche, Henri (1979) *The Sociology of Hope* (London: Routledge & Kegan Paul).

Eriksen, Thomas Hylland (1993) *Ethnicity & Nationalism: Anthropological Perspectives* (London: Pluto Press).

Geertz, Clifford (1973) *The Interpretation of Cultures* (New York: Basic Books).

Giacaman, George (1995) 'Civil Society and Authority' in M. Budeiri et al., *Critical Perspectives on Palestinian Democracy* (Ramallah: Muwatin Publications; in Arabic).

Giacaman, George (1996) 'What is Political Action? On the Crisis of Political Parties at the Present Juncture' in *Pluralism and Democracy: The Crisis of the Palestinian Political Party* (Ramallah: Muwatin Publications; in Arabic).

Gresh, Alain (1988) *The PLO. The Struggle Within* (London/New Jersey: Zed Books).

Habermas, Jürgen (1989) *The Structural Transformation of the Public Sphere* (Cambridge, MA.: MIT Press).

Hammami, Reema (1995) 'NGOs: the Professionalization of Politics', *Race and Class*, Vol. 37, No. 2.

Harris, William Wilson (1980) *Taking root: Israeli settlements in the West Bank, the Golan, and Gaza-Sinai, 1967–1980* (New York: Research Studies Press).

Heller, M. A. (1993) *A Palestinian State: The Implications for Israel* (Cambridge, MA.: Harvard University Press).

Henriksen, Georg (1973) *Hunters in the Barrens: The Naskapi on the Edge of the White Man's World* (St. John's: ISER, Memorial University of Newfoundland).

Henriksen, Georg (1993) *Life and Death Among the Mushuau Innu of Northern Labrador* (St. John's, Newfoundland: ISER Research and Policy).

Herzl, Theodor (1941) *Old New Land* (New York: Wiener Publ./Herzl Press).

Hilal, Jamil (1995) 'PLO: Crisis in Legitimacy', *Race and Class*, Vol. 37, No. 2.

Hiltermann, Joost (1991) *Behind the Intifada* (New Jersey: Princeton University Press).

Hitchens, Christopher (1995) 'Foreword' in Edward Said, *Peace & Its Discontents: Gaza-Jericho 1993–1995* (London: Vintage).

Holland, Dorothy and Naomi Quinn (eds) (1987) *Cultural Models in Language & Thought* (Cambridge: Cambridge University Press).

Hornby, A. S. with A. P. Cowie, and A. C. Gimson (1974) *Oxford Advanced Learner's Dictionary of Current English* (Oxford: Oxford University Press).

Institute for Palestine Studies (1994) *The Palestinian–Israeli Peace Agreement: A Documentary Record* (Washington DC: IPS).

Jaffee Center for Strategic Studies (1989) *The West Bank and Gaza: Israel's Options for Peace* (Tel Aviv: Jaffee Center for Strategic Studies).

Jayyusi, Lena (1984) *Categorization and the Moral Order* (London: Routledge and Kegan Paul).

Johnson, Michael (1977) 'Political Bosses and their Gangs; Zu'ama and Qabadayat in the Sunni Moslem Quarters of Beirut' in Ernest Gellner and John Waterbury (eds), *Patrons and Clients in Mediterranean Societies* (London: Duckworth).

de Jong, Jan (1996) 'To Save What Can Be Saved: Reading Between the Lines of Palestinian Strategy On Jerusalem', *News from Within*, May.

Kaminker, S. (1994) *Planning and Housing Issues in East Jerusalem* (Jerusalem: St. Yves Centre).

Keesing, Roger M. (1981) *Cultural Anthropology: A Contemporary Perspective* (New York: Holt, Rinehart and Winston).

Lavie, Smadar (1990) *The Poetics of Military Occupation. Mzeina Allegories of Bedouin Identity Under Israeli and Egyptian Rule* (Berkeley, Los Angeles, Oxford: University of California Press).

Lønning, Dag Jørund (1995) *Bridge over troubled water. Inter-ethnic dialogue in Israel–Palestine* (Bergen: Norse Publications).

Lønning, Dag Jørund (1995) '"Are we Friends or Enemies?" The management of enemy images in a new political situation in Israel-Palestine'. Ph.D. project description. University of Bergen.

Mooney, J. (1896) *The Ghost Dance Religion*. Bureau of American Ethnology, Annual Report 14 (Washington DC: US Government Printing Office).

Muslih, M. (1990) 'Towards Coexistence: An Analysis of the Resolutions of the Palestine National Council', *Journal of Palestine Studies*, Vol. XIX, No. 4.

Obeyesekere, Gananath (1984) *Medusa's Hair: An Essay on Personal Symbols and Religious Experience* (Chicago: The University of Chicago Press).

Price, Monroe (1995) *Television, the Public Sphere and National Identity* (New York: Oxford University Press).

Qleibo, Ali H. (1992) *Before the Mountains Disappear: An Ethnographic Chronicle of the Modern Palestinians* (Jerusalem: Kloreus).

Rabin, Yitzhak (1979) *The Rabin Memoirs* (Boston: Little, Brown).

Rosen, Lawrence (1984) *Bargaining for Reality: The Construction of Social Relations in a Muslim Community* (Chicago: The University of Chicago Press).

Sayigh, Yezid (1995) 'Sovereignty and Security of the Palestinian State', *Journal of Palestine Studies*, Summer.

Scott Jr, George M. (1992) 'A Resynthesis of the Primordial and Circumstantial Approaches to Ethnic Group Solidarity: Towards an Explanatory Model', *Ethnic and Racial Studies*, Vol. 13, No. 2.

Seligman, A. (1992) *The Idea of Civil Society* (New York: The Free Press).

Shlaim, A. (1994) 'The Oslo Accord', *Journal of Palestine Studies*, Vol. XXIII, No. 3.

Swedenburg, Ted (1990) 'The Palestinian Peasant as National Signifier', *Anthropological Quarterly*, Vol. 63, No. 1.

Taraki, Lisa (1989) 'Mass Organizations in the West Bank' in Naseer Aruri (ed.), *Occupation: Israel over Palestine* (Belmont, MA.: AAUG Press).

Taraki, Lisa (1990) 'The Development of Political Consciousness among Palestinians in the Occupied Territories, 1967–1987' in J. Nassar and R. Heacock (eds), *Intifada: Palestine at the Crossroads* (New York: Praeger Publishers).

Usher, Graham (1995) *Palestine in Crisis: the Struggle for Peace and Political Independence After Oslo* (London: Pluto Press/ MERIP).

Usher, Graham (1995) 'What Kind of Nation? The Rise of Hamas in the Occupied Territories', *Race and Class*, October–December.

Usher, Graham (1996) 'Closures, Cantons and the Palestinian Covenant', *Middle East Report*, April–June.

Usher, Graham (1996) 'Has Arafat Gone Too Far?', *Middle East International*, 16 August.

Usher, Graham (1996) 'Oslo 2: Frenzied Efforts Falter', *Middle East International*, 22 September.

Usher, Graham (1996) 'West Bank Towns under Arafat's Control', *Middle East International*, 5 January.

Van Teeffelen, Toine (1996) 'Development Discourse. The Case of Palestine' in Inge Boer, Annelies Moers and Toine Van Teeffelen (eds), *Orientations. Changing Stories. Postmodernism and the Arab World* (Amsterdam).

Weber, Max (1947) *The Theory of Social and Economic Organization* (New York: Oxford University Press).

Weinberger, Naomi (1995) 'The Palestinian National Security Debate', *Journal of Palestine Studies*, Spring.

Wood, Ellen M. (1995) *Democracy Against Capitalism* (Cambridge: Cambridge University Press).

Worsley, P. (1957) *The Trumpet Shall Sound: A Study of 'Cargo' Cults in Melanesia* (London: MacGibbon and Kee).

Ya'ari, Ehud (1994) 'Can Arafat Govern?', *The Jerusalem Report*, 13 January.

Index

Index compiled by
Auriol Griffith-Jones